TRAINING TO WIN

TRAINING TO WIN

The Complete Training System
for the Modern-Day
Event Rider

CAROLINE MOORE FBHS
FOREWORD BY ROSALIND CANTER

KENILWORTH
PRESS

Copyright © 2023 Caroline Moore

First published in the UK in 2023
by Kenilworth Press

British Library Cataloguing-in-Publication Data
A catalogue record for the book is available from the British Library.

Paperback ISBN 978-1-910016-44-2
E-book ISBN 978-1-910016-45-9

The right of Caroline Moore to be identified as the author of this work has been asssserted in accordance with the Copyright, Design and Patent Act 1988.

All rights reserved. No part of this book may be reproduced or transmitted in any form or by any means, electronic or mechanical including photocopying, recording or by any information storage and retrieval system, without permission from the publisher in writing.

Disclaimer of liability
The information in this book is true and complete to the best of our knowledge. All recommendations are made without any guarantee on the part of the Publisher, who also disclaims any liability incurred in connection with the use of this data or specific details.

Front cover photo by William Carey
Back cover photo by Ben Clarke

Book design by Becky Bowyer
Becky@becbowyer.com

Printed in China

Kenilworth Press

an imprint of Quiller Publishing
The Hill
Merrywalks
Stroud GL5 4EP
Tel: 01453 847800
Email: info@quillerbooks.com
Website: www.quillerpublishing.com

Appointed GPSR EU Representative: Easy Access System Europe Oü, 16879218
Address: Mustamäe tee 50, 10621, Tallinn, Estonia
Contact Details: gpsr.requests@easproject.com, +358 40 500 3575

Contents

Acknowledgements	9
Foreword	11
Introduction	13
1. What Makes a Champion	**15**
1.1 The correct training system	16
1.2 A podium mentality	16
1.3 A positive mindset	19
1.4 Confidence	21
2. The Athlete's Philosophy	**27**
2.1 Understanding good practice	27
2.2 Effective goal-setting	35
2.3 The 'no-excuse' culture	37
2.4 Performance over outcome	38
2.5 Understanding the equine	38
2.6 Looking after yourself – 'the busy fool'	39
2.6a Managing your health and fitness	40
3. Training to Learn	**45**
3.1 How a horse learns	45
3.2 The training zones	48
3.2a Comfort zone	48
3.2b Learning zone	48
3.2c Pressure zone	49
3.3 Creating a work ethic	49
3.4 Useful equipment	50
4. Annual Training Plans	**55**
4.1 Planning the workload	55
4.2 'Taking the horse to the gym'	57
4.3 The training seasons	57

    4.3a End of season rest period — 58
    4.3b Winter work (11–12 weeks) — 58
    4.3c Spring preparation (6 weeks) — 59
    4.3d Maintenance at short format throughout the season (ongoing) — 61
    4.3e Building up to a long format or championship event (6 weeks) — 62
  4.4 Trot-up training — 63

5. Responsibilities and Jumping Rules — 65
  5.1 Rider's responsibility — 65
  5.2 Horse's responsibility — 65
  5.3 Rider's position and rules for jumping — 66
  5.4 The three points of approach — 71

6. Training to Learn Exercises — 73
  6.1 Developing stride length — 74
    6.1a Developing stride variation — 74
    6.1b Raised canter poles on a circle — 77
    6.1c Four-stride exercise — 78
    6.1d Developing the jumping canter – three cavalletti — 80
    6.1e Raised trotting poles on a circle — 82
    6.1f Suppleness and control: pole-parallel-pole related distance — 84
  6.2 Developing straightness — 86
    6.2a Using tramlines — 87
    6.2b Narrow poles to hold a line — 89
    6.2c Introducing the narrow fence — 90
    6.2d Training the steering aids — 93
    6.2e Leg-yield in canter — 95
  6.3 Change of direction over a fence — 97
    6.3a Directional changes over raised poles — 97
    6.3b Cavalletti bounces — 99
    6.3c Bounce-parallel-bounce — 100
    6.3d Cavalletti cross — 103

Contents

    6.4 Working on different terrain and ground conditions   104

7. TRAINING TO COMPETE   107
    7.1 Dressage skills required at all levels   107
    7.2 Showjumping skills required at all levels   109
    7.3 Cross-country skills required at all levels   111

8. TRAINING TO COMPETE EXERCISES   113
    8.1 Flatwork   113
        8.1a The square exercise – parallel poles   113
        8.1b The square exercise – parallel poles with counter-canter   115
        8.1c The square exercise – parallel poles with shoulder-in   118
        8.1d The square exercise – parallel poles with medium trot   121
        8.1e The square exercise – parallel poles using 10m circles into medium canter   122
        8.1f Training the square halt   123
        8.1g Training the rein-back   127
        8.1h Short side training – square exercises with corners   128
        8.1i Centre line training   133
        8.1j Training straightness – leg-yield into counter shoulder-in   136
    8.2 The developmental system to train flying changes   138
    8.3 Jumping exercises   142
        8.3a Training the turn to a fence   143
        8.3b The angled fence   145
        8.3c The corner fence   149
        8.3d Reaction training for horse and rider: bounce-24yards-bounce   156
        8.3e Developing the skills to jump narrow fences   159
        8.3f Training the shoulder brush fence   163
        8.3g Training steps up and uphill fences   166
        8.3h Training fences on a mound   168
        8.3i Training steps down and downhill fences   168
        8.3j Training confidence at water questions   172
        8.3k Ditch training with additional questions   177

8.4 Riding to a cross-country fence at the correct speed	179
8.5 First-minute training and riding to the time	183
8.6 Riding the last minute on the cross-country	184
8.7 Effective use of the showjumping warm-up	185
9. TRAINING TO WIN – THE MAKING OF A CHAMPION	**189**
9.1 Marginal gains	189
9.2 Performance profiling	190
9.3 Training in the pressure zone	194
9.3a Stride reduction around a track of showjumps	194
9.3b Exercise to develop ability to task-load	196
9.4 Training high degrees of accuracy	196
9.4a Turning tight into a line and exiting straight	196
9.4b Jumping into a line on a curve and exiting straight	200
9.4c Precision training with three cavalletti	202
9.5 Improving the horse's jumping technique	203
9.5a Improving bascule	204
9.5b Developing lift	206
9.5c Jumping out of counter-canter	208
10. COMPETITIONS	**209**
10.1 Competition planning	209
10.2 Developing the working system leading up to an event	212
10.3 Effective course-walking	213
10.4 Clean sport	221
10.5 'In the zone'	223
10.5a Nerves and how to combat them – creating a strategy	223
10.6 Riding at a championship	228
10.6a Preparation leading up to a championship	228
10.6b At the event	228
10.6c The trot-up	229
10.6d Dressage day	230
10.6e Cross-country day	232
10.6f Showjumping day	235
INDEX	**237**

Acknowledgements

My thanks to the following people for providing their photos and diagrams that appear in this book. Other than those credited below, the images are my own.

Ben Clarke
Photo numbers 1, 16, 17, 19, 21, 23, 24, 25, 26, 27, 28a, 30, 31, 32, 33, 34, 35, 36, 37, 39, 40, 41, 44, 45, 46, 48, 49, 51, 54, 55, 57, 58, 59, 60, 61, 64, 65, 66, 67, 69, 71, 72, 75, 76, 80, 81, 82, 84, 85, 86, 87, 88, 91, 92, 93, 97, 98, 99, 102, 103, 104, 108, 110, 111, 112,116, 119, 124, 126, 127, 128, 129, 130, 131, 132, 133, 135, 136, 137, 138, 139, 140, 141, 142, 143, 144, 145, 146a,b,150, 151, 152, 153, 154, 155, 156, 157, 158, 159, 162, 163, 164, 166,169, 170, 171, 172, 174, 175, 176, 177, 178, 179, 180, 181, 182, 184, 185, 186, 194 (back cover)

Hannah Cole
Photo numbers 5, 117, 149, 189, 191

Nico Morgan
Photo numbers 7, 8, 9, 29, 56, 79

William Carey
Photo numbers 10, 70, 83, front cover

All-Action Sports Photography
Photo numbers 38, 95

Abbie Kyte
Photo numbers 28b, 53, 68

FSVEO Fotografie
Photo number 6

Trevor Holt
Photo numbers 11, 106

Scott Matthews
Photo numbers 14, 15

Zsuzsi Vajanski
Diagrams 2, 42, 43, 47,48, 50, 62, 63, 66, 67, 71, 73, 74, 77, 78, 84, 87, 88, 89, 90, 94, 96, 107, 109, 113, 114, 115, 121, 125, 147, 161, 165, 166, 167, 168, 173

Adam Fanthorpe
Diagram 193

Foreword

Caroline is not only my trainer, but my mentor in every aspect of becoming a successful performer. Above all else, she is a great friend. She has been instrumental in all aspects of my eventing career, and in my reaching the pinnacle of becoming Team and Individual World Champion in 2018 on our own Allstar B.

In this book she covers all the bases, from building a successful relationship with your horse and learning the importance of the correct basics, to handling pressure and nerves in competition – all of which are relevant to riders from Grassroots through to top level professionals.

Caroline writes in the same clear and concise way that she trains. There is no stone left unturned in her training, and she explains this methodical approach to working with both riders and horses to create successful partnerships.

Every time I train with Caroline she encourages me to be my own critic, to question and analyse myself and my horse in order to reach our training and competition goals. She imparts her knowledge and training methods in a way that will encourage you to do the same.

Caroline is one of my greatest inspirations. Her thirst for learning and improving continues to motivate me every day. This book can be picked up whenever direction is needed in the training of our horses as well as in rider confidence.

Thank you, Caroline, for helping me to achieve my dreams. Together we are always learning and striving for those marginal gains, and haven't we had fun along the way!

Rosalind Canter

Training to Win

Introduction

Horses are great levellers. The journey that is taken to train them to be the best in their field takes patience, empathy and refined skills, but most of all a correct, workable system. This book will help you develop your own training strategies thereby giving you the simple, fundamental exercises that will improve the all-important basics. Progression needs to be a passion that you strive for, a goal to be reached with the knowledge that the horse will only improve as the rider hones their own techniques. This book will take you on that journey of training the young horse to learn new skills, to develop as an athlete and to thrive in competition.

I hope that you get as much pleasure out of using this book as I had writing it.

1. Being the best isn't about luck on the day, it's about being incredibly well practised in every area of training.

Chapter 1

WHAT MAKES A CHAMPION

Success isn't always about greatness. It's about consistency. Consistent hard work gains success.
— Dwayne Johnson

Being a champion in any sport, but especially the sport of eventing, is not just about luck on the day. To be a champion you need to be more mentally and physically prepared than your competitors, able to perform at the highest of levels and to react to all the scenarios that competition might throw at you. The partnership between you and your horse needs to be explicit and the horse needs to be fully trained and prepared for all the questions involved.

I have worked with many riders in the past who have natural flair or what some might call talent, but they have not managed to be successful or stay in the sport for various reasons. At the same time I have also had the pleasure of working alongside riders who have had to overcome problems with their own skills and come out the other side to become champions. Why is that, we wonder? What are the ingredients of a champion? Why do some athletes make it and others fall by the wayside? The four main attributes the athlete needs to possess are:

- The correct training system.
- A podium mentality.
- A positive mindset.
- Confidence.

Responsibility is something that is crucial when developing high standards and a podium mentality.

Most of the text of this book is going to look in depth at a training system that is proven to produce athletes to become champions, and it will offer you an opportunity to build your own successful system.

We all know that eventing is the sport of three disciplines; dressage, showjumping and cross-country and they are all very separate in their own ways. However, within this book you will discover how interlinked the three disciplines become within the training, and the impact that can have on the efficient use of time.

1.1 Correct training system

A correct training system requires necessary understanding of the subject and a simple but disciplined approach. We will look at how you and your horse learn and develop strong foundations in your skills so we can build on them as you move up the levels together. I put the training system into three categories.

Training to learn
The first category is to develop the basic skills correctly and to coach the partnership to understand the procedure of learning. This is the most important part of training the horse and it is the foundation that we use to build everything else on.

Training to compete
The second and largest category of training is to coach all the skills required for the partnership to compete successfully at the appropriate level of competition. There are at least seventy skills that your horse will need to learn and become competent at. To develop good foundations it will often take five years to go from starting the 3- or 4-year-old to competing successfully at 4* level as an 8- or 9-year-old. Within the following chapters we will visit a lot of these skills and help you develop each one.

Training to win
The third category is progressing your horse and yourself to the level of having the edge over other competitors by bringing your competition work into your training. This develops mental and physical skills so that high performance is well within your comfort zone.

1.2 A podium mentality

Although the sport of eventing is often thought of as fast and furious, the modern day competition is highly precise, with medals won and lost in millimetres and split seconds.

Developing a podium mentality within your training is the key to developing high performance at the level at which you compete, whether it is at 90cm (3ft) or top senior level. A podium mentality is a way of working whereby you put 100 per cent into everything that you do to create a high standard. It's about having strict discipline with yourself, your own riding posture, your preparation, your expectations, your daily system and developing a quality in your horse's training that is of a high level of thoroughness. In Chapter 9 *Training to Win* we will look at marginal gains and how you can improve your long-term performance.

Changing your habits to have a podium mentality is a crucial part of your new system. Here are some examples of this:

- Every transition needs to have thought, preparation and a planned place to execute it. With good repetition your horse should have the will to perform it correctly each time.

- Every halt transition should be corrected so it's square and consequently your horse never learns to halt incorrectly.

- Every jump must stay on the line that you have approached the fence on, with a focal point to continue the straightness afterwards.

- When trotting over poles or jumping a showjump always line up specific stripes on the poles to be exact to the millimetre.

- Taking your own fitness and health as seriously as the horse's.

2. Podium mentality.

Responsibility is something that is crucial when developing high standards and a podium mentality. If you take responsibility for your own actions you will develop the all-important no-excuse policy that will allow you to be a learner in life. This mental attitude will also be the key to developing yourself as a champion in your own right.

Here is an acronym on which I base my own coaching philosophy. This reminds me that everything that I do needs to have thought, preparation and be performed to the best of my ability.

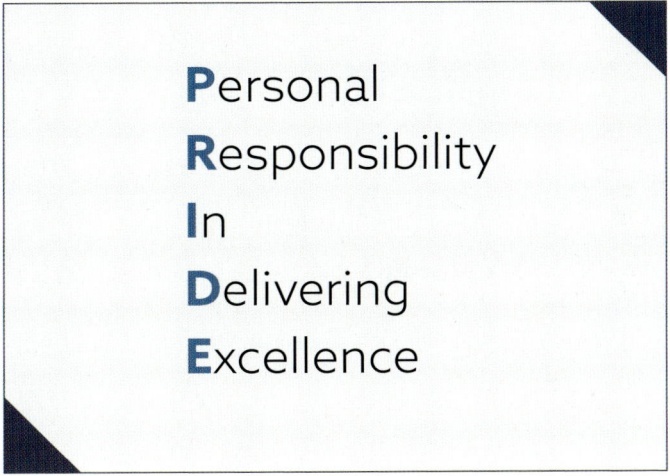

1.3 A positive mindset

In life we are either learners or non-learners. We are either happy and excited to be challenged by the unknown, or we would prefer to stay in the safety of our comfort zone. Challenge doesn't always mean bigger, higher or wider. Sometimes tasks that are out of the ordinary will offer a new learning experience – a necessity for an extensive toolbox. Where does our mindset come from? It is generally in our personality, but is also often influenced by an upbringing of beliefs, not just programmed into us by parents, but also by our role models, teachers at school, or coaches in sport. I have found when working alongside younger riders that the parental influence can have a massive implication on whether the athlete succeeds in the sport (or not, as sometimes the case may be). Here are some examples of how parental influence affects the rider.

1. If the parent was a high achiever in sport, or previously a sports person, they are often highly motivated and pushy and, when empathy is needed, it often isn't forthcoming. This behaviour can have a negative impact by making the rider feel unmotivated as they are always trying to live up to expectations. Sometimes this

type of parental influence can cause the rider to self-criticise too much and only put their belief in coaches who are pointing out their weaknesses rather than their strengths. The negative impact all this can have is creating nerves around poor performance and might make the rider either take unnecessary risks or even become risk averse.

2. If the parent has little equine knowledge or a lack of interest this will pose a big challenge for a younger athlete at the onset. They will often have to take responsibility for themselves to learn about all aspects of horsemanship and stable management. They will often be involved in sport from pure love of horses rather than parental pressures. This generally bodes well in their long-term involvement in the sport and creates the growth mindset from an early age.

3. The division between wealth and being financially challenged can have an impact on the athlete's mindset from early stage. If, at an early age, the rider gets to partner expensive horses they will often refrain from challenge in the fear of potentially devaluing or reducing the performance. Equally, a rider who is financially challenged will learn early about values, equality and respect which, although it may be tough in the early stages of their career, will stand them in good stead for later years.

In my experience the following physical and mental attributes are ideal for an athlete to develop if they want to be successful.

- Being concerned about improvement.
- A passion for stretching themselves and sticking to the plan if things go wrong, instead of abandoning it.
- A desire to overcome deficiencies rather than hiding them.
- Not wasting time proving themselves over and over again when actually they could be upping the challenge.
- Being happy to reveal inadequacies occasionally when having to put effort or risk into a challenge.
- Being willing to learn how to deal with problems. When things don't go to plan having a strategy, good basic building blocks and a sound, well-practised system.
- Feeling privileged about pressure and using it as a positive rather than a potential enemy.
- Having the ability to turn a problem into a positive by embracing something that doesn't go to plan and creating success from it.

1.4 Confidence

Confidence is a mental state of mind that derives from the ability to perform a physical skill. Undoubtedly, confidence is the key to success in any sport, but it has to have a structure and system that sits behind it. Yogi Breisner FBHS always talked about a 'cup of confidence' that needs topping up regularly with work that is cemented with positive repetition. Then, if a bit of confidence is dropped, you have a system to fill the cup back up again and the combination will continue to be successful.

How to develop a horse's confidence

A horse isn't born with the skills to win a championship; skills need to be developed into the horse's training. Using a step-by-step building block system (see photos 3, 4 & 5) you can develop good deliberate practice which, in turn, will create confidence with that particular skill. For your horse to feel confident the training needs to be comfortable, safe, unthreatening and enjoyable. When the skill is easy to replicate it is time to make the training more challenging. If, at any point, the horse looks to be worried by the question, a good trainer will drop the challenge back to a lower level, height or technicality. This will top-up confidence levels before repeating the challenge again. This will ensure that your horse always has belief in his own ability and scope.

3. These three images demonstrate a building block system. Start with the narrow flags and ditch.

4. Add a fence to the question.

5. The question in competition.

> **Rules to develop the horse's confidence**
> - Make sure that your horse is comfortable, sound and happy in the work.
> - Maintain a system of pressure and reward in training.
> - Use a small step-by-step approach.
> - Repetition, repetition, repetition and repetition of good practice.
> - Move the challenges up in small increments of height, technicality or intensity.
> - Regularly go back to skills that the horse can perform easily and well.

How to develop the rider's confidence

Just like a horse's, your confidence will come from the knowledge that you can perform the skill successfully. A successful system would be starting the skills in a familiar training area, before moving to a more challenging environment and then eventually performing the skill to a high level in competition. Confidence and belief can become very fragile in the sport of eventing, so it's very important to have a good balance of success in your comfort zone and challenge in your pressure zone. If you are confident in a competition environment you can deliver a 'can-do' attitude that will allow you to handle what comes in your way. If you fall victim to self-defeating thoughts this can have a huge impact on your performance, so make sure that you have a good system in place and a responsible team around you to prevent this happening.

> **Rules to develop the rider's confidence**
> - Develop a systematic approach.
> - Aim for small improvements in all the basic work.
> - Build up and regularly practise all the skills required for competition.
> - Focus on performance rather than results.
> - Surround yourself with people who believe in you.

Chapter 2

The Athlete's Philosophy

What is a philosophy and why is it so important? It is a group of beliefs that you use to guide yourself to developing a successful system, which is often made up from positive experiences that you have had in the past. As a coach I find it is important to be open-minded within a training system as there are many alternative ways and techniques that work for different horses and riders. However, there are a certain number of beliefs to which, in my opinion, an athlete should adhere and these I class as the winning ingredients. You can call these beliefs 'rules' and they will encourage discipline, maintain good practice with a competitive outlook and provide a way of coping with outside interferences. Throughout this book you will learn how to develop your own system and rules that work specifically for you.

2.1 Understanding good practice

This is very simple in that we need to understand what it is we are striving towards. What does 'good' look like? What is 'quality'? What is our ultimate aim in training? Why it is important only to follow 'good deliberate practice' and refrain from repeating poor or even detrimental practice. The following points offer some guidance on these issues.

1. Choose a reputable coach with whom you can discuss good working practice and who will focus on your performance so that, in turn, your horse will make improvements. It is the athlete's responsibility to learn and the coach's responsibility to promote good practice and facilitate the learning environment.

2. Familiarise yourself with the scales of training and their

The training scale is the most important guideline for riders and coaches.

6. The author coaching.

relationship to flatwork and jumping. The training scale is the most important guideline for riders and coaches. It is a programme of systematic physical education of the horse that helps to develop the physical and mental aptitudes of the horse. By following these principles the rider can train the horse to be obedient, supple and happy to work in training and competition. The essential principle for the event rider to consider is that the scales of training are used to train all three phases, dressage, showjumping and cross-country.

● Rhythm

Regularity and tempo (speed of the rhythm). The strides should be equal in distance, regular and remain in a consistent tempo.

Relative to jumping
Riding towards and away from a fence in a level, regular rhythm allows the horse to adjust himself whilst staying in balance and harmony.

● Suppleness

Elasticity and freedom from anxiety. The horse should have a soft range of movement, stretching across the back and laterally from side to side. The horse should look happy and relaxed in his work and follow the rider's aids easily without tension.

Relative to jumping
The horse is able to make turns from either direction, staying obedient to the rider's aids. The transitions that are made whilst jumping should have engagement and be through from behind. A good jump is a consequence of elasticity in the neck and body.

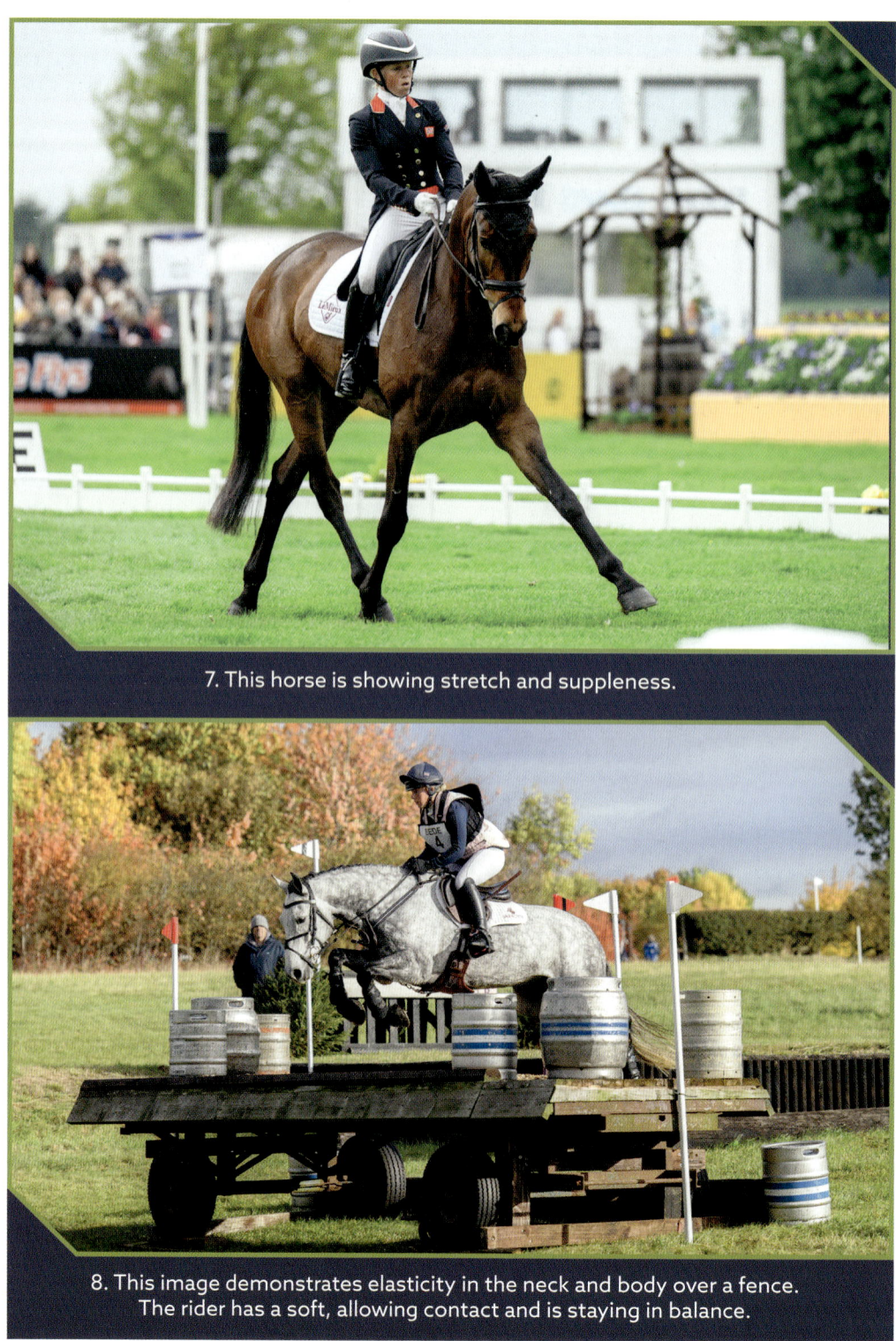

7. This horse is showing stretch and suppleness.

8. This image demonstrates elasticity in the neck and body over a fence. The rider has a soft, allowing contact and is staying in balance.

● CONTACT

The contact is where the energy travels across a swinging back from active hind legs to the bit. The rider should accept the contact by allowing the forward momentum to continue with small, elastic half-halts and a doorway that is slightly ajar.

Relative to jumping
Endeavouring to maintain a lovely contact whilst jumping is an ultimate goal. Having the ability to produce the energy required but keep the mind and body soft will have a huge impact on performance. The 'contact' is ultimately the main directional aids used through all of the rider's body. These aids need to be given in a way that allows the horse to keep travelling towards a fence.

> Imagine the rein contact being a door. If it is left wide open the energy will escape onto the forehand, with little balance. If the door is closed tightly the energy will often 'hit' the hand and the horse will become an anxious coiled spring, resulting in crookedness and anxiety. If the rider allows the door to be left slightly 'ajar' it has the effect of maintaining a contact with elasticity to allow a forward feeling.

● IMPULSION

Impulsion is the degree of contained energy within the horse, which should come through a soft back and be guided by the rider's light rein aids. The desire should be to go forwards and eventually, through training, the rider can use the horse's natural gait to add looseness, forward trust and suppleness.

Relative to jumping
Producing the right canter to jump out of is always an ongoing training goal. To jump with effort, the horse needs to be mentally active, but with a degree of controlled impulsion. The rider should measure the canter energy on a scale of one to ten, ten being the most energetic. The jumping canter should always be based on a canter measured around eight, otherwise the mental energy is possibly not good enough.

9. A straight horse across the diagonal in an extended trot.

● STRAIGHTNESS

Developing a horse's straightness is always an ongoing goal. As the rider asks for more energy the straightness can become fragile and will need correcting. The rider always needs to have an awareness of the horse's weight distribution so that when the horse loses the straightness the rider can correct it instantly. The horse should be trained to offer equal bend to both directions.

Relative to jumping
Keeping the horse in an upright, straight balance around a turn, on the approach, landing and getaway from a fence will allow the rider to train him up through the levels without putting undue pressure on one limb more than another. As well as improving his performance this will hopefully increase his longevity in the sport. Taking off and landing in the corresponding spot is essential for the accuracy required at all levels and this can only happen with established straightness in the horse's initial training.

● COLLECTION

Collection occurs when the horse is working correctly through from active hind legs, staying supple across the top of his back, accepting an elastic contact, and the impulsion is directed to a slightly shorter frame.

Relative to jumping
Eventually, through correct training, the horse can offer a canter that can move effortlessly up and down through transitions, showing different stride lengths whilst maintaining the impulsion out of which to jump.

10. This partnership is showing total straightness and symmetry even when jumping out of a 5* water question.

11. This image demonstrates a partnership staying straight and engaged around a tight turn after a drop into water. The rider shows a leading directional aid but stays in balance.

3. Watch, read and learn. There are so many social media platforms where you can find relevant information and good techniques – for example you only need to type in 'rein-back' and it comes up with ten or more different short videos of top coaches demonstrating how to do a correct rein-back. One very useful exercise I encourage athletes to do is write for a dressage judge at the level that at which they are competing, just to recognise how a dressage test is judged and to learn more about what the judge actually requires.

4. Remember, '*correct*' is what keeps the horse in the sport for a long time. It is the horse working in a way that builds up his muscles to perform comfortably and carry the rider readily. It is what the dressage judge is looking to mark well and is in line with classical training. It is having an understanding and empathy with the horse and making him feel happy in his work.

2.2 Effective goal-setting

Rather than talk about weaker areas I like to describe the deficiencies as 'work-ons'. Your 'work-ons' are a realistic group of small daily goals related to essential skills that will allow you to become a more proficient athlete. Let's take a very common example of a rider who sits with the hips slightly to the left of centre, therefore collapsing the right hip, which leads to a dropping of the right shoulder, a stronger pull on the right hand and consequently the horse will prefer to drift his body away from the pressure, escaping his body to the left. This leads to crooked centre lines, running left into jumps and inevitably running out at left-handed corners. So, in this case, the 'work-ons' need to be taking the left seat bone into the centre of the saddle, the right seat bone sits right and light, the shoulders need to turn slightly towards the left, the rider may need to look through the horse's left ear and relax the right upper arm. Just by doing these positional corrections at every corner, before every transition and before every turn to a fence, a rider can create good practice in a short space of time. The rider who doesn't put effort into these 'work-ons' will have a drift at a left-handed angled fence in a crucial championship and risk penalties by being the wrong side of a flag. Knowing your 'work-ons' is a result of *profiling your performance* regularly, which we will cover in Chapter 9 *Training to Win*. It is essential that, whilst you are riding, you are regularly reminded of your 'work-ons', not by a coach, but by a personal trigger. This can be in the form of a whiteboard 'rules' list in the tack room or even a plaiting band in the horse's mane to consistently remind you until it becomes good practice.

12. A rider collapsing the right hip. You can clearly see the drop of the right shoulder and the effect it has on asymmetry and the rider's weight distribution.

> ### Training journal
> A training journal is a great way of recording everything that you do to take yourself and your horse up through the levels. Making the time each day to fill in the training programme for each individual horse will build up a picture of a progressive work plan, fitness plan and skills training. The journal can also keep a record of veterinary problems, medications, feed changes and other management issues that have an impact on your horse's performance. It is also a great way of setting daily training goals to improve your skills by the ever-important 1 per cent and will raise your awareness of good deliberate practice.

2.3 The 'no-excuse' culture

If it's important to you, you will find a way. If it's not, you'll find an excuse.

– Ryan Blair

In your philosophy, having a 'no-excuse' culture is a way of breaking through the barriers of things going well for you. If you have a well-implemented plan with good preparation it is more likely that unexpected issues can be dealt with efficiently and be overcome quickly. If, on the other hand, you create an excuse for every small problem it will give you a mental way out for things going wrong. Unfortunately, when this happens you will not learn from your mistakes and the issue is likely to recur repeatedly.

Every time you find yourself starting to make an excuse for something, turn it around and find the real reason why it went wrong. This will give you a chance to embrace the problem, put a new plan in place and act upon it.

> ### For example
> A rider complained that she didn't receive the dressage score that she was hoping for because the horse spooked in a corner and lost 3 marks. The horse spooking is the excuse. Actually the real reason is that the rider hasn't trained the horse to be connected between leg and hand so consequently has the allowance to spook. The real reason falls to the rider, who should then implement a better training system to prevent it happening in the future.

2.4 Performance over outcome

It is very easy to become obsessed with winning or always being in the prizes, but having the mentality that a good, correct performance comes first is very important for your horse's future. Each competition needs to have a small performance goal, whether it is maintaining a better rhythm in the showjumping, staying straight across fences on the cross-country or maybe showing more relaxation in the warm-up for the dressage. Each competition needs to be on an improvement scale so, as well as gaining the essential MERs (Minimum Entry Requirements) you are, in fact, educating your horse at the level ready to eventually move up. Every competition needs reflection with feedback from either/or yourself, a coach, or any qualified onlooker just to make sure mistakes aren't repeated and that plans are put in place to make subtle improvements in all phases. After a weekend of competition I will often have riders calling in for a debriefing. Those riders who are concerned with the performance during each phase, often giving me in-depth feedback and self-critique, are the riders who will make improvements throughout the season. It's irrelevant to me as their coach whether they say they won or were highly placed, as I can see that in the results. Although a win at a National competition is an added bonus, it wouldn't be what I would encourage over and over again as it can lead to complacency in training, and going at top speed in every competition will risk long-term soundness of the horse.

2.5 Understanding the equine

Equine athletes come in all shapes, sizes, breeds, conformation, colours and, most importantly, they all have different temperaments to work with. In Chapter 3 *Training to Learn* we will look at how a horse learns and develops skills and how different problems can arise with horses with different temperaments. They are fascinating animals who, in general, love to work, gallop and jump, but all have a brain, muscles, tendons, ligaments and a nervous system and will react to discomfort in many different ways. To become a champion athlete in eventing you will need to have the ability to train your horse to be the best in his field, which we will cover in the next three chapters – but it's highly important that you understand 'how your horse works'. To be an effective equine trainer you will need to understand how your horse is put together, and this includes understanding flaws in horses' conformation and how that might affect their performance and soundness. You will need to understand how the horse's body develops when starting to get fitter for purpose, and be able to relate to the connection of the vet, the physiotherapist and the farrier. This is achieved by having a thirst for knowledge and learning through the experience of keeping horses.

Here is just a small list of questions that, as a rider and trainer of your horse, you need to research and understand:

The Athlete's Philosophy

13. Understanding equine biomechanics is an important part of being your horse's trainer.

- Why can a poor hoof-pastern axis predispose to tendon injury?
- Why can firm ground conditions have an effect on some horses and not others?
- Why should you warm your horses down sufficiently after any form of strenuous exercise?
- What is the difference between a muscle strain and a ligament sprain and how would you recognise and treat each?
- Why do some horses with straighter hind leg conformation struggle with engaging exercises and how should you work with this in training?
- Why might your horse start twitching his head in sunlight and how might you deal with it in an empathetic way?

There are so many areas that need knowledge and understanding when training the equine athlete and it is our responsibility to learn how to deal with each situation so we can keep our horses comfortable in their training.

2.6 Looking after yourself – 'the busy fool'

Time management is one of the biggest contributors to whether you achieve success as you wish. Time is extremely precious and should be managed in a way that gives you the space to deal with the necessities that allow you to do your job to the best of your ability. Plan time to:

- Eat and drink.
- Think about and plan your daily activities.
- Think and plan for the longer term.
- Be aware of others around you.
- Train each horse dependent on his needs.
- Have a home life and down time.
- Manage business activities.
- Follow your own continuous personal development.

To be successful in time management you should ideally regularly reflect and review, preferably with the input of an outside party or coach who can look objectively at your lifestyle.

2.6a Managing your health and fitness

Managing your own health and fitness requires you to understand the degree of fitness necessary to be your best in the sport. We consider the horse to be the athlete as far as physical fitness is concerned, but actually the rider's fitness plays a large part in the high-performance end of the sport. Take the following points into consideration:

- Aerobic fitness. Slow work but long distances. Course-walking.
- Anaerobic fitness. Short, sharp, high heart rate work. This is rarely needed in the sport apart from at the end of a cross-country course on a strong horse. Anaerobic training will intensify your heart rate and is a good fitness tool, especially for weight loss.
- Core strength work using Pilates or instruments to develop strength and control, riding posture and balance.
- Resistance training. This work in the gym can really help develop your strength and endurance. The number of repetitions you do will have an impact on developing short-term, intermediate-term or long-term endurance. Having a personal trainer to advise you on a training programme would be ideal. All of this work will help security and safety in the saddle.
- Training your eye muscles (see photos 16 & 17). The muscles in the eyes are the first to fatigue when the athlete starts to get tired. The eyes are obviously a very important part of riding, especially when jumping, and it is possible to train your eyes to be quicker at reading information and improve their stamina so that they can work for longer periods. A good exercise is to hold your arms out straight in front of you, slightly wider than your shoulders. Raise your index fingers and, keeping your head still, look from one finger to the other as many times as you can within 1 minute. You will probably notice that your eyes get tired towards

The Athlete's Philosophy

14 & 15. Two riders working on their core with EQ Bands.

16 & 17. A young rider developing strength in the eye muscles.

The Athlete's Philosophy

the end and start to slow down. Repeat this exercise regularly to monitor your progress, also with the arms a little higher (head staying straight so that your eyes have to look up).

▸ Find a type of fitness exercise that you enjoy doing and fits into your daily lifestyle. This way you are more likely to keep it up on a regular basis.

18. A selection of healthy food for a busy rider.

Management of your own nutrition

This very important as it is the fuel that gives you the energy to be the best. The physical work that is done with horses takes up a lot of energy and it can be a very fine balance of eating enough to fuel the work without increasing your weight. Riding at your minimum weight is always going to benefit you as a rider, just for the pure advantage of your horse carrying less weight. Having a good all-round education about nutrition is crucial to you as the rider and it is your responsibility to find out more information to develop the correct diet for yourself. To maintain a healthy riding weight with the right amount of energy the following rules can be followed:

- **Bread, cereal, rice and pasta 6–11 servings/day.**
  Serving sizes include 1 slice of bread, ½ bagel, 1 cup of cereal, ½ cup cooked rice or pasta, 3–4 small plain crackers.
- **Veg group 3–5 servings/day.**
  Serving sizes include 1 cup of raw leafy veg, ½ cup of other veg, ¾ cup of veg juice.
- **Fruit group 2–4 servings/day.**
  Serving sizes include 1 medium apple, banana or orange, ¼ cup dried fruit, ½ cup canned fruit, ¾ cup of fruit juice.
- **Meat, poultry, fish, eggs, nuts group 2–3 servings/day.**
  Serving sizes include 5 oz cooked lean meat, poultry or fish, ½ cup cooked dry beans, 1 egg, 2 tablespoons of peanut butter.
- **Milk, yogurt and cheese 2–3 servings/day.**
  Serving sizes include 1 cup of milk or yogurt, 1.5 oz natural cheese, 2 oz processed cheese.
- **Fats, oils and sweets should be eaten sparingly.**
  This category includes salad dressing, cream cheese, chocolates, snack foods, etc.

Seven rules for eating right

- Eat a variety of foods so that all nutrients are provided.
- Eat a diet high in wholegrain products, veg and fruit. This type of diet is low in fat but provides the energy needed for athletic work and is good for the health.
- Eat a diet moderate in fat and cholesterol. Foods high in fat can be high in calories and lead to unwanted weight gain.
- Eat a diet moderate in sugar. A diet high in sugar will often be low in nutrients and high in calories.
- Eat a diet that is moderate in salt or sodium.
- Drink lots of fluids. Water is essential to all bodily functions and intense physical activity can lead to dehydration, which can limit performance in many ways. For each 1 per cent of bodyweight lost by dehydration the ability to work is reduced by 2 per cent. Dehydration will cause irritability, headaches, dizziness, nausea, feeling weak and will reduce performance in athletic situations.
- Drink alcohol in moderation. Alcohol contains lots of calories, almost no nutrients and will increase the likelihood of dehydration.

Chapter 3

Training to Learn

Remember – we are our horse's coach. It is never their fault. It is our inadequacy in their training if they don't understand the question. What can we do to improve their understanding and mental health?

3.1 How a horse learns

Training your horse to learn and to receive and understand aids from you is one of the most important ongoing lessons. All animals, horses included, learn from previous experiences and association. Using the right amount of pressure and a well-timed reward by relief of the pressure creates a clear system so the horse understands what is being asked of him. To do this effectively, you need to develop the following attributes:

- An independent balanced position, with self-awareness.
- An empathetic understanding of how your horse is feeling.
- A disciplined approach, with attention to detail.
- Patience.
- A clear understanding on what you are aiming to achieve.
- A good knowledge of your horse's anatomical conformation with an understanding of how any weaker areas could have an effect on the willingness to perform the task.
- Understanding the value of confidence.

The following points should be your rules:

1. *Plan* your training around your horse's needs.
2. Start with the *absolute basics*.

Once a skill is understood you must practise, practise and practise again if you want it to be second nature.

19. Remembering to praise where required. A pat will also help relax a horse when anxious.

3. Progressively create *building blocks* that you can 'add on' to.
4. Have *clear reasons* to reward and reprimand.
5. Recognise *the effect* that the training is having on your horse both physically and mentally.
6. Once a skill is understood you must *practise, practise and practise again* if you want it to be second nature.

Understanding how a human learns through experiment will help you have an understanding of how to train your horse correctly. The following briefly explains the Kolb Model of Experimental Learning developed by David A. Kolb in 1984.

Experience – making mistakes.

Reflection – recognition, self-awareness and coach intervention.

Plan – think and put an action plan together.

Practise and experiment – action.

By using this model of learning you will train your horse with a system that makes you think before poor repetition. This training is far superior in the long run and will prevent your horse learning poor habits.

> ### Example
>
> **Experience** – produce an action such as a canter strike-off. The horse misinterprets this, runs and picks up the incorrect lead.
>
> **Reflection** – think about why it happened, what you could do to prevent it recurring and what could you do to improve the understanding.
>
> **Plan** – for a better preparation by using walk-trot transitions, 15m circles to develop a better balance.
>
> **Practise and experiment** – ride the canter transition again and, if correct repeat, repeat and repeat.

What can go wrong within the training process?

Most training problems are human error resulting from a poor understanding of reward and reprimand. For example, if a rider asks a horse to perform an activity without correct preparation and complete understanding, the horse is more likely to make a mistake. If a horse runs past an obstacle because of a poor approach, this will become a learned association if it is allowed to be repeated without good immediate correction, and is detrimental to the horse's long-term performance. Stepping back to the first building block of riding the approach correctly with a lower fence or even a pole on the ground is far better than reattempting with an equally poor approach to the larger fence.

Choices and consequences

When you ask your horse to perform an action that has been learned previously he will have a choice of whether to perform it correctly or not. If your training has been effective he will understand that if the action is performed willingly he will be praised, but if he decides to opt out there needs to be a small consequence. The actual consequence may be up to your discretion, but a small correction with added pressure is often enough before giving the horse the choice again. For example, if your horse decides, even with a correct approach, to run past a narrow fence you should retrace your steps and stand in front of the fence and, with a small amount of pressure with leg and rein aids, explain to him that he should have jumped it. (Often people will use a whip at this stage, but actually that can take the focus off the learning.) Then approach the fence again with a light pressure to give the horse the choice. If he is confident he will jump the fence 90 per cent of the time without an issue, in which case huge praise is needed. If he constantly refuses to jump the fence then you will need to go back a few steps to consolidate the training. Remember to think how the horse thinks and do not get angry with your horse.

3.2 The training zones

3.2a Comfort zone

Being in a comfort zone within your training is essential in order to increase the important confidence levels in your horse. Aim to maintain the training in a way that produces only low stress levels and anxiety, such as concentrating on good-quality basics within the levels of competence. This includes jumping exercises that develop stamina and technique without the challenge of height. This sort of practice should always be established and built up so that you have a clear idea of what activities are comfortable and familiar. It is essential that the work in the comfort zone is eventually free from mistakes and it should be performed at a high level, with focus on attention to detail.

What is a 'no mistake culture' in the comfort zone?

A 'no mistake culture' is a state of mind where, within your training, you can put in so much good quality, deliberate practice and preparation that you can eradicate the errors that occur through inattention to detail and a lack of preparation. The work in the comfort zone should be 100 per cent mistake free as the only mistakes will often result from poor preparation and idleness.

3.2b Learning zone

The learning zone is where we start to challenge the horse with new skills that are added to the strong foundations and correctly developed building blocks that are already in place. If problems occur at any stage, drop back to the previous building block to restore confidence before moving on again. Initial mistakes are, and should be, a naturally occurring process when learning a new task. They are part of the learning zone and should be expected when training your horse. Ideally any mistakes need correcting with thought and clarity as soon as they occur and in some cases an experienced rider may make a correction before the mistake actually happens, preventing it from being a learned experience. To help manage your horse's confidence through the learning zone it is important to keep the technicality without stress – for example when introducing a technical jumping question, keep the height very low so your horse doesn't lose confidence. On the other hand, if you are developing your horse's eye for more height, keep the technical questions easier to interpret.

Embracing a mistake

A mistake is feedback. It needs embracing when learning new skills and should be used wisely rather than being turned into a negative. Why did it happen? How can you learn from the mistake? How can your horse learn from the mistake? What personal rule can you put in place to prevent it recurring? If a mistake is made as a result of your weakness it can be turned into a *super skill* because it should be corrected and practised repeatedly.

3.2c Pressure zone

Once you and your horse have learned new skills that are within your comfort zone, the last area of training, called the pressure zone, can be introduced. This is often called the panic zone because it should include challenges that create high levels of anxiety similar to those that may be found in competition. The partnership should be stretched in training to mimic competition stress levels by pushing boundaries to the limit. This area will be covered more in Chapter 9 *Training to Win*, and is relevant to all levels if you want to become a champion.

3.3 Creating a work ethic

It is crucial to instil into your horse a healthy work ethic throughout his career. The will to do his best and put effort into his work derives only from the training. Initially, the discipline of being in front of the rider's leg, both mentally and physically, is high on the priority list and is the first boundary. If your horse stays mentally and physically forward in all of his work your leg aids should be kept light and comforting, with minimal pressure. As soon as the effort goes out of the forward momentum it should be reinforced with a sharp and reminding leg aid that has an impact, rather than a continuous nudge, which will desensitise the effect of the aids. When the forward momentum is resumed the leg aids must become light again, offering an instant reward. Use the aids to generate power, then balance the horse, followed instantly with a rewarding softness. This will enable your horse to work in the correct way with energy and relaxation. It is a good idea to do small increments of good-quality work

> *Remember that the trainer is responsible for the horse's desire to 'offer' and the will to perform.*

Power button – generating mental and physical energy with seat and leg aids.
Balance button – containing the energy with small, 'talkative' half-halts using upper body, contact and seat.
Soften button – relaxing the aids to allow the horse's body to breathe.

with the reward of a stretch and a break whenever your horse has performed well, asking for longer periods of top-quality work only as the horse's fitness and stamina improve. By using this method your horse will be keen to offer more and learn to enjoy the work. The desire to canter down the centre line in an obedient fashion or dig deep into his reserves towards the end of a demanding cross-country course and then focus ultimate care and attention in the showjumping arena on the third day of a long format competition will be a reflection of your training.

Fatigued, or evasion?

How do you know whether your horse is fatigued or not putting the effort into the work?

A horse will become *fatigued* through his muscles and develop soreness if he is asked to work beyond what his fitness levels are. The following symptoms will often occur:

- Respiration will often increase.
- Sweating may occur, more in one area specifically.
- Performance starts to drop.
- Response to the aids tends to become slower.

A horse who is being *idle* in his work may use different methods of evasion such as avoiding straightness, using inattention to avoid responding to the aids correctly and a reluctance to travel forward when the challenge becomes more testing. It's quite important to have the ability to recognise the two different body states so that you can react fairly. Once a horse has learned that reduced effort is possible it may become an association with work in certain training areas, or with different types of flatwork, and we would often class it as the horse being bored.

3.4 Useful equipment

If you have just a small training area it's essential that you maximise your facility with equipment that is easy to manoeuvre but sturdy enough to withstand the wind and weather conditions through the winter months. It would be sensible to keep your arena corners free from any equipment so as to maximise the size of the arena and to create a work ethic within your horse by insisting on good-quality corners.

Markers of some description are an essential aid for the rider for accuracy training, whether it is in an arena or a field, otherwise it's really easy to lose attention to detail when training school movements.

Poles used to trot or canter over should have coloured stripes to continue the degree of accuracy required in the sport. Wooden poles will teach the idea of choice and consequence once your horse has started his training successfully. Plastic poles are colourful, low maintenance and fabulous for longevity. They are ideal for showjumping training with a competition-weight pole as a top rail, and for guiding rails and ground-poles, and are essential for any rider with outdoor facilities throughout the winter. Half-round poles painted white can easily be cut into different lengths for different purposes and are very safe because they don't move if a horse stands on them. However, they are not practical for raised poles as they may break easily if a horse stands on one.

Wing weights. Keeping jumps up in the wind can be very frustrating and using some form of security is essential for training in the winter. The wing weights pictured are weighted at 28kg / 62lb and can withstand 65mph winds.

Pole raisers are only really useful if they don't move when touched by the horse. This is for two reasons. The first very obviously is that, if you are working by yourself, you would need to dismount to relocate the poles if they were getting regularly moved but, more importantly, if a horse kicks a raised pole that doesn't move he knows where the boundary is and will make an effort to draw his shoulders back and up to prevent touching it next time. Pole raisers are easy to make out of 4x4in square posts purchased from a local wood merchant by cutting them into 30cm / 1ft foot segments and then sawing out a 5x10cm / 2x4in section where the pole will rest. These pole raisers are inexpensive and will rarely move if a horse kicks the pole.

20. Essential wing weights.

21. Homemade pole raisers.

22. Dressage boards used as ground-lines.

Dressage boards. Triangular free-standing plastic dressage boards are a versatile addition to your equipment for many reasons:

- Marking out an area such as a dressage arena, corners or an exercise with boundaries.
- Creating safe tramlines either side of a fence to ensure straightness.
- To trot over, set at 1.10m / 3.5ft apart.
- As a safe ground-line in front or behind a fence.

Short telescopic training flag posts with plastic flags are an essential addition to your equipment when training the event horse to be straight, accurate and comfortable with narrow areas. The main reason for using the plastic flags is that they are safe, non-threatening and won't break or splinter if a horse were to hit them hard. Using flags with narrow fences creates a boundary that is very clear to the horse, therefore backing up your disciplined system.

Corner cups. Having an adapted cup that can offer a place for two poles to sit is a very useful and inexpensive piece of equipment to help train the event horse.

Simulated cross-country fences are non-threatening, often quite small and are a great way of coaching 'good association' by allowing the horse to come to no harm whilst challenging technical lines. These cross-country lines, which are discussed in Chapters 8 and 9, are a way of training the partnership to read different questions that they are likely to come across on track.

23 & 24. Short telescopic plastic training flag with a corner cup, manufactured by Jump4Joy.

Practising challenge will breed confidence into horse and rider which, in return, will promote positive course-walking and riding.

Cavalletti. Portable cavalletti are extremely useful as a training aid. Throughout the book I refer to cavalletti use: although small jumps can have the same impact, they are just more work to set up. Cavalletti can be set up using three different heights, the lowest at 15cm / 6in for raised pole work, the middle height, which is approximately 38cm / 15in, and the top height of 43–50cm / 17–20in that would be used for canter work. They are an extremely versatile training aid used for all different levels and abilities, but ideally the ones that split apart from the pole if a young horse gets his legs in a muddle are the safest to use. (As a matter of interest, since it's not widely known, cavalletti is a plural and an individual one of these is correctly known as a cavalletto. This is the term used later in reference to a single one, when discussing various exercises with this equipment.)

25. Cavalletti used on the smallest height for raised poles. Note how this exercise encourages the engagement and push from the hind limbs to raise the shoulders.

Chapter 4

Annual Training Plans

4.1 Planning the workload

Planning your horse's daily, weekly, monthly and annual workload should be done with a lot of thought and preparation. If you take an average of five weeks off in your horse's work through the twelve-month period, which allows for snow, Christmas, enforced and off-season rest, then an average of ten days competing and one day off a week, this leaves you with 272 riding days. Within those days your horse will need approximately twenty fast work days either galloping, swimming or on a treadmill, which leaves you 250 training days a year. Breaking each week up into different work is essential for the horse's physical and mental state and how it's done should vary depending on the time of year. However, using the following categories will help you plan the workload. By putting your training sessions into categories you will maximise the development of your horse, and it will ensure that you plan and prepare your sessions wisely.

- Learning a new skill.
- 'Taking the horse to the gym.'
- Practising a skill within the comfort zone.
- Recreational riding and relaxation.
- Fitness and stamina work.

Winter is a good time to look at your own positional weaknesses and start to focus on yourself as an athlete...

'Your major training rule should be that you always come out of a jumping session having improved the flatwork.'

26. Trotting over a raised board is part of 'taking the horse to the gym' training.

4.2 'Taking the horse to the gym'

This is a phrase that I use for low-impact muscle-building work twice weekly through the winter work and once a week in the competition season. After a 20-minute warm-up routine that should consist of transitions, stretching with circle work, 4–5 minutes of canter work with some transitions within the gait and some comfort zone lateral work, give your horse a minute or two to breathe before starting the gym work. Using specific exercises relevant to your horse, start with one exercise repeated on both reins four or five times before moving on to another exercise that will use a different band of muscles. Repeat on each rein (duration depending on fitness), then move on to another less demanding exercise before giving your horse a break. By moving from one exercise to another you will allow the horse's muscles to get some relief, but will still be improving fitness and stamina. One of the exercises should involve raised poles or boards, one should involve transitions at a specific marker and the third exercise should involve changes of direction for suppleness. Using different floor plans is a good way of thinking outside the box and developing your own ingenuity. This type of work is also classed as *circuit training* and, if performed correctly, it will have a big impact on your horse's movement, stamina and outlook on his work. Once the main part of your training is completed, use a warming-down technique that again suits your horse to take his heart rate and muscle use down to a more idling state so that he finishes his work in no discomfort and in a relaxed state of mind.

Warm-ups

Wherever possible, use the same warming-up and warming-down routine for your other riding days and this will bring routine and continuity into your horse's training which, by association, will develop confidence and contentment in his work. If you are at a competition where there is a lot of atmosphere and possibly tension, using a familiar routine will put your horse back at ease and into the right mental state to perform. Changing your normal work routine can have a detrimental effect on performance and should be avoided if at all possible.

4.3 The training seasons

Splitting the year into different training seasons is a good way of developing a structure into the work plan. Although every day should be a progression there are different periods during the year when new skills are introduced and other periods when practising excellence within a comfort zone is of the utmost importance for confidence. There are times within the competition season when tapering the workload has a huge benefit to performance, and other times when tick-over work is useful. Generally speaking, the ground is quite good within the early spring events but, as the summer creeps in, the ground can get firmer and not always suit all horses. It is important to keep the option of having a short period away from competition mid-season to avoid potential concussive injuries.

4.3a End of season rest period

The timing of this and the actual extent of a rest period will ultimately depend on specific circumstances such as age of the horse, any minor injuries that have occurred, turnout facilities available, the following year's season plan and any other domestic issues. A rough guide to time off is as follows:

A sound, lower-level horse who has finished with a strenuous long format should have three weeks completely off work and three weeks coming back in slow work. This should be slow hacking and strengthening walk and trot work.

A sound, higher-level horse who has finished with a strenuous long format should have three weeks off and four weeks coming back in slow work.

A sound horse who has had a continuous season with short formats should have two weeks off and two to three weeks back in slow work.

Horses who have had an intermittent season because of interruptions won't have a necessity for time off as long as the work doesn't include strenuous, high-impact work.

4.3b Winter work (11–12 weeks)

In the UK this period will generally run from the middle of November through to mid-January. It is an ideal time to train new skills and use low-impact, high-strengthening work to develop the core muscles ready to move on to the faster work in February. Training new skills may require two to three days of intensive work, so allowing the horse to have a physical and mental rest for a couple of days following is ideal. This allows muscles to repair and time for the skill to be absorbed before practising it again. The work programme needs to relate to the results of the performance profile and the aim would be to strip some of the skills down and improve them in small increments so that the

27. Road work is very important when getting the horse fit.

overall quality improves in the long term. Winter is a good time to look at your own positional weaknesses and start to focus on yourself as an athlete by getting into a fitness programme that suits your lifestyle, which you can manage to keep up throughout the year.

A typical winter work week would be:

- Day 1. 'Taking the horse to the gym' day.
- Day 2. Skill training.
- Day 3. Skill training/practice.
- Day 4. Relaxation riding day.
- Day 5. 'Taking the horse to the gym' day.
- Day 6. Rest day or relaxation riding day.
- Day 7. Skill training.

This will often need a Plan B approach with weather conditions varying – however, try to stick to a programme wherever possible.

4.3c Spring preparation (6 weeks)

Depending on the planned start of your season you will need to add a fast work aspect to your winter training plan. The ideal length of time to build up to your first event is a six-week period, which will allow for eight to nine fast work sessions with a built-in 'buffer' week to allow for any poor weather conditions or minor injuries that may occur – so ideally during mid-January if you are planning to start at the first event of the season in March. Everyone will have a different method of getting their horses fit depending on age, facilities, level of competition, etc. Plan your individual programme to be specific to your horse and your circumstances. Here are some basic rules that will help maximise fitness training:

★ Plan your fast work with another horse and rider partnership. This will allow you to teach your horse to want to gallop alongside another horse, therefore increasing his natural stamina and work ethic. If he is naturally quite lively and forward-thinking it is a good time to take him as lead horse and use the session as control work.

★ Use the fast work session to train your horse to move up and down the gears, noting how many strides it takes you to go from a top speed down to a short, energetic, rounder stride. Practise using preparation points so your horse gets to recognise your 'top speed' position and your preparation point position with shoulders and eyes coming up.

★ To help with your own strength, practise your fast work with your stirrups shorter. This will help you develop more balance over the top of the withers, security through your lower legs and mobility through the hip, knee and ankle joints.

- ★ Try to do your fast work training every fourth day to maximise fitness levels without putting undue stress on your horse's body.
- ★ Try to vary the fast work to include short sprints and longer, slower work sessions but always make sure there is a full warm-up and cool down session.

Alongside introducing the faster work sessions you will also need to use these six weeks to prepare for the first events. This will include:

- ▸ Practising dressage test riding with feedback from coach/judge.
- ▸ Practising in the showjumping ring under competition atmosphere.
- ▸ Cross-country schooling on grass, with undulations and different footing.

A typical working fortnight within the spring preparation training may look like this:

- ▸ Day 1. 'Taking the horse to the gym' session with some small jumping exercises.
- ▸ Day 2. Fitness day.
- ▸ Day 3. Relaxation riding day.
- ▸ Day 4. Dressage training, test riding practise.
- ▸ Day 5. Jump training skills day.
- ▸ Day 6. Fitness day.
- ▸ Day 7. Relaxation riding day, or day off.
- ▸ Day 8. Flatwork skills training session.
- ▸ Day 9. Showjumping competition: two classes.
- ▸ Day 10. Fitness day.
- ▸ Day 11. Flatwork and 'taking the horse to the gym' session.

28a. Fast work on an artificial surface.

28b. Fast work on grass.

- Day 12. Cross-country schooling session.
- Day 13. Day off.
- Day 14. Fitness day.

So there's a lot to fit in …

Going into your season confidently is down to correct foundations, structured winter training, getting the fitness levels up to requirements and keeping the skills simple. Try not to overload the workload, which can cause soreness in the horse and induce a poor work ethic.

4.3d Maintenance at short format throughout the season (ongoing)

Once the competition season has commenced it is a time to use the short format competitions as training events leading up to your main goal. To keep the learning progressive and to make improvements throughout the season you need to have a strict process of positive reflection and feedback that you can use continuously to update your training plan. This is part of performance-profiling that is done throughout the year, which we will look at in Chapter 9 *Training to Win*. The workload changes slightly during the competition season and the training turns into formulating what will be your competition practice.

There are no hard or fast rules as to how many events you ought to do, as this will depend on age and level of the horse, but a typical competition programme is fortnightly intervals at the beginning of the season and, when into a regular routine or if the ground starts to firm up, a competition every three weeks. This gives you an adequate opportunity to keep progressing the training alongside a fitness level that doesn't increase; it should just stay at a maintenance level.

A personalised routine needs to develop leading up to a competition that prepares your horse to perform at his absolute best on the competition day, and it may be different for each individual. This might include some fast work four days before the competition, ensuring that it is done using ground conditions that are suitable and not too firm. Also some good-quality skill training, which may include transition work, centre line training, practising movements that are in your test and generally working on accuracy and suppleness. A quiet day to allow the horse to go to the event feeling comfortable in his muscles and looking forward to his work, and a jumping session either one or two days before the event to get the partnership's eye in, to open the jumping muscles and to back up the confidence levels, are other requirements. The jump training session needs to be non-threatening and not too technical, but it may be useful to get the height up with some straightforward exercises with which both you and your horse are confident. Tapering the work by giving the horse a few days to a week off any sort of strenuous work – even giving some field rest – can have a positive impact on performance. During the 2020 competition season, when it stagnated because of the coronavirus pandemic, the workload became very light through the summer months and riders either let their horses down or focused a lot on the training programme that would normally be conducted in the winter. The result was that, when competitions resumed, the performance overall was a lot higher than usual, partly because of the focus on training but mainly because the horses had had lighter work and were feeling rested. There was definitely a lot to learn from that period and allowing the horse regular rest from periods of hard work has, in most cases, a very positive impact.

4.3e Building up to a long format or championship event (6 weeks)

This is another part of the training plan and workload during the competition season. In the UK, long format competitions don't usually start until May, and run through to October, whereas in other parts of Europe and elsewhere in the world they are in the FEI calendar as early as March and will run through to November and December. Whatever main goal you choose, if it is a long format it will require a six-week period of progressively increasing the fitness workload to cope with the extra time on the cross-country. Long format fitness training needs to be the basis of your training programme, with the other training sessions fitted around it. It can become quite difficult to fit all the training sessions into your plan, so you have to be strict in order not to overload the training schedule and ensure that your flatwork training is done within the realms of all your other work. By focusing on the quality of the work and having the discipline to do 1 minute of flatwork, including a transition to trot, to walk and to a square halt after every jumping exercise, you can move your dressage score percentage up really efficiently.

4.4 Trot-up training

A very important area to introduce into your weekly training schedule is practising the trot-up. This is obviously an essential phase of a long format competition, as well as useful for your home vet and farrier, and it is quite crucial to develop the training early on.

Make sure that you are using a suitable, flat surface with plenty of space. Have your horse in a snaffle bridle with the reins over his head and be on his left side, standing at his shoulder facing forwards. The skill is to get the horse to walk and trot alongside you by staying at his left shoulder, so practise initially by walking with a second person in a safe place far enough away on the right side with a very long schooling or piaffe whip. Every time you make a single click, get the other person to lightly flick the whip so as to touch the horse's hindquarters at exactly the same time. This process will create an association so that every time you make the click, the horse will expect a light flick from behind and should travel forward. Once this process is established in halt to walk and walk, try the same technique for the walk to trot transition. Soon the horse should become obedient to the click and your positioning without the second person behind – although backing up this training technique regularly would be important with an idle horse. Whilst trotting up in hand be mindful to look straight ahead, not at the horse. With your right hand, hold the reins doubled over and, with no actual contact, placed about 15cm / 6in underneath the horse's lower jaw.

When trotting on a road with a camber make sure that the horse gets the opportunity to trot in the centre and run yourself on the slope. When turning around, first make a smooth downward transition to walk, ensuring that the horse doesn't fall behind your body position, then turn towards the right so that the horse is between you and the observer. Sometimes it's a good idea to slowly raise your left arm in front of the horse's right side on the turn to keep the turn smooth then, making sure that you re-straighten the horse into the centre of the trot-up strip, use the click to repeat the process back again, this time trotting straight past the person observing wherever possible. The downward transition needs to be trained to be smooth and forward so the horse doesn't drop behind you, which can make a sound horse look unsound.

29. Running at the left shoulder with a relaxed rein under the jaw. Horse and rider looking forward. Horse trotting in the middle and the rider running on the camber.

Chapter 5

Responsibilities and Jumping Rules

Before we look at the first few training exercises, let's take a look at some of the responsibilities of the rider and the horse.

5.1 Rider's responsibility

- To offer clear training through a system of pressure and reward.
- To follow the scales of training principles.
- To offer helpful riding skills that aren't a hindrance to the horse in any way.
- To ride in a good balanced position, always using a focal point to maintain straightness.
- To offer direction with good preparation.
- To promote a level, rhythmical stride pattern on the approach to a fence.
- To set the gait and speed.
- To keep resetting a good balance, keeping the horse in a 'box'.

5.2 Horse's responsibility

- To be obedient and accept instructions – *trained* skill.
- To react to ongoing situations using natural ability and *trained* skills.
- Desire to put effort in to please the rider – *training* the attitude to work.

Training your eyes to look beyond the fence will give you all sorts of additional skills.

5.3 Rider's position and rules for jumping

Learning to develop your own 'feel' to a fence is something that we are always building on. Riding styles are very habitual and it's very important that you keep revisiting your 'rules' to make little improvements whilst working with your horse daily. By making these small changes in training they will filter through to your competitions and you will start to feel the major benefits.

Head and eyes

Training your eyes to look beyond the fence will give you all sorts of additional skills. First, it will prevent you from focusing completely on the approach, which can get any rider anxious about being on the perfect stride pattern. Being stride-obsessive has a detrimental effect on the natural rhythm and prevents the horse from reading the fence for himself. Keeping your eyes up will, in turn, keep your head up and immediately that will enable your upper body to be in a better balance on landing and this will help you ride onto your next line effectively. This will bring many advantages, including time consumption in competition, staying on the ideal line and a quicker recovery on the landing side. To help you develop the process of keeping your eyes up, always decide upon a focal point beyond the fence whilst on the approach so even if things don't go quite to plan you are in a good solid position and can have your thoughts on the next line.

30. This is a sequence of images demonstrating the importance of keeping your head up and your eyes on the next fence. As the horse takes off at the 'A' element the rider has her eyes firmly on the line of the approach to the 'B' element.

31 & 32. Throughout the landing the rider demonstrates a longer rein length, a strong lower leg position and maintains secure eyes. Whilst the horse is working for her balance in the water the rider allows time but is continually looking at the next element.

33. Although the rider has moved her outside rein towards the withers to manoeuvre the shoulder through the turn she is showing a weakness with her inside hand that has risen up through the aid. This can be detrimental and cause the horse to run through the left shoulder.

34. A successful completion of the question. However, you can see how the inside (right) rein has become stronger than the loose outside rein, which is releasing the outside shoulder in a detrimental way. This is a 'work-on' for this rider.

Responsibilities and Jumping Rules

Rein length

Rein length is very important as it will affect your body position and the pressure applied to the bit. Allowing the reins to slip out slightly longer after the preparation area will allow the horse's nose to go out to the fence and prevent him leaning into the reins and rushing. With slightly longer reins your body will have more independence in the air and, more crucially, you won't get pulled forwards on landing. With shorter reins the upper body will follow the horse's shoulders down. Your horse will jump much better with a horizontally positioned neck on the approach to the fence.

Photo 35 shows the rider keeping his elbows locked and reins short, which takes away the horse's natural balance of being able to use his neck and back correctly.

35 & 36. These two images demonstrate what can happen with the rider's balance if the reins are too short whilst jumping.

Photo 36 shows how the rider gets pulled forwards with the tight reins on the landing, which acts as a fulcrum as the lower leg becomes weak and slips back.

37. This rider shows how the longer length of rein still maintains a great connection but allows her balance to stay correct as the horse negotiates the landing in the water.

The single-bridged rein

If you struggle to maintain a regular, even contact on the approach to a fence, putting a bridge in your reins will often help. You make a single bridge by crossing or folding the extra length of rein from one hand and placing it under the opposite hand so that both the reins are linked together with a slack section of rein. Straight away you will find that the turning aid alters slightly as you use both reins together at the withers. To turn right, for example, your right hand will open slightly and your left hand will follow towards the withers as the hands work as a pair rather than independently. Your upper body will alter slightly too as your shoulders become more influential as you turn with your rein aid to the new direction. With all three of those aids coming into play you will find your horse much more willing to turn.

Lower legs and stirrup length

The strength and security of lower legs comes with practice, discipline, a stirrup length that suits your conformation and finally a saddle will play an important role in your balance so it is important to find one that suits your thigh length. Having a saddle that is too short for your thighs, or knee rolls that have big blocks in front of your knees, will encourage a knee pivot and an automatic slipping of the lower legs. In this situation, to create a secure lower leg position you will need to open the knees significantly to prevent a pivot. The strength of a lower leg ultimately comes with lots of practice and a thought process on the last few strides towards the fence. I would encourage any rider to put effort into their leg position once the focal point has been picked up. Initially a large

Responsibilities and Jumping Rules

38. The single bridge. This was a tight-turning fence and the rider demonstrated the turning aid of the horse's withers before the nose. Both reins work in unison. The lower leg is secure and the rider is showing the intent of direction with her bodyweight to the inside.

proportion of the brain will need to be on the thought process of knees and toes turning out slightly on the take-off, with more weight going down the inside heels. Slowly, after lots of self-discipline, it will become a natural correct habit and you won't need to put any thought into it. You should play around with stirrup length until you find a comfortable place that suits your conformation and balance.

Using intention with your body

Having a forward intention with your legs and soft rein aids will always produce a happy horse who wants to jump. Using an upper body direction by turning your shoulders, head and pelvis to the new direction will show an intention to the horse, and a slight lean inwards to a turn will encourage a definition of where you want to go.

5.4 The three points of approach

To become more systematic in your approach to a fence follow these three simple points, which are fairly failsafe and will also create a routine for your horse.

The preparation point

39. The preparation point. This rider is demonstrating going from top speed to a canter where the hind legs become engaged and the withers raise up. You can see how the rider's body becomes taller.

This is the area where you tell your horse that a fence is coming up. In the showjumping ring it is done in a subtle way within your stride length and it may be just an engagement of the hind legs and a half-halt to calibrate the stride length. On the cross-country you will be going from top speed down the gears to the gait and speed suitable for jumping the obstacle. Whilst riding cross-country the point at which you do this preparation will depend on different factors. These include the experience and balance of your horse, the terrain, the ground conditions, the point at which you are on the course and how your horse is feeling underneath you. The most important aspect is that, when you make a gear change, it must derive from your upper body becoming taller, by keeping the hands low into the withers area and the lower legs becoming active. This will allow your horse to engage his hind legs with a back position that is not inverted or hollow, which should promote a better-quality jump.

The turning point

This is the point where you create a line of approach that is correct for that fence and beyond. Using an active inside leg into the turn will allow your horse to have the quality and power in the canter, then a supporting outside leg out of the turn will help hold the line across the fence. Keeping your hands together and low, turn the withers before the nose, then allow the horse to pull his nose out once the turn is completed. This method ensures that you get the horse's shoulders around the turn and gives the horse great balance to complete the approach.

The focal point is the area that your eyes should pick up beyond the fence on the turn. If you stare at something in the distance it will keep your eyes up, your body in a good position, create awareness of any deviation on the line and help you ride away from the fence efficiently.

Chapter 6

Training to Learn Exercises

The first training year of the horse's career is vital to his performance and ability to learn new skills later on in his competition life. As previously mentioned, the process of pressure and reward or release is essential to whether a horse understands the question. Think carefully before you apply aids.

In this training to learn section we will look at various exercises that will help you develop the fundamental building blocks essential for event horses and riders to build on as they progress through the levels. The list of skills is very long, but the starting points are as follows:

- Staying level in a rhythm when judging distance.
- Maintaining straightness.
- Transitions within a gait.
- Developing effective hoof-brain coordination.
- Staying in balance in different frames.
- Taking off and landing on the corresponding line.
- Holding a line with support aids.
- Negotiating narrow fences.
- Directional changes when negotiating an obstacle.
- Landing on a preferred lead.

*Remember, whilst training, challenge yourself **always** to finish each period of work, however long or short, with a transition to trot to walk and then into a square halt before relaxing the aids. This will breed discipline and a naturally correct halt as long as you ride it through from the hind legs to the front.*

Check your own balance and position by doing some canter work without stirrups.

Building distances accurately

As a prerequisite for building exercises it is crucial that you get your showjumping walking step calibrated to a yard (3ft / 90cm). The common denominator for the stride length of a horse in the showjumping arena is 4yds (12ft / 3.65m). If you regularly walk correct competition distances in a showjumping arena you will get a feel for what a yard in distance is like, but it is good to calibrate your steps occasionally over a long distance to make sure that your distances are accurate.

> ### Exercise
> Use a tape measure and mark out a distance of say, 24yds / 22m. Then walk the distance over and over again until 24 steps become comfortable each time. Then, from a pole on the ground, walk a distance of what you believe to be 24yds / 22m then, using your tape measure, record the correct distance to see how accurate you have been.

Exercises are only worthwhile and productive if they are done with thought, planning, preferably some way of measuring the success of the work and then reflection before moving on. So I have put my exercises in a simple format:

1. Understanding the reasons and outcomes of the exercise.
2. Setting up the floor plan.
3. The warm-up, build-up and correct introduction.
4. Working through the exercise.
5. How the exercise relates to competition.

6.1 Developing stride length

One of the most important skills that an event horse has to master is the ability to alter his frame and stride length either from a short stride to a controlled and balanced expansion, or from a top-speed gallop down through the gears to a round, soft, engaging power stride with obedience and yielding. This has eventually to become seamless and almost instantaneous, with minimal pressure from the rider, so it's important to start the process very early on in the event horse's development. It should be initiated with half-halts and be built up in an everyday training plan on the flat, using poles and training jumps. The focus should be on the rhythm, balance and levelness within the step through the change in the stride length. The following exercises will help this process.

6.1a Developing stride variation

This exercise is designed to develop the rider's 'feel' for stride length, eye for a pattern, and rhythm. It will teach the horse to be obedient, stay level and develop different

Training to Learn Exercises

canters for all disciplines. It is also great for fitness work for the horse. In a 20x40m arena, one circuit equates to 120m / 132yds, and ten circuits around the arena to 1.2km (about three-quarters of a mile). Repeating ten times on both reins without a break (twenty times in all) would be a good stamina test for the horse and excellent for the rider without stirrups.

You can turn this into a reaction skill by someone else deciding how many strides (stride number) you are going to fit in between the two poles just as you pass over the centre line. This develops a skill in which you interpret an instruction and react immediately by changing the canter before you reach the first pole (see set-up and equipment below).

The beauty of this exercise is that it takes little equipment, can be done in any size arena of 40m length or more and it can have a high impact of training if executed successfully.

Set-up and equipment
Start by laying four poles around the arena on small blocks so the poles don't move, two on each long side opposite each other so the distance in between is identical down each long side. Leave at least 10–12m / 11–13yds from each corner to be able to ride a good turn.

Warming up
First develop a good working canter and, using your core and balance to encourage the horse to keep the pole in the middle of his stride, canter over both sets of poles down each long side. Whatever stride pattern you put in on one side, match it with the opposite side. This will ensure that you develop a rhythmical and level canter with an even length of stride.

Working the exercise
Once you are satisfied that the canter is balanced and level, start to shorten the canter stride on one side and lengthen on the other. For example, if you start with eight strides on each side move to develop nine on one side and seven on the other. If you lose the balance at any time, go back to the eight on both sides again. Then work towards ten and six. The alteration of the stride length needs to be whilst passing over the centre line so that it is established by the first pole and should not change for the whole line.

Relevance to competition
This exercise relates to competition when you need to have the correct stride length for the profile of the fence in the showjumping arena and, more importantly, on the cross-country.

40. This image demonstrates the collected canter required for ten strides between the poles.

41. This image demonstrates the more extended canter required for the six strides between the poles.

Training to Learn Exercises

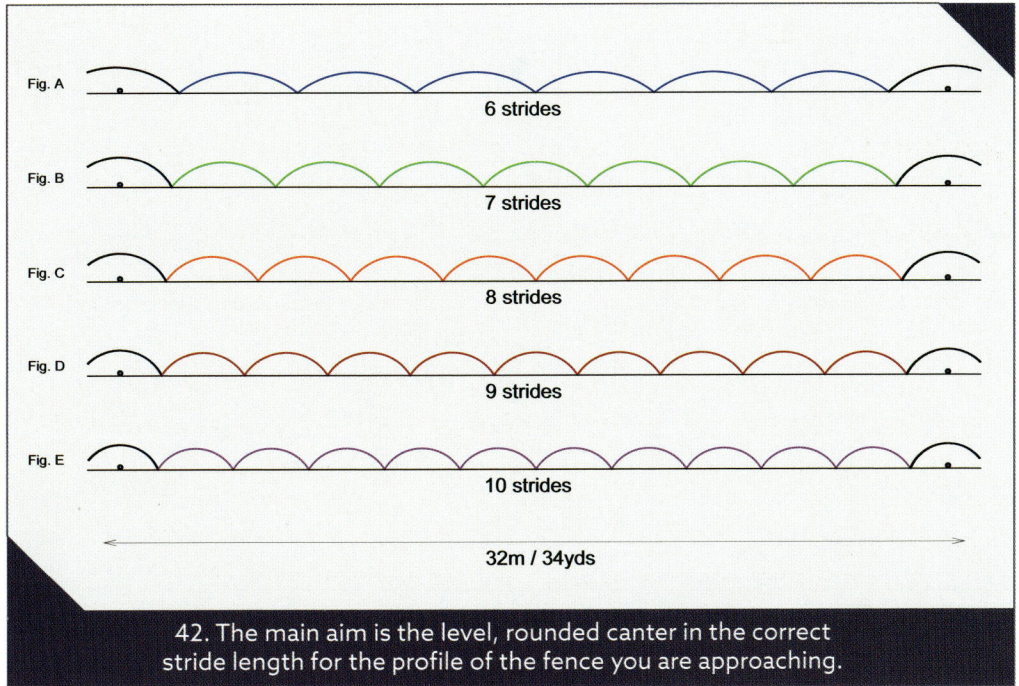

42. The main aim is the level, rounded canter in the correct stride length for the profile of the fence you are approaching.

6.1b Raised canter poles on a circle

This exercise can be used in any arena size of 20x20m and above. It is a multi-discipline exercise to develop the rider's reactions, the horse's obedience and athletic ability and is a great exercise to do when you want to add something extra to your flatwork session.

Set-up and equipment
You will need nine poles, three placed on each third of a 20–30m circle, (see diagram 43) preferably on small blocks to prevent unnecessary movement.

Have three poles set at a working canter distance 2.7m / 3yds apart at their middles (on a curve following the circumference of the circle so you can choose an inside, middle or outside line). The next three poles need to be set a third of the circle away on a collected canter distance of 2.3m / 2.5yds in the middle and the third set of poles need to be set at a medium canter distance of 3.2m / 3.5yds in the middle of each pole.

Warming up
This should involve some suppling work such as serpentines, smaller circles and leg-yielding to produce some engagement and connection. Use lots of transition work to refresh the half-halt aids before starting the exercise.

Working the exercise
First do this exercise in trot, making sure the horse puts two steps of trot between each pole, which requires you to ensure that you change the length of each step for each set

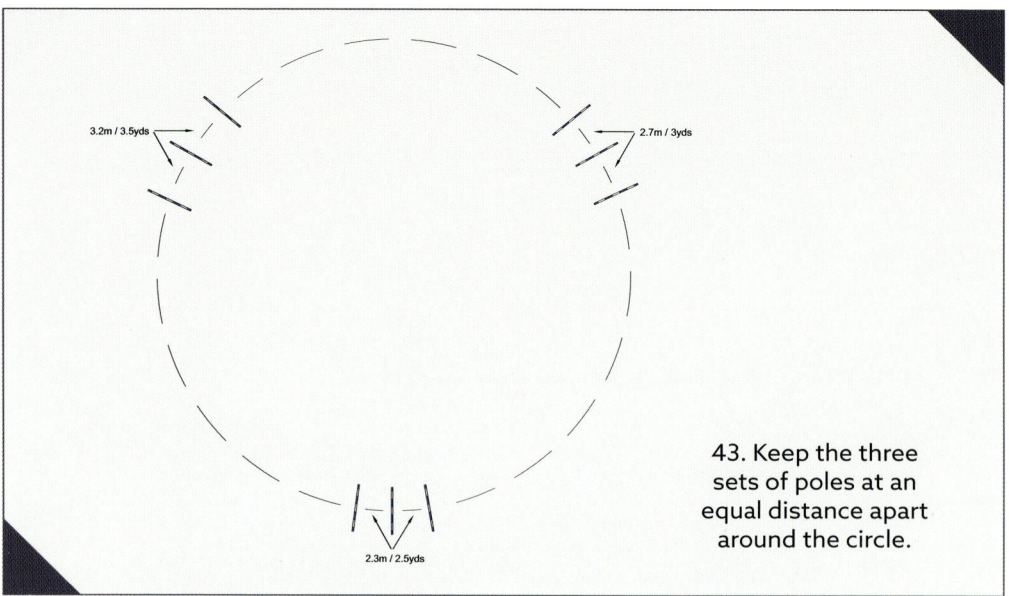

43. Keep the three sets of poles at an equal distance apart around the circle.

of poles accordingly. Then, after developing some transition work and warming up in canter outside of the exercise, start the circle in canter with the working canter poles, then move on to the collected canter poles and then the medium canter poles, which brings you immediately back to the working canter poles. The success of the exercise relies on riding a smooth transition to the new canter as soon as you've gone over the last pole of your current circuit. Use your shoulders and seat aids to influence the canter before using the rein aid. If the horse loses balance, drops behind your leg, or rushes into the contact, re-establish the canter outside of the exercise before starting again. The more advanced way of riding the exercise is to go from working to medium back to collection, so do it this way after establishing this progression on the easier rein first. Keeping your eyes up will help develop more 'feel' and spatial awareness (see photos 44, 45 & 46).

Relevance to competition

This exercise relates to competition when you have to make effective gear changes in the showjumping arena, and develops the transitions for the dressage arena and obedience and reactions for the cross-country. By having the poles fixed on blocks it will develop a good hoof/brain coordination and encourage the horse to become more careful and independent.

6.1c Four-stride exercise

This is a flatwork and jumping-based exercise that I encourage riders to do regularly in their training. It has lots of advantages, such as improving reaction skills, developing engagement, energy, balance and suppleness. It also heightens awareness of different canters.

Training to Learn Exercises

44. Training the shorter stride using the poles set at 2.3m / 2.5yds. Note that the rider is looking at the poles, which is incorrect.

45. Showing an 'uphill' working canter with the raised poles set at 2.7m / 3yds. The rider looks to the new direction.

46. The poles set at 3.2m / 3.5yds show how the exercise helps to raise the shoulders in the medium canter.

Set-up and equipment
There are no props at all to this exercise and it can be ridden anywhere suitable such as an arena, field, gallops or even out hacking on suitable ground.

Warming up
Make sure you and your horse are sufficiently warmed up for this exercise as it is mentally and physically tough. The warm-up needs to consist of regular little transitions, half-halts and balancing work. I would often work the horse laterally with some leg-yield and shoulder-in to prepare him for the positioning in the downward transitions.

Working the exercise
Start by using some half-halts within the working canter and ride some shorter strides every time you pass A, B, C and E. (If you are riding in a field or elsewhere, pick out suitable landmarks.) Then, when you have produced a good canter that has self-carriage, start to ride four strides of collected canter followed by four strides of working canter followed by four of medium canter then back through four of working canter and four of collected canter, then immediately repeat moving through collected, working, medium, working and back to collected. Your horse will start to get used to the pattern of the exercise and anticipate, which enables you to use more subtle and lighter aids. Initially, make the change of stride length just a little longer or shorter either side of the working canter, but as you get more skilled at this exercise the collected and medium strides become more pronounced. You can do this exercise around the arena or within school movements, depending on your horse's balance.

Relevance to competition
The exercise relates to competition through the quality of transitions in the dressage test, gear changes for both jumping disciplines and the development of the softness required in good downward transitions to keep the horse obedient within his work. I call this procedure 'refreshing the canter' and it's great to get the horse mentally ready for the first fence or cantering down the centre line.

6.1d Developing the jumping canter – three cavalletti
When we train horses to jump into a related distance we are aiming to jump in with a level canter at the appropriate length of stride for the distance. If we jump in too short the horse has to expand out and the rider will lose control. This exercise coaches the rider to control stride length through a related distance with the upper body and core, and thus to train the horse to become obedient and balanced on the landing side of a fence. It is one of my favourite exercises to develop any level of rider and horse and has multiple uses.

Set-up and equipment
Place three cavalletti in a straight line with 15m / 16yds) between each, setting the height on the tallest at approximately 50cm / 20in).

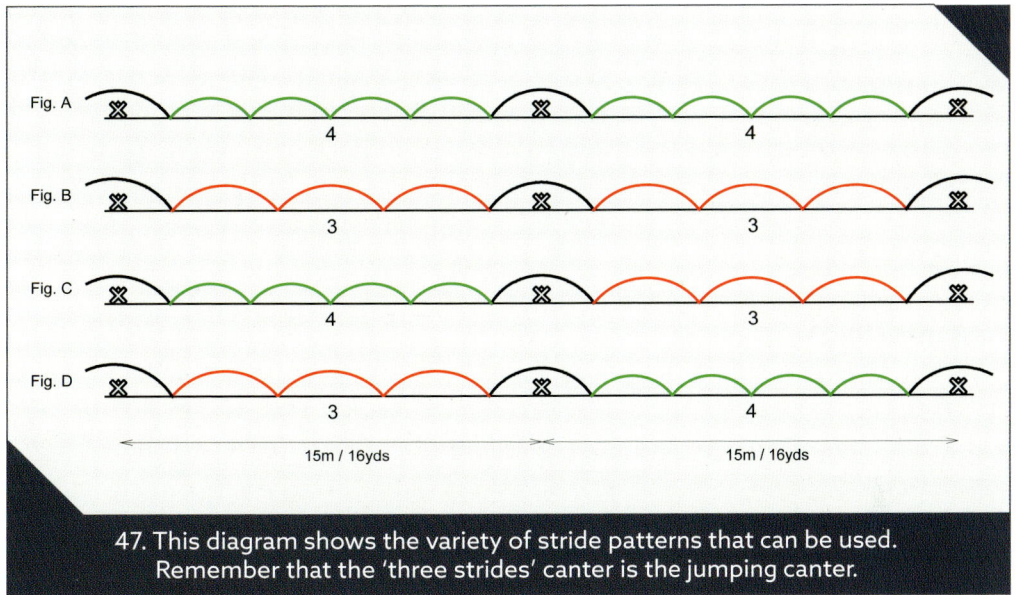

47. This diagram shows the variety of stride patterns that can be used. Remember that the 'three strides' canter is the jumping canter.

Warming up
Warm up your horse for the jumping exercise through the usual 20-minute routine, making sure you have focused on transitions within the gait. Allow the horse to canter over all three cavalletti in a good working canter, allowing him to make his own decisions on stride pattern and canter length (see diagram 47).

Working the exercise
Ride the exercise in a straight line and work in either a shorter frame to put *four* level strides in between each of the cavalletti or a longer frame to put *three* level strides in between each. Work hard on the shorter strides being level, rounder and high-powered without expanding. Work hard on the longer strides being up to the bridle and connected across the back without becoming flat or on the forehand. Use seat and shoulder aids that relate to each canter: upright dressage seat for the shorter strides and a lighter, softer, allowing position for the longer ones.

Once you have mastered both of the canters, develop an exercise with three strides between the first and second of the cavalletti and four strides between the second and third. The success of this exercise is about having a big enough canter into the first element so that the horse covers the ground to become closer to the second element, so that you can adopt the 'four-canter' position and land in the 'four-canter' rather than landing in the big canter then trying to control the stride. If you have a slow-reacting horse you can also teach him to expand if needed by jumping into the distance in the four strides and jumping out in three strides.

Relevance to competition

This exercise relates to top competition when the course designer gives you a big, soft-profile fence into a distance then asks you to have maximum control on the landing to make a turn to an accuracy fence. If you jump into this type of combination in a canter that is too short you will either have to add a stride for control or, in most cases, the horse will have to expand to get the distance out, therefore you are likely to lose control and balance on the landing which, in turn, will make the turn to the second element difficult. Training the horse to jump into the distance in a big canter but land immediately in a balanced short frame will give you a great tool for cross-country riding at all levels.

6.1e Raised trotting poles on a circle

This is an exercise that develops a degree of suppleness, tests accuracy and produces forward-thinking transitions. I would use it as a warm-up exercise before jumping, or just as one of the weekly gym exercises.

Set-up and equipment

Set out five to eight raised poles, 5cm / 2in off the ground, or use the triangular dressage boards on the outer arc of an 18–20m circle (or larger for the younger or less balanced horse). Because the poles are on a circle their inner aspects should be set at approximately 1.05m / 3.4ft apart, so that the centres will be at approximately 1.10m / 3.5ft and the outer aspects at 1.15m / 3.8ft apart.

Warming up

Before doing any work that involves raised poles/boards it's important to have your horse fully warmed up through his muscles and using his full range of movement, as this exercise will often ask him to reach and stretch. Pay particular attention to good-quality circles, riding marker accuracy and an awareness of equal number of strides either side.

Working the exercise

Start by riding a circle around the poles and making progressive walk, trot and canter transitions to create obedience and engagement of the hind legs. Then, in a working trot and making sure that you ride the correct size circle, introduce the poles, ensuring that you ride to every pole in exactly the same part of the pole as the previous pole so that the circle doesn't go off line. After trotting over the last raised pole, prepare for and pick up a working canter. Canter the circle until an appropriate point where you have enough time to do the downward transition and prepare for the first pole again.

Training to Learn Exercises

48. A drone image of the exercise set up, showing the transition areas.

49. A young horse trotting over raised boards on a circle to improve suppleness.

Regularly change the rein by going out of the circle area and refreshing the gait with some medium work. The exercise can also be used with other transitions, for example, after the poles, balance the canter and ride a trot to walk to halt transition. Ride three or four steps of rein-back then move straight forward into trot and go to the first pole again.

Relevance to competition
This exercise tests accuracy of the strides, which is essential for all three phases. However, it really helps to get the horse accustomed to receiving aids to perform a transition at a particular place, which is essential for the dressage arena.

6.1f Suppleness and control: pole-parallel-pole related distance
This exercise needs to be kept quite small because it is fairly difficult to perform as it asks the horse to read a lot of distances, sit back on his hind legs, stretch across an oxer, and then it asks the horse to immediately maintain his balance on the landing and keep a short, round stride. It teaches the horse to develop his hoof-brain coordination and it prevents the horse from expanding through a distance. I will often keep this grid at no more than 90cm / 3ft) even for a more advanced horse. I would specifically use it for horses who rush, lose their balance on landing or have particularly long strides, and need educating to become obedient and more adaptable on the landing. It is particularly good for training the rider to look up and use their upper body in a taller position that supports the horse's balance whilst approaching a fence. Horses who have a poor bascule will benefit from the poles either side of the parallel to help develop a better jumping profile.

Set-up and equipment
Build two small square parallels with a ground-pole either side in a straight line with a distance of 22m / 24yds between the two fences. Then, either side of each parallel, at 3m / 10ft, place a pole raised up off the ground by 5cm / 2in.

Warming up
Warm up the horse ready to jump and use some randomly placed poles in the arena to canter over, maintaining the rhythm and balance and focusing on the evenness of the strides. Use some transitions within the canter to produce engagement and softness in the work. Check your own balance and position by doing some canter work without stirrups.

Working the exercise
When ready to jump, start with one of the pole-jump-pole combinations by itself, by turning into it inside of the other fence. Focus on staying completely straight

Training to Learn Exercises

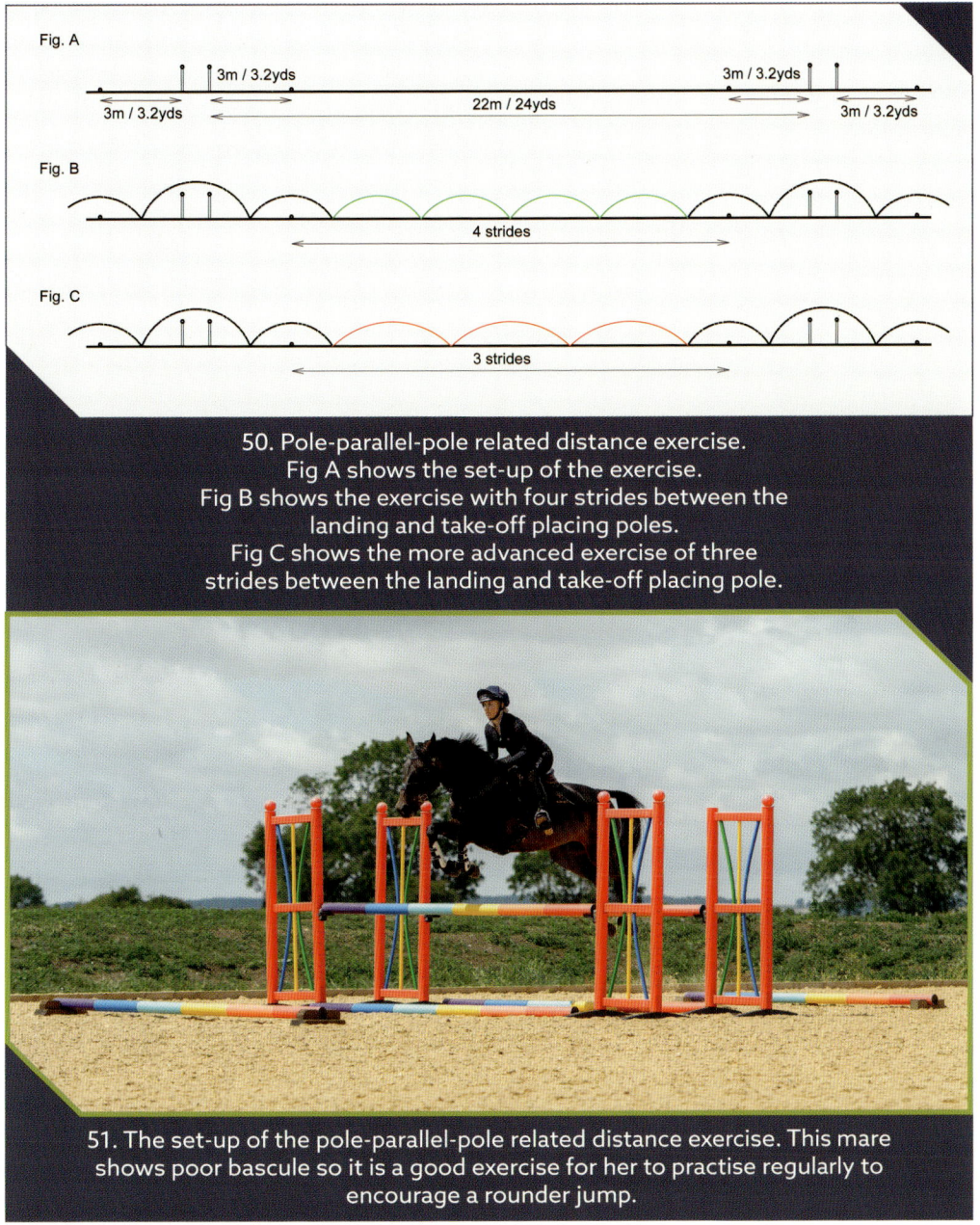

50. Pole-parallel-pole related distance exercise.
Fig A shows the set-up of the exercise.
Fig B shows the exercise with four strides between the landing and take-off placing poles.
Fig C shows the more advanced exercise of three strides between the landing and take-off placing pole.

51. The set-up of the pole-parallel-pole related distance exercise. This mare shows poor bascule so it is a good exercise for her to practise regularly to encourage a rounder jump.

throughout the approach, jump and getaway. Then build up to both fences in a straight line. You are aiming to jump the pole-fence-pole followed by four short strides before the second pole-fence-pole. What may happen is that the four strides will initially feel very short, but the more you practise the exercise the more the horse will recover his balance between the two fences. With the help of the landing poles you are teaching the horse to put six strides in the five-stride distance. In contrast to the above you may want to jump pole-fence-pole and move forward for the three strides between the two poles to land and expand, which is also an important skill.

Remember to keep a count of how many times you use the grid as it can be very demanding on the horse. I would suggest a maximum of five to seven times from each direction, with a small increase in the height of the fences if your horse is comfortable with the exercise. Straightness within this exercise is paramount; choose either the middle or inside of the midline and make sure you look through the line and keep your eye on a focal point. Using tramlines with this exercise would be an addition to the degree of difficulty.

The result of this exercise is having the ability in a 22m / 24yds distance to be able to land and move forward on five strides or land and have the obedience to put six strides in comfortably if this is ever necessary.

Relevance to competition

The exercise will relate to competition if the course designer gets you into a distance in a big canter from a forward previous distance, or from a wide fence followed by a shorter distance to a vertical. You will always need to land and collect or land and expand at some point whilst showjumping and cross-country riding.

6.2 Developing straightness

Teaching your horse to stay straight on a line, a curve, a circle or around a corner should be ongoing within your daily training. As your horse's trainer you need to be ultra-sensitive and aware of any loss of balance, wilful or not, which can lead to crookedness and evasion. The importance of staying straight and balanced in your own position and looking up through the horse's ears to a focal point of your choice is crucial as a rider. With the help of a coach, get familiar with your own positional faults and set up a system to help eradicate them. You may perhaps need to change your natural focal point, altering your comfortable seat positioning to something that feels less familiar. Use objects around your training area, such as a gate post or a dressage marker which, as you pass them, will remind you to physically correct your faults. Training yourself in this way will help your self-awareness and you will become more sensitive to your own immediate weaknesses.

Once you are riding straighter you can really start training your horse to put effort into his own balance. Using tramline poles in and out of the centre line will focus awareness of straightness and, as you move through these chapters, you will learn different exercises that will challenge and test ongoing straightness. This will help you achieve your competition goals.

Training to Learn Exercises

> To help correct a horse who doesn't naturally stay straight you need to use the pressure and reward aids. Create an equal feeling from left leg to left rein and right leg to right rein with the horse down the centre of your aids, hopefully in a balanced way. The pressure aids should be kept light if the straightness is maintained but, as soon as the balance wanders, the pressure aids should become stronger to correct and then lighten again when the horse has moved back onto his line. Remember, pressure and release/reward is the only training method that the horse understands.

6.2a Using tramlines

Tramlines should be used at all levels as they teach the horse to take off and land in the corresponding spot without moving to the left or right in the air. They are a great reminder for the rider to deliver the horse to the fence in a way that he is straight and balanced and continue riding the straight line well away from the fence. To perform this exercise successfully it is necessary to be riding with a level contact and have a secure focal point throughout the whole line.

Set-up and equipment

Initially it would be advantageous to do this exercise over poles in the trot before cantering to a small fence. The poles can be raised or on the ground, in a straight line or on a zigzag pattern and need to be approximately 1.05m / 3.4ft apart in the centre. Initially the tramlines should be approximately 15m / 16yds before and after the poles, sitting at only 1m / 3.3ft wide, so the line is quite long and the horse has to make an effort to maintain a straight line and balance. With more advanced horses you can place the tramlines closer to the poles/fence, as shown in the photograph. Have four wings ready for when you're ready to jump.

Warming up

Make sure that your horse is well warmed up ready for jumping, and use exercises that encourage you to ride straight lines to a focal point. Ideally use a square exercise (see Chapter 8 *Training to Compete Exercises*), or even do work on an inside track with lots of half-halts and transitions.

Working the exercise

Working on both reins and from both directions, ride through the line of the tramlines in, over the poles and through the tramlines out. Get ready to correct the horse's balance

Training to Win

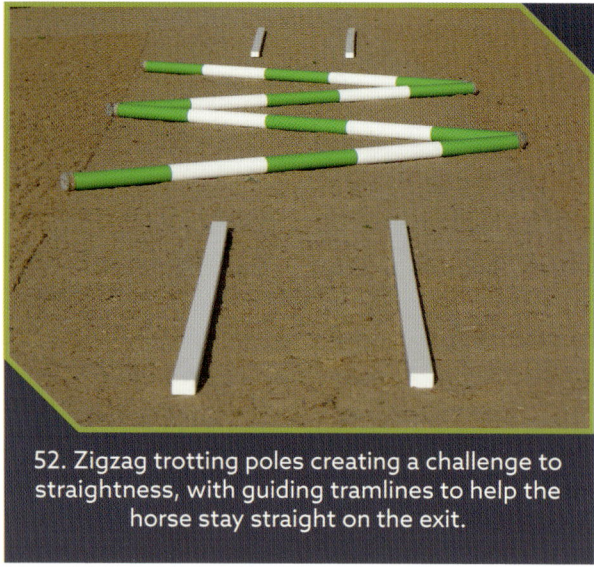

52. Zigzag trotting poles creating a challenge to straightness, with guiding tramlines to help the horse stay straight on the exit.

and straightness to either side immediately with the wall of aids (leg, seat bones and reins), which are light if he stays on his line but become more pressurised if you feel him starting to veer off the line. Once he is staying straight without too much help, change the poles to a small fence. Establish an active canter, focus on staying level within a good balance and ride through the tramlines to the fence, making sure that you land on the same line for the tramlines out. Build the fence up to a spread and maybe a double to make the exercise more challenging, but never allow the boundaries to change.

Relevance to competition

Clear rounds are built from correct approaches and a good balance, so this is the base exercise for all others to be built on. It is imperative that a horse can stay on a desired

53. Using tramlines to help the three straight strides: the take-off stride, the mid-flight stride and the landing stride.

line from the approach, mid-flight and on landing and getaway without drifting and losing balance.

6.2b Narrow poles to hold a line

This is an exercise to develop steering aids and a partnership between horse and rider. It secures an immense accuracy, discipline and strength in your core to hold a horse on a very narrow line of poles without allowing any deviation. It's a great warm-up exercise to switch on your muscles and mind before anything more challenging (see photo 54).

Set-up and equipment

Very simply you will need four wooden 90cm / 3ft half-round poles, preferably painted white (two will work just as well but it's more advantageous to have the lines down both long sides of the arena). Set the poles on a straight line 2m / 6.5ft in from the track or on the centre line with as much room between them as your arena allows.

Warming up

Keep to your normal warm-up routine but specifically focus on leg-yielding, both to develop the engagement and suppleness, but more importantly to get your horse within a good lateral connection.

Working the exercise

Ride over the two poles on a straight line, making sure that the turns both onto and off the line is are correct ninety-degree turns (see Chapter 8 *Training to Compete Exercises* parallel poles exercises) and work your horse in trot and canter on both reins. Once you are able to hold the line with no loss of balance or straightness you can start to test your own real accuracy by using different movements between the poles. In trot, start by riding straight over the first pole then turning into shoulder-in, paying particular attention to keeping the hind legs on the line between the poles before straightening up again for the second pole. This exercise challenges you to deliver the aids with the whole of your body and move the withers rather than just the horse's inside leg and losing the shoulder to the outside. Do the same with travers, really focusing on the horse's forelegs and face staying straight on the line of the poles, which will create superb precise positioning. In the canter, the two exercises could be a give and retake of the reins halfway along the line, and also using medium canter between the two poles hugely challenges the straightness of both horse and rider when doing the transition down before the second pole. For more information about shoulder-in and travers, see Chapter 8 *Training to Compete Exercises*.

Relevance to competition

Having the skill to hold a line straight by having the horse connected between the aids is crucial for future success in competition. It will affect your marks in the dressage, your ability to jump clear within the time in the showjumping and is essential for staying straight between the flags in the cross-country.

6.2c Introducing the narrow fence

This is a top priority to introduce into your horse's training as early as possible so that it becomes familiar, enjoyable and eventually second nature. He needs to be established in the ability to hold a straight line on the flat and over fences and have a good understanding of your steering aids. If you introduce this work before the basic aids are in place, or by not following a clear, progressive system, your horse may learn to run out. It's crucial that you take this training step by step, starting only with flags. Although this exercise is in the 'training to learn' section it is a useful exercise for all levels, including Advanced level, just to reassure a horse that it is correct and harmless to stay straight through and over a narrow obstacle.

Set-up and equipment

You will need at least one pair of short wings, preferably with a plastic flag on each one. Following on from this, you will need some form of fence that can fit between the flags, such as a plastic block or a little hurdle filler, or even a free-standing soft brush type of fence. Set your wings and flags up on a straight line in your training area approximately 2m / 6.5ft apart.

Warming up

Develop a warm-up routine where your horse is attentive, loosened through his muscles and ready to jump. When your horse becomes accustomed to going through narrow flags, I would use these wings and flags within the warm-up routine, either on the centre line, off a turn or even on a curving line such as a circle.

Working the exercise

Start by walking your horse in a straight line through the middle of the flagged wings, ensuring that you use a focal point, and carry on riding for at least three straight strides after the flagged wings to train your horse to stay straight on the landing. Repeat this in trot and canter, including using a directional change. Initially when going through a narrow area some horses can become claustrophobic as they pass objects close to their eyes – this is why we practise and reward many times whilst the exercise is non-threatening. Once he is confident with the exercise, bring the flagged wings in narrower to a measurement of 1.2m / 4ft apart. Then use the flagged wings as part of a jumping combination, such as a line of fences, by using a small fence, followed by one non-jumping stride to a set of flagged wings, followed by another one non-jumping stride to a second fence. If you have the room you can add another set of narrow flagged wings and another fence to jump out. Soon, your horse will feel really confident and comfortable going through these narrow areas and the effect will actually encourage

Training to Learn Exercises

54. A 5-year-old in the initial stages of developing straightness. These are the first building block aids to staying straight at top level and should be revisited if problems occur.

55. The first building block of the narrow fence.

56. Developing a small jump between the flags.

Training to Learn Exercises

a will to stay straight. When introducing the first narrow jump as a single fence, I recommend using a narrow pole initially so that the horse gets used to going over a narrow obstacle then, once he is comfortable, introduce a small 70cm / 2.3ft fence, either a plastic block or small filler, first in trot and then in canter. Your horse will become very confident using this build-up system and really enjoy this non-threatening work, so it's highly important that it is brought into your work in a regular routine. Maybe every time you do jump training you might use a narrow fence somewhere in your floor plan. Even whilst training without fences, the flags are a useful method of training your horse to stay straight.

Relevance to competition
Promotes confidence and belief in negotiating narrow fences.

> **Question – poles to prevent a horse running out at a narrow fence or not?**
>
> The correct training philosophy would be that if you have to use something to prevent the horse running past the fence then you need to drop down to the previous building block and ensure that the initial training is put in place correctly. Your horse should have the will and basic knowledge to complete the task and generally it is human error if the horse makes a mistake.

6.2d Training the steering aids

Set-up and equipment
Use little panel fillers or similar approximately 70cm / 2.3ft in height and 90cm /3ft in width. Place two side by side in a straight line in your training area.

Warming up
Keep to your normal warm-up routine for jumping but work largely on accuracy, with precise transitions and accuracy on the centre line to develop straightness. Also use leg-yielding in trot and canter as a corrective aid if, whilst using this exercise, your horse wants to deviate off the line of approach.

Working the exercise
Initially just trot to the fillers, concentrating on your focal point with your eyes up and ahead then, on the approach, get prepared to initiate a stronger pressure to maintain the straightness and react quickly to any deviation off the line. If your horse stays straight,

57 & 58. Young horses enjoying the exercise of the narrow panels.

keep the pressure low, but if he goes to deviate, apply a stronger leg-to-rein 'wall' pressure until he is back on the line. Once he is confidently jumping the little obstacle in trot and canter in the centre, start to choose either the left or the right filler to demand more precision. Use slight pressure aids on the approach so that the horse feels and accepts the steering aids comfortably. It's at this point that you can halve the width either by taking one panel out or putting the fillers together to make a little spread fence. Again, approach in the same way of maintaining a level, balanced trot or canter, keeping the pressure aids light until they are needed to correct straightness should any deviation occur. To me, this is one of the most important exercises to master.

Starting at an early stage within the training, this super exercise is used all the way up through the levels, even as a warm-up exercise for horses and riders before a senior championship. Successfully jumping three 90cm / 3ft narrow fillers on a 20m circle with no stirrups is, even for an experienced rider and an advanced horse, a skill that will challenge without danger and be invaluable.

Relevance to competition

Training your horse to be confident at narrow fences plays a large part in whether he will be a champion or not. Most course designers will use narrow fences in all sorts of questions, whether in a water combination, up on top of a mound or even at the bottom of a long slope down, where the horse is likely to be less balanced. In all scenarios it is essential

Training to Learn Exercises

that the question to the horse is not the width of the fence – he should be able to read it and jump it like any other obstacle. Now, of course, the big factor is whether the horse is straight or not and this comes down to meticulous training, correct preparation for a fence and a rider who is balanced in their own position.

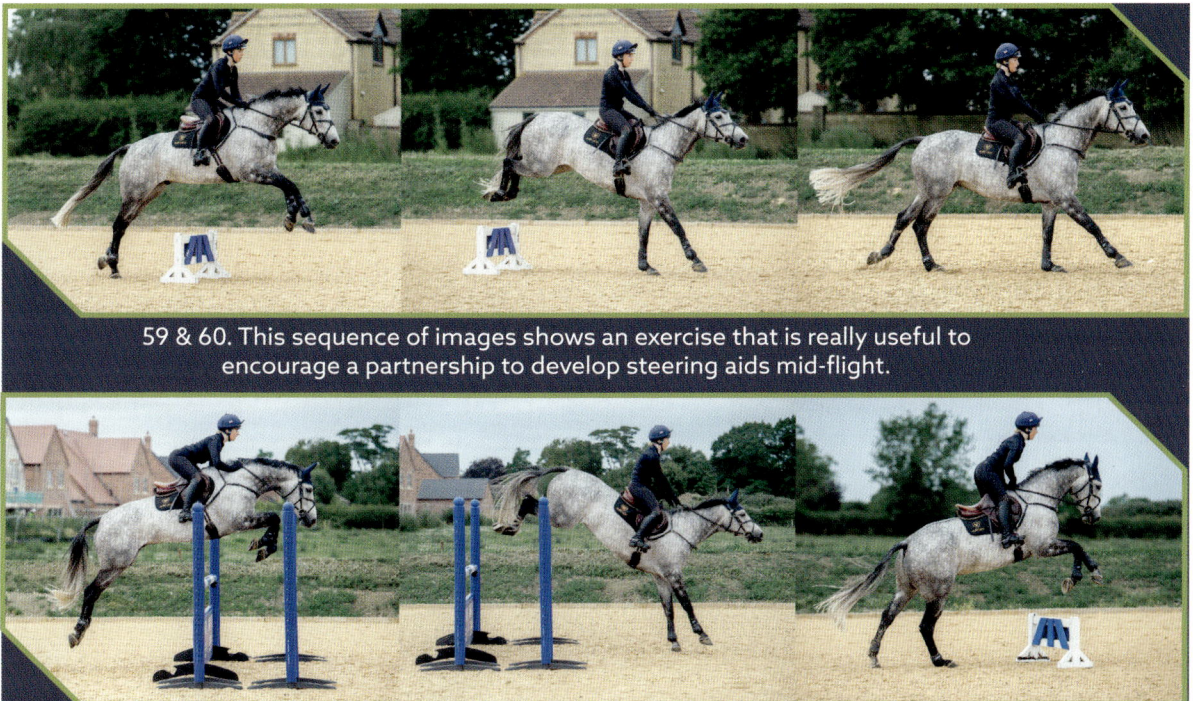

59 & 60. This sequence of images shows an exercise that is really useful to encourage a partnership to develop steering aids mid-flight.

6.2e Leg-yield in canter

Leg-yielding is an exercise to develop suppleness and engagement and is normally performed in the trot as it's easier for the horse to do the movement in the symmetrical two-time gait. However, having the ability to move a horse sideways in the canter to transfer balance and move onto a line with the body staying straight is an essential skill required for jumping. Imagine that you are moving through your preparation area for a right-handed corner and you accidentally turn too late. Having the skill to leg-yield back to the correct line of the approach will have the added bonus of supporting the horse's balance through the middle of the flags. Your horse is then less likely to drift towards the part of the corner that is angled away from the line of approach – a common fault. Having the ability to transfer the horse's balance from slightly left to right or vice versa is an aid you can use to prepare the horse to land on the correct lead.

Set-up and equipment

There are no props at all to this exercise and it can be ridden anywhere suitable, such as an arena, field, gallops or even out hacking on appropriate ground.

> ### Aids
> When teaching a younger horse to leg-yield in canter towards the leading leg your aids will need to carry a large pressure of your outside leg as the aid to move away, with a secure opposite rein to train the horse to stay straight. Focus on keeping your balance equal and riding tall through your ribcage. Eventually, these aids should become less pressurised and the horse will move his withers and body in response to your body's intention.

Warming up

Develop your normal warm-up routine, but pay particular attention to using serpentine suppling exercises and transitions within the canter work to prepare the horse for the exercise. Then start by doing some leg-yielding in trot, moving away from the wall or fence then riding straight onto a line with a focal point. Balance the trot before the corner with some half-halts and make sure that you come out of the corner with the balance evenly between both sides. Allow the horse's inside shoulder to lead into the movement and then ride parallel away from the track in four or five strides of leg-yield before straightening up onto your focal line. You can add to this exercise in trot by moving into counter shoulder-in when on your focal line, or leg-yielding back to the outer track.

Then establish the working canter and ride some subtle transitions within the canter, moving towards collected and medium canter just to engage and connect the horse before riding the leg-yield in the canter.

Working the exercise

Start in a working true canter and ride a corner onto the long side of the arena. Then, using subtle leg-yield aids, move the horse both straight and sideways away from the track from your outside leg towards the horse's leading leg. Make sure this is done slowly and gradually, and initially only ride to 2–3m / 6.5–10ft in before straightening up onto your focal line. Then prepare and ride the leg-yield back to the outer track, but focusing on staying in a very minor shoulder-fore position to prevent the horse falling back onto an outside shoulder. It is quite hard for a horse to do this movement in an asymmetrical gait like the canter, but it's an important skill to have in his toolbox and should be built into the daily routine of working exercises to develop balance, engagement and straightness.

Relevance to competition

Having the ability to correct and put a horse back onto a line in canter and at speed is crucial in competition and is a baseline movement that will be used at all levels.

6.3 Change of direction over a fence

Giving directional aids before a fence is something that is used all the time in the showjumping arena, more than ever on the cross-country and needs to be well established from an early stage. Training directional aids into the horse's vocabulary should be done with balance in mind and with subtle, light, seamless aids that derive from the mind of the rider and get transported through to the mind of the horse with body positioning. Just turning your eyes can show the horse your preferred direction and should be backed up with the rein aid guiding the withers and the legs supporting the trunk and the hind legs. Your weight should pass through your inside heel, which will give security to you, but also suggest direction to the horse.

The horse has a three-time canter beat with the sequence of legs working from the outside hind leg, then the inside hind leg and the outside foreleg together then the inside foreleg as the leading leg before a moment of suspension. As a horse jumps he takes off with both hind legs pushing off together then, as he lands, the trailing foreleg hits the ground first, followed by the leading leg. To land on his left lead he needs to put the right forefoot down first, and to land on his right lead the left forefoot needs to hit the ground first. So this is down to balance. Think of an old-fashioned set of scales with an even amount of weight either side and relate that to the horse. Once he has started loading to one direction the bodyweight transfers across and he loses his balance, with symptoms of speeding up, going crooked, loading into the rider's hand and, when jumping, drifting across the fence sideways.

To land on a desired lead your horse needs to develop the skill of staying balanced, straight and taking off and landing on the corresponding line. Once that is achieved by using the exercises in this chapter, you can teach him how to land on a specific lead by positioning him to the new direction and balance on the way into the fence. This teaches him to anticipate a landing direction and land correctly, with good balance and rideability. The following exercises take you through different methods of training the horse to land on the desired canter lead.

6.3a Directional changes over raised poles

This is an exercise that would nearly always be set up in my training area as a warm-up for jumping. It has many benefits, the first of which is to establish directional aids so that the horse gets accustomed to reading and following them in a relaxed fashion. Next, it will warm up and loosen the horse's jumping muscles, and finally it activates the joint movement. From the rider's perspective it will offer a chance to work in the lighter seat and challenge balance before jumping.

Set-up and equipment
Using three to five 5cm / 2in raised trotting poles or triangular dressage boards set up a

line over the centre either at X or, if you have more equipment, use two lines to develop a serpentine. Set the distance between the poles/boards at 1.10m /3.5ft as this is ideal for the right height of lift.

Warming up

Use a regular warm-up routine of transition work, some loosening lateral work and plenty of canter work before asking your horse to lift and stretch.

Working the exercise

Start by making sure that your trot work is connected and in balance with some transitions and half-halts, then ride over the poles making sure that you look up, not down at the poles, to feel and react to your horse underneath you. Then start to make a figure of eight or serpentine to change direction and start decreasing the width of your loops until you are riding a 10m half-circle onto the poles. As you move through the exercise you can add more bend to stretch the outside of your horse, thus emphasising the change of direction. Add a slight leg-yield positioning to the new direction as you move through the exercise to create the balance into the outside rein. You can also add more cadence and collection by adding a touch more energy before riding a slower tempo over the raised poles to create height and engagement. Remember always to look up to the new direction early. If there is a loss of balance, repeatedly half-halt so that the hoofprints are made exactly halfway between the poles and not close to the following one.

Relevance to competition

This exercise is to educate the horse through a change of direction whilst engaging in an obstacle. It is the very first building block to directional aids involving turning over fences, the ability to stay in balance through a turn and responding to your half-halt aids.

61. This sequence of images shows the directional change over raised boards, which is the prerequisite before going over a fence. Note the rider's eyes and the horse's change of bend over board three.

6.3b Cavalletti bounces

This is an essential exercise to work into all horses' regimes, whether it is a young horse starting this skill for the first time or an older horse practising his footwork and balance. The art of being able to ask your horse for a change of direction and canter lead over a fence, especially when not on a sharp turn, requires a system that is personal to you and your horse. The pressure aid needs to be applied on the approach and you should aim for a line that is right of centre if approaching from the right rein and left of centre if approaching from the left rein.

Set-up and equipment

Use three small fences or cavalletti in a straight line going across the centre line where there will be an obvious change of direction to the horse. Place them at a distance of 3.2m / 3.5yds apart, set on their highest setting approximately 50cm /20in.

Warming up

Warm up in the normal routine with emphasis on leg-yielding in the canter as mentioned in exercise 6.2e. Using some cavalletti placed singly, let your horse warm up his jumping muscles, focusing on maintaining the rhythm and staying level in his stride.

Working the exercise

Create an active, upbeat canter that is round and fairly short-striding. Approach the three cavalletti in a straight line off the left rein with an emphasis on slightly overshooting the turn, but use a leg-yield aid to move back to left of centre. So, applying a stronger right leg at the girth area, sitting up through your core and turning your eyes to the right, jump through the three cavalletti with two bounces and change direction. Make a point of staying on your line

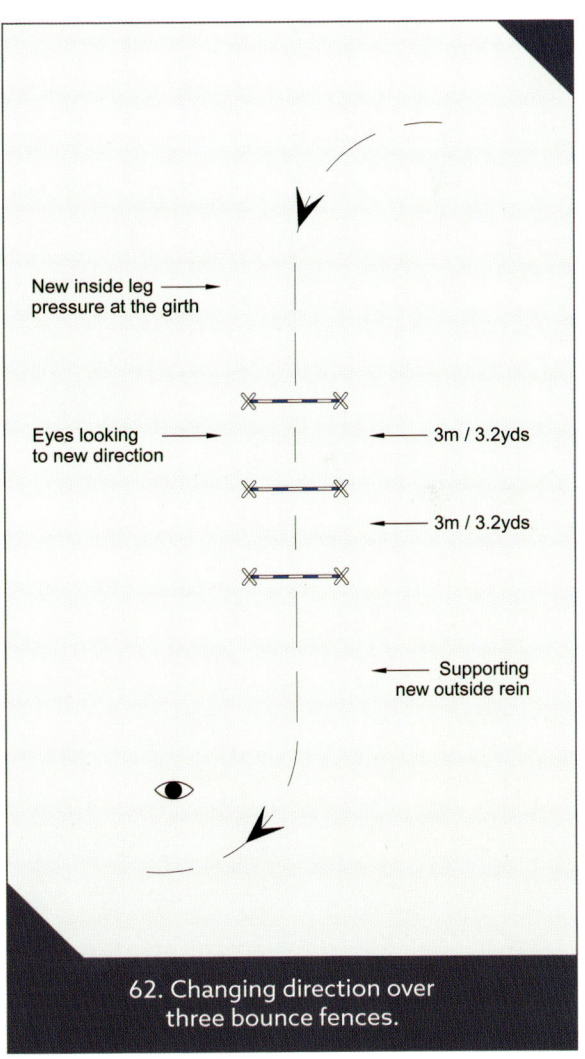

62. Changing direction over three bounce fences.

for the first cavalletto, introduce the change of direction over the second and allow the horse to turn right over the third. Repeat the exercise at least three times to both directions until the aids have become an 'association' and a learned habit for the horse. The more you repeat this exercise in your basic training, the more your horse will know that a change of direction is coming up and he will prepare himself by getting his body ready to land in a new direction. The idea of indicating the new direction on the approach is the crucial building block, which is then used in competition later on. Once familiar with the aids, the horse will eventually perform his change of lead over the first cavalletto but maintain his balance in an upright stance.

Relevance to competition

It is essential to be able to do a change of direction over a fence and land in a balanced, 'uphill' canter, on the correct lead and ready for the new fence immediately. This is clearly important in the showjumping arena but is an essential aid whilst running at speed cross-country, especially when the course designer has given you a big table on a turning line to a very angled corner.

6.3c Bounce-parallel-bounce

This exercise covers the following training skills and is an essential part of training the event horse.

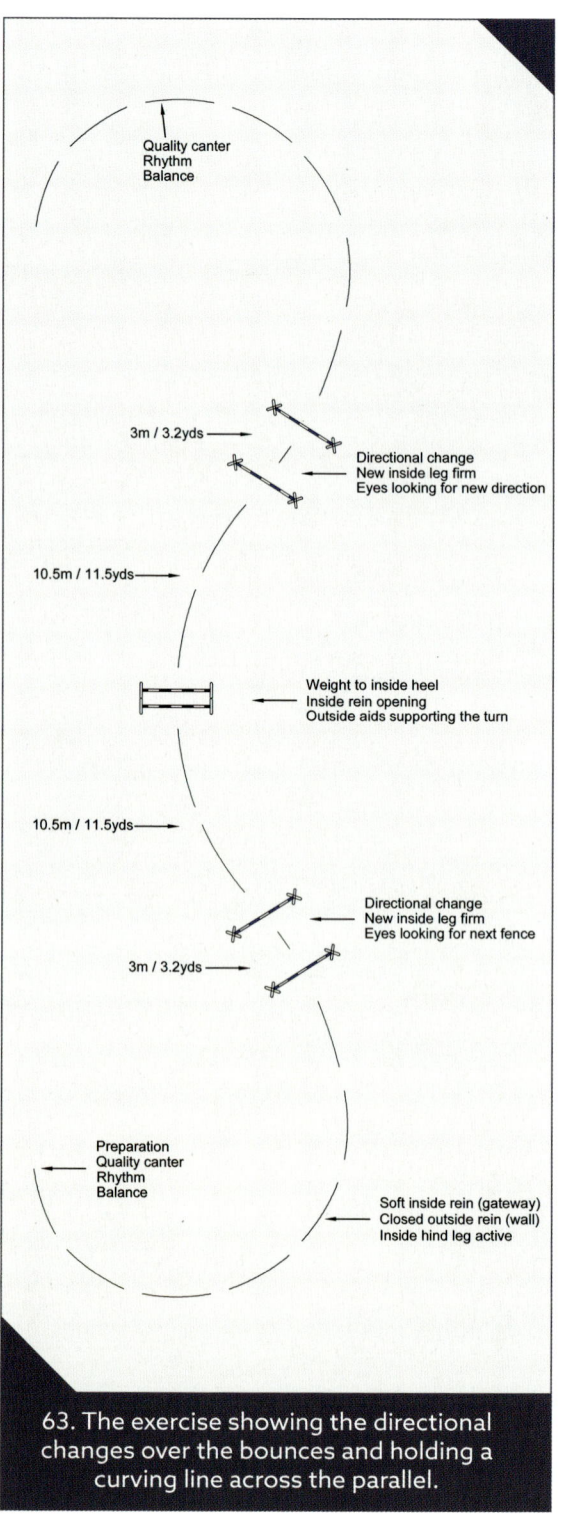

63. The exercise showing the directional changes over the bounces and holding a curving line across the parallel.

Training to Learn Exercises

64 & 65. The value of using cavalletti for bounces. Note the engagement and hind leg activity.

- ✦ Rider's directional aids are challenged by the need to steer with eyes, rein aid, bodyweight and legs throughout the whole exercise.
- ✦ Rider's position and weight distribution are improved by encouraging the rider to be inside-leg dominant and keep the eyes up.
- ✦ Directional changes for the horse include two lead changes, leading to improved jumping technique and developing hoof-brain coordination.
- ✦ The ability to stay level and not rush through the jumping exercise is improved as the bounce out needs control and the correct speed.

Set-up and equipment

Set up the exercise by initially placing a small square parallel that can be jumped from both directions in the centre of your training area. Make sure that you include good ground-poles. Pace out 10.5m / 11.5yds for two non-jumping strides on a sensible curve to a bounce, made either from cavalletti set at 3m / 10ft apart and at the highest setting, or small verticals at approximately 50cm / 20in in height. Then repeat the same to the other side of the parallel on the same curving line (see diagram 63).

Warming up

Follow the same warm-up routine ready for jumping an exercise like this by including transitions within the canter from collected-working-medium-working-collected to develop engagement and obedience. Also use plenty of leg-yielding and circles to promote suppleness and straightness before starting to jump. If you have some raised poles on a circle they are another ideal way of warming up your horse for this exercise.

Working the exercise

Start in a working canter going around the parallel on a curve and jumping the cavalletti to change direction. Practise giving the new directional aid on the approach with a slight overshoot on the approach line, weight down the inside heel, slight leg-yield off the new inside leg and eyes to the new direction. Use both sets of bounce cavalletti a few times until the canter is level in a good rhythm, the horse is responding to the directional aid and is landing correctly in balance. Then, using the full line, approach off a left turn (or out of the corner of your training area), jump the first bounce but, as you do so, give your directional aid to the parallel, aiming to jump it right of centre whilst giving your directional aid to the third element (second bounce) and turning back onto the left rein again. Repeat on both reins, building up the height in the middle parallel if required.

The rider's responsibilities are to give correct directional aids:

- ▸ Eyes look to the following element and direction.
- ▸ Inside rein aid opens to the new direction like a 'gateway' and the outside rein closes towards the withers like a 'wall'.

- The rider's weight should stay down the inside heel for security and to keep the seat slightly to the inside.

The horse's responsibilities are to follow the rider's aids:

- To follow the directional aids without rushing or resisting.
- To land on the correct lead in a good balance.
- To jump with a good technique without losing balance to the outside shoulder over the middle fence.

Relevance to competition

The middle element is a turning fence, which is required as the horse moves up the levels, but is essential to introduce as a basic building block in the early stages. The horse needs to acknowledge and respond to directional aids without it affecting the quality of the approach or jump.

6.3d Cavalletti cross

This is a useful exercise to train the ability to turn to a fence off a short distance, to train the development of quick reactions from both horse and rider, and it also improves stamina and fitness depending on how many circuits are done.

Set-up and equipment

Ideally you need four cavalletti or, if not, just four 50cm / 20in verticals set in a cross with the distance between the insides set at 4.1m / 4.5yds. When I set this exercise up for someone the first time I would number the cavalletti one to four clockwise with jump numbers if I had some to hand, but you can also use dressage letters instead.

Warming up

Use your routine warm-up for jumping, but focus on using trot-canter-trot transitions for obedience and balance. The majority of the work is done on turns to a straight line so use some 10m circles in canter at specific markers to develop three strides on each quarter of the circle, which is the basis for your turn to a fence.

Working the exercise

Start by picking any of the cavalletti and using it for a change of direction as a warm-up. Pay particular attention to allowing the horse to look after his own stride pattern and use his own hoof-brain coordination. Then stop and think about the exercise before getting started, as it requires you as the rider to plan and think about your next cavalletto. Starting on the left rein, set up the working canter on a 20m circle with correct balance-power ratio and jump *number one* then, staying on the left rein, jump *number two*, again staying on the left rein jump *number three* then go around to *number four* but use number four for a change of direction to the right. Straight away follow

Training to Win

the exercise through on the right rein, but this time going from *number four* to *three* to *two* to *one*, where you can repeat with a directional change to the left and start again. It sounds hugely complicated but actually all that you are doing is jumping then missing out two cavalletti then moving to the next with a directional change every fourth fence. Keep the turns fairly tight, focusing on the rhythm and balance.

It could be easy to lose the quality of the canter and become less disciplined on your turns so, if you feel that this happens, move out of the exercise then introduce more quality with some transition work before rejoining the cavalletti again.

Relevance to competition

This is a crucial exercise for any event horse for suppleness, obedience, footwork and stamina. It should be brought into the winter training but also used regularly as a skill educator through the competing season. It essentially helps the ability to turn into a fence from a short distance, which is important for tight times and reducing time penalties.

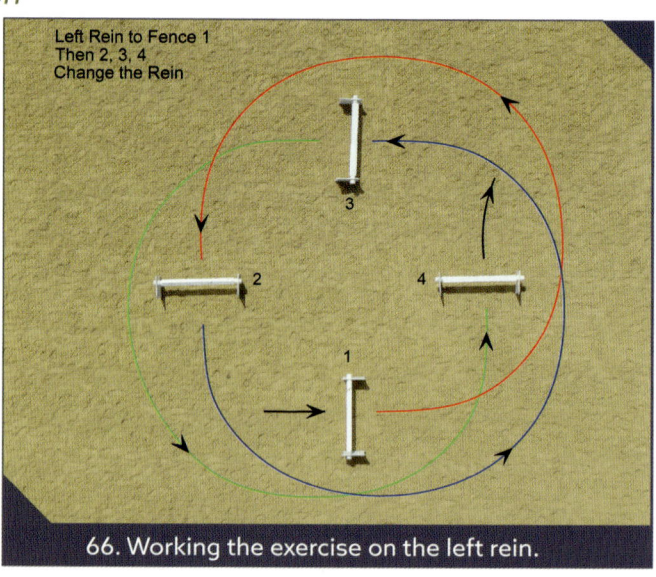

66. Working the exercise on the left rein.

6.4 Working on different terrain and ground conditions

One of the most important skills a horse needs to learn is how to balance and use his footwork when on land that is changeable in gradient and ground conditions. Where horses spend the first two to three years of their life can have an impact on how they handle less than perfect

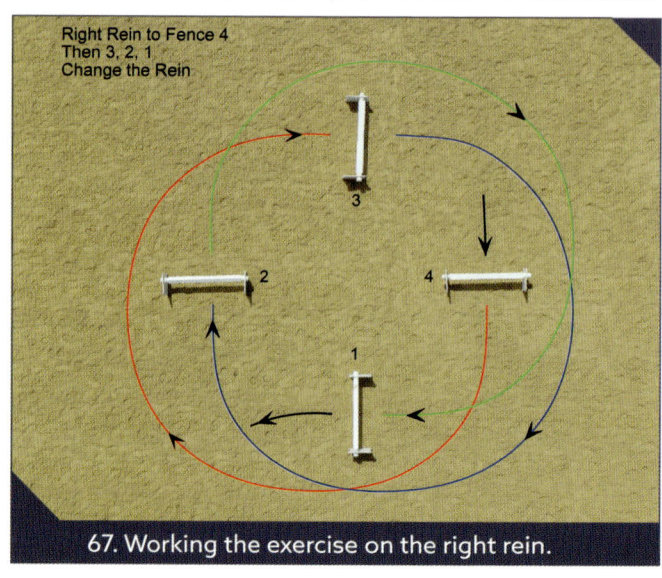

67. Working the exercise on the right rein.

ground conditions. Horses who have been kept out on pasture that has slopes, mounds, streams and other natural hazards will generally have a better idea how to shift their weight and balance to stay upright compared to horses who have been reared on flat pasture or kept in enclosed pens where youngstock can be housed together through the winter. Once ridden away, for the first few months it is fairly important to spend less time in an arena with perfect footing and more riding time on bridleways, hacking through woodland and letting your horse deal with natural obstacles so he learns how to use his hoof-brain coordination with a rider on his back. Then, when the first cross-country schooling comes along, allowing him to look, use his eyes, discover the safety of water and small ditches by following another horse will ensure that he develops his levels of confidence from the very beginning.

Ditch training is the time to really develop the trust and partnership between horse and rider. Rarely will a young horse just pop across their first ditch without bothering to look, so often this is the first time that a horse has to really trust the rider and often it can be the first small argument. Be well prepared by having another horse to follow or someone on the ground to offer a lead. Start by using a small, narrow ditch and allow the horse to look with his neck down and assess the situation. Encourage him quietly with your legs and reassure with a directional rein aid, getting ready to drop the reins to the buckle the first time so that your horse doesn't get an uncomfortable tug on the reins if he puts in a large jump. Repeat many times from both directions so the horse realises that it isn't going to hurt and that it is very safe. Bring ditch-hopping in whenever you get the chance at an early age so that your horse becomes accustomed to it as a normal occurrence. Be strict with straightness and back-up aids if he ever hesitates. If you get the opportunity to train over ditches going down a slope it can be advantageous for the future. Moving downhill to a ditch offers a different visual appearance and can initially be a cause for concern so again repeat regularly until it is a learned skill.

68a & b. A young horse improving his natural balance and footwork working on different terrain.

Chapter 7

Training to Compete

There is no obvious crossover of when you stop training your horse to learn, as this should stay ongoing throughout your horse's competitive career, but now it's time to increase the skill level. You have hopefully introduced clear basics in his first year of learning. Your horse should be willing to put effort into his work, because he knows it will be rewarded. He will understand how to go forward, be able to interpret the aids to work rounder, alter direction, feel comfortable about jumping fences in a straight line, know how to hold his balance at a working gait and, amongst other things, have a greater awareness of where his feet are. The exercises that you have built up should have given him correct muscular development so that he will be able to cope with the more technical work needed for his job as an event horse. All of the training from now on should come in small increments, so you build up layers of understanding, ability and ultimately confidence. If, at any point, your horse fails to understand the question or becomes uncomfortable in his work he will possibly not perform the task correctly and start evading in one form or another. It is your job as the rider to recognise this lack of understanding and to rephrase the question, making it simpler for the horse to understand and reinforce the building blocks. Let's look at the skills that the partnership needs to compete successfully.

Your horse should be willing to put effort into his work, because he knows it will be rewarded.

7.1 Dressage skills required at all levels

Novice 2* level and below

- Medium, extended and free walk on a long rein.

- Working and medium trot.
- Working and medium canter.
- Transitions within the gait.
- Progressive and direct transitions.
- Square halt and salute.
- Rein-back.
- Centre line with transitions.
- 10m and 12m half-circles and return.
- 15m and 20m circles.
- Serpentine loops and 10m loops in trot and canter.
- Counter-canter.
- Leg-yielding to and away from the track in trot.
- Stretching the frame.
- Give and retaking the reins.

69. A medium trot in a 4* test.

Intermediate 3* level
All of the above plus:

- Collected walk, trot and canter.
- Centre line in canter.
- Shoulder-in.
- Half-pass, to include travers and renvers.
- Simple changes.
- Walk pirouettes, to include working pirouettes and turn on the haunches.

Advanced 4* and 5* level
All of the above plus:

- Single flying changes.
- 8m circles.
- Extended trot.
- Extended canter.

At all levels the following skills will be required
- Half-halts.
- Knowledge of number of strides for all circles and each movement. As a guide, these would be:
  - Corner strides = three.
  - Canter strides short side = seven straight strides collected canter, six working canter.
  - Extended and medium canter to collected canter = two or three strides.
  - Medium canter 12m marker long arena = four strides.
  - Walk demi-pirouette = five or six strides.
  - 10m circle canter = twelve or thirteen strides (approx. three on each quarter circle).
- Arena craft and use of corners.
- Routine outside of arena.
- Warm-up routine.

7.2 Showjumping skills required at all levels

- Landing on a required lead.
- Landing and opening the stride.
- Landing and closing the stride.
- Holding a line to the inside of centre.
- Jumping on a curve.

Training to Win

- Using the fence to turn.
- Competent track jumping. Verticals, ascending spreads, parallels, triple bars, water trays, related distances, doubles and treble combinations.
- Developing an eye for and confidence with height (10cm / 4in a year).
- Working at 325mpm, 350mpm and 375mpm.
- Turning in on five, four and three strides to a fence.
- Warm-up routine for specific purposes. Short and long formats. Artificial surface and grass.
- Course-walking and understanding design.

70. Preparing a turn in the showjumping arena in a 5* long format. Note the longer bridge rein.

Training to Compete

7.3 Cross-country skills required at all levels

- Riding in a posture that is in balance, has independence of the reins, can react quickly to ever-changing conditions.
- Different seat positions. 'Top speed' position, preparation position, light seat travelling to a fence position, deep seat travelling to a fence position, problematic position and landing position.
- Riding in a rhythm in the different gears and speeds required.
- Holding a line jumping at speed.
- Being confident to jump angles, narrow fences, brushes, ditches, tables, coffins, water, bounces, steps, drops, all types of corners, shoulder brushes, gates, bullfinches, fences with lids, slices and fences on mounds.
- Riding up and down gradients, including ridge and furrow.
- Start box routine.
- First minute riding.
- Last minute riding.
- Visualisation skills.
- Warm-up and warm-down routine.

It may be that you won't require all of the above skills in competition, but bringing them methodically into your training programme within the realms of your horse's ability will give you the tools to compete successfully – and ultimately with confidence.

Chapter 8

Training to Compete Exercises

8.1 Flatwork

8.1a The square exercise – parallel poles

There are two square exercises that are useful to the training of an event horse, each with different exercises for flatwork and jumping. The main movement an event horse has to do is to turn smoothly onto a straight line. This is used in the dressage arena, to a showjump and of course, when riding cross-country. The skill of using three upright, balanced strides to negotiate a turn is something that should be practised every time you ride, as it is an essential preparation for every movement or jump. This exercise will enforce the boundaries of the three strides around the turn and deliver three straight strides before the next turn. It is an exercise that should be brought into the training programme slowly and built up over days and weeks, as it is mentally and physically strenuous.

Set-up and equipment

You will need eight poles or half-rounds to set up the exercise. If you have a 20x40m arena, set the exercise up just off the track at one end. If you have a 60m long arena (or bigger) you can set the exercise up in the centre to use both sides of it. Place the poles 1.5m / 5ft apart on four sides of a square as in the diagram. For the more experienced horse use a span of 17m / 18.5yds from the outside poles across the square and for a less balanced or less experienced horse use an 18m / 19.7yds span.

Check your own balance and position by doing some canter work without stirrups.

71. Drone image showing the exercise of the parallel poles.

Warming up

Use a normal warm-up routine in walk, trot and canter, but introduce travelling through one set of poles whenever possible to get your horse familiar with the narrow space of the poles. Introduce transitions and some smaller circles to increase attention levels and engagement of the hind legs.

Working the exercise

Start by walking the square, ensuring that you stick to your own rules that you have so far developed in your training regarding your position. Head and eyes up, seat bones to the inner side, opening the inside rein, support with the inside leg at the girth area, outside rein staying close to the withers and outside leg actively in use to produce the thoroughness and straightness. Then pick up the working trot and repeat the square two or three times on one rein and then on the other before moving out and letting the horse go on to a larger area. Remember, it's a straight, turn and straight exercise, so don't allow yourself to forget the discipline around each turn. Once the horse is established and comfortable with the exercise in trot, move away from the square and develop some canter work. Ride a few transitions within the gait (maybe the exercise where you ride four strides of collected canter, four strides of working canter, four strides of medium canter then back down through working and collected canter again). Then pick up the square in the working canter, focusing on three strides around each turn, followed by three straight strides between the poles and three strides again on the next turn. Your horse will become fatigued with the exercise very quickly so recognise that early and move away from the square before returning on the other rein. This is a base exercise that is useful to have in your arena throughout winter training as it can be a platform on which to build other exercises.

72. A rider training the turn using the parallel poles.

Relevance to competition
The turn that this exercise embeds within your horse's toolbox is the base for everything technical that you need to do in competition.

8.1b The square exercise – parallel poles with counter-canter

Counter-canter is a movement that is crucial to help suppleness and straightness in the true canter. It is the same three-time beat, balance and positioning as the true canter but travelling away from the direction of the leading leg. The reason that this exercise is useful to the horse/rider partnership in competition is because it challenges the balance

> **Building blocks for counter-canter**
>
> 1. Develop the true canter, which should be established with straightness and balance.
> 2. Establish shallow then deeper loops.
> 3. Establish the half-circle and return with counter-canter on the track.
> 4. Establish 20m half-circles in counter-canter.
> 5. Establish smaller circles in counter-canter.
> 6. Establish the counter-canter strike-off.

when moving into the counter-canter and again as you move back into the square in true canter. Initially you and your horse need to have worked thoroughly through the building blocks of counter-canter within your training so that the exercise is not too difficult to perform.

Set-up and equipment
As in the previous square exercise, lay out the four sets of parallel poles with a span of 17m / 18.5yds from outside pole to outside pole. If using a training arena of less than 50m in length, put the square at one end of the arena.

Warming up
Ride through your normal warm-up routine but focus on direct walk to canter and canter to walk transitions. Then ride some counter-canter strike-off work, being clear to your horse using slightly more exaggerated aids to reinforce your commands. Use the square exercise in the trot and, every time you get to the set of poles that are over the centre line, circle away from them in a change of direction, using 20m, 15m and 10m circles. Focus on the horse's balance staying completely upright and not falling out through a shoulder or the hindquarters, by sitting straight yourself and keeping your focal point directly through the horse's ears and where the horse is moving towards. Resume the square after each circle to establish the straight-turn-straight mode again.

Working the exercise
Start by using the square for the working trot and canter work, moving in and out of the square whenever required to give the horse a few strides of relaxation. Use tiny transitions within the canter to energise and activate the horse's brain and the hind legs before starting the counter-canter exercise. Then, if you feel that the canter is satisfactory, ride one square but, as you move through the centre line poles, as you did in the trot, move off on to a large circle in the counter-canter. Initially gauge the balance

Training to Compete Exercises

underneath you and, if it feels too fragile, just make a transition to trot before restarting the exercise again. Keep your aids clear and slightly pressurised until the horse gains the confidence to stay in the counter-canter to resume the square again. Add to this by making the circle smaller if your horse has the balance. Test the flexion away from the leading leg to challenge balance, but also to put maximum stretch through the outside part of the horse's body when the diagonal pair is just about to leave the ground. All of these exercises are part of the building blocks for flying changes.

Relevance to competition

The skill to be in perfect balance in counter-canter relates to all levels of competition. For the dressage it is introduced at 2* level and runs right through to Olympic and 5* level, albeit to prepare for the flying change. But having the ability to be able to

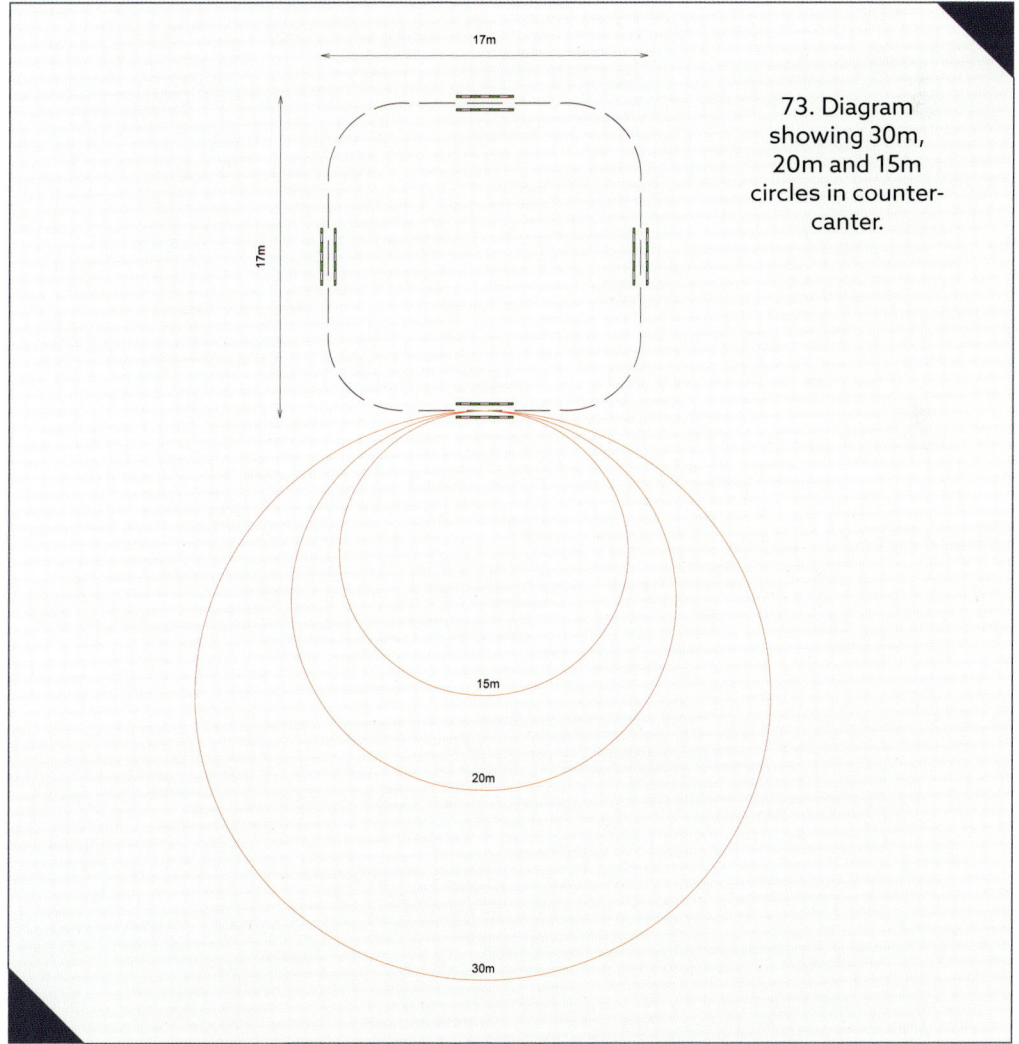

73. Diagram showing 30m, 20m and 15m circles in counter-canter.

approach a fence and jump out of counter-canter needs to be high on the list of skills as this may be required in competition if your horse fails to land on the correct lead and flying changes aren't yet established. Dropping back to trot in competition is not the preferred option as this will often result in time penalties.

8.1c The square exercise – parallel poles with shoulder-in

Using this floor plan to move in and out of shoulder-in without using a wall or track is hugely beneficial, but relies on the rider being very disciplined regarding a focal point. Shoulder-in is ridden correctly when the rider uses the whole body aids to turn the horse's withers and shoulders, and using a line with no boundary will ensure that the aids are collaborative rather than just a strong pressure with the inside leg, which pushes the quarters out. Having the ability to ride different degrees of shoulder-in within the training programme is an important skill, for example:

- Less angle with more expression in the trot.
- Less bend around the rider's inside leg then applying a controlled amount of bend and softness at the rider's discretion.
- More angle with bend but less expression in the trot.
- Walk-trot transitions holding a small shoulder-in angle.
- Shoulder-fore in collected, working and medium canter.

All of the above relies on the rider having ultra-awareness of what is required and a feeling for what is happening underneath them. Mirrors and video footage really help, but if the rider's eyes stay on the line, progress will escalate.

Set-up and equipment
Use the same square of parallel poles as for the previous two exercises.

Warming up
Using a routine warm-up plan, but focus on riding good-quality transitions and use leg-yielding to develop the initial suppleness before moving on to the work in shoulder-in.

Working the exercise
Start the work within the square of poles to produce the initial engagement and accuracy and to establish your own correct position. Use trot and canter with some subtle transitions to keep your horse attentive to the aids. Then ride out of the square onto the long line with a disciplined focal point and, after a well-prepared turn at the end of your training area, ride a long line back to the square with your focal point being the two poles leading back into the square. Carry on with this floor plan but prepare with more power and half-halts, then each time you ride onto the long line, turn your body into the shoulder-in movement with your eyes on the focal point ahead. This instruction of using your whole body to turn into the shoulder-in will ensure that the

horse stays on his line. The withers should turn slightly to the inside and the outside part of his body should be supported with your outside leg, seat, rein and positioning aids. At a suitable point, turn your body back onto the straight line again and allow your horse to straighten back up onto a straight line. Repeat on both reins with an awareness of how much bend, angle and type of trot you are asking for. Practise the skill of being able to turn in and out of shoulder-in at will, noting how many strides it takes you to do so. You can use 'add-ons' to this exercise when your horse feels secure in his balance and positioning by increasing aspects in tiny increments, such as a little more energy, maybe a little rounder, a touch more angle, or perhaps a little more softness around your inside leg. Be sensible and ask only within the boundaries of your horse's training so as not to lose his confidence. Riding a 10m circle off your line and then picking it accurately back up again is a really important skill to develop and involves spatial awareness and using peripheral vision.

Relevance to competition

Riding a good-quality shoulder-in should be a continuous 'work-on' as it's required at 3* level and above, but the shoulder-fore should be brought in at an early stage and used to help downward transitions within the gait and, of course, to help develop straightness in the canter for all three phases.

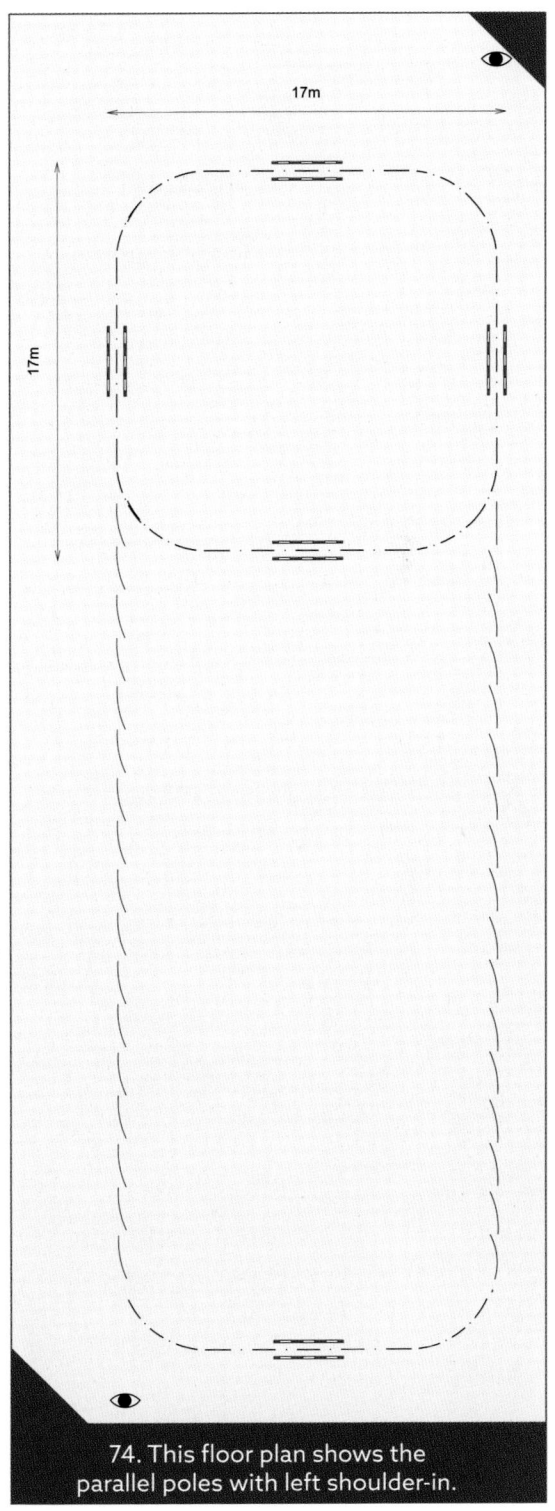

74. This floor plan shows the parallel poles with left shoulder-in.

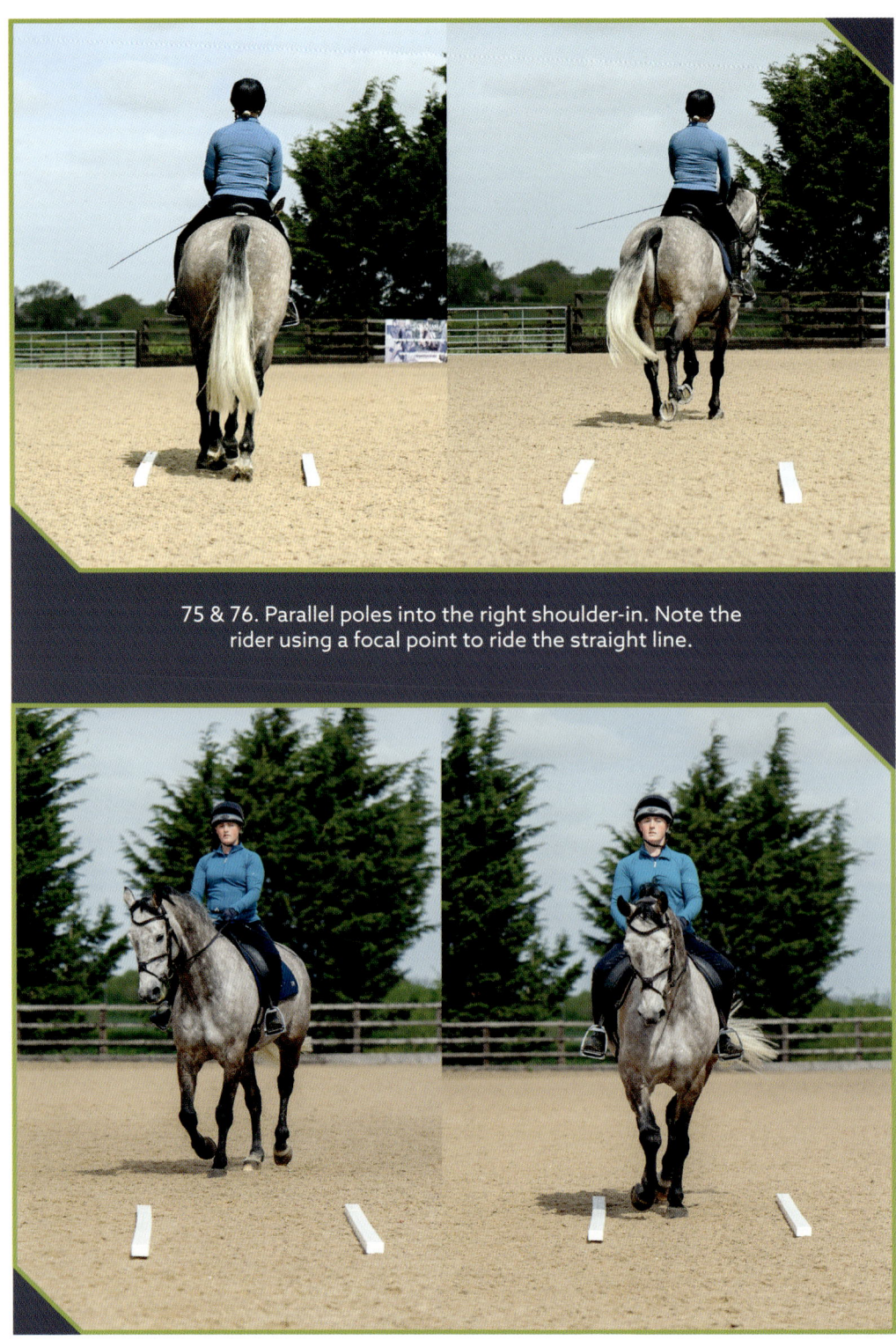

75 & 76. Parallel poles into the right shoulder-in. Note the rider using a focal point to ride the straight line.

8.1d The square exercise – parallel poles with medium trot

Using this floor plan to develop accuracy into and out of the medium trot can have a big impact on the softness that your horse develops through the transitions.

Set-up and equipment
Use the same square of parallel poles as for the previous three exercises.

Warming up
Use your regular warm-up routine but focus on including some leg-yielding work to produce suppleness and engagement in the trot and some medium canter work to open the top line and develop the stride length.

Working the exercise
Start by working the square exercise in trot and canter with some transitions as you pass through the poles to keep the horse's brain active and sharp on the aids. Then start to ride three-quarters of the square before coming out onto the straight line down the long side and riding straight to a focal point at the end of your training area. Then, making a correct turn at the end, focus on the line back into the square area of poles before riding back straight and rejoining the square. Once you have established the floor plan, start to produce more engagement on the square so you start to 'coil the spring' ready to open the stride into the medium trot as you pass out of

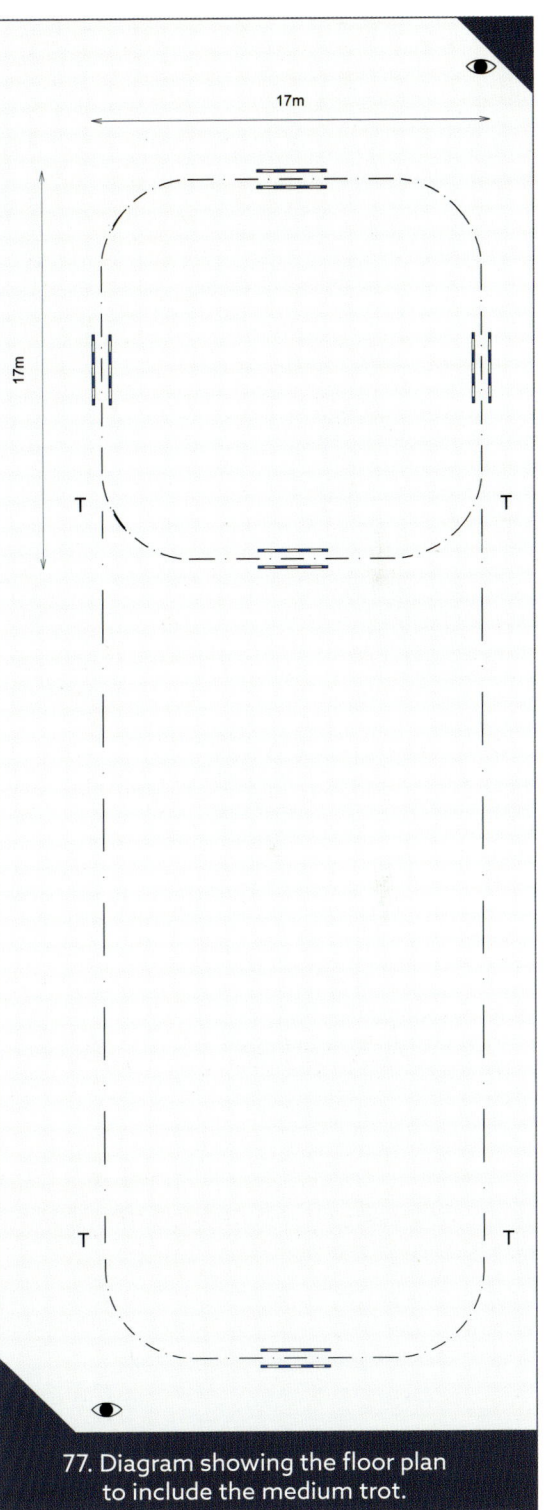

77. Diagram showing the floor plan to include the medium trot.

the corner onto the straight. Be in charge of the horse's frame so that your horse doesn't get too long and lose his balance onto the forehand. Set the number of strides that you require before riding a good half-halt and then the downward transition. To improve the downward transition, ride into some shoulder-in or a leg-yield as you use your collecting aids. This gives the horse's hind leg a job to do in the transition and helps maintain the balance in a more 'uphill' form. If the medium trot is not developing as you wish, rather than practising a poor medium trot, return to good-quality transition work to develop roundness and connection, which will help when you ask again. Sometimes, if your horse doesn't have the natural lift and cadence required for an expressive medium trot, he will need to be trained in a way that will really improve the trot in the long term. The medium and extended trot can only develop from initial engagement, so that is the area to focus on. Using a few strides of shoulder-in or leg-yielding before the medium trot can also set up the hind legs and prepare the horse for more lift through the shoulders.

Relevance to competition
Training the medium trot and canter out and then back into the square will really benefit the work in a test environment by training the correct engagement from a turn and increasing awareness of preparation for the downward transition.

8.1e The square exercise – parallel poles using 10m circles into medium canter
This is where you start becoming immensely accurate in the number of strides you are riding for each movement. It can be a strenuous exercise, so a regular change of rein and stretch are required for any level of horse. Using a correctly ridden 10m circle in the canter to set up a medium canter is a great way of keeping the horse's shoulders coming up and out rather than down and forwards. Then, using the 10m circle to collect the canter after the medium helps prevent the horse running onto the forehand and losing his balance.

Set-up and equipment
Use the same square of parallel poles as in the previous exercises, but ideally place them in the centre of your training arena so there is enough room to work around the outside comfortably.

Warming up
Use your regular warm-up routine, but focus on riding around the outside of the square in the trot and canter with small subtle transitions to give more quality and height to the strides. Ride some changes of rein using 12m half-circles to develop the stretch in the outside of the horse's body, which is key to lateral suppleness.

Working the exercise

Ride the floor plan in trot to start with to get a feeling of how it works and where to look for your focal point, then work some transitions in and out of the canter to prepare for the exercise. Start by riding four 10m circles, each one starting from the outside of the square as you are passing a set of parallel poles circling inwards. The 10m circles should be approximately three strides on each quarter of the circle (twelve or thirteen in all), which will increase your awareness of size and also highlight in which part the circle loses its shape. Between each 10m circle ride part of a 20m circle to the next point at the poles before riding the next 10m circle. Once this is established within your horse's balance on both reins, start to ride the canter between the 10m circles in a medium canter; this should be four strides.

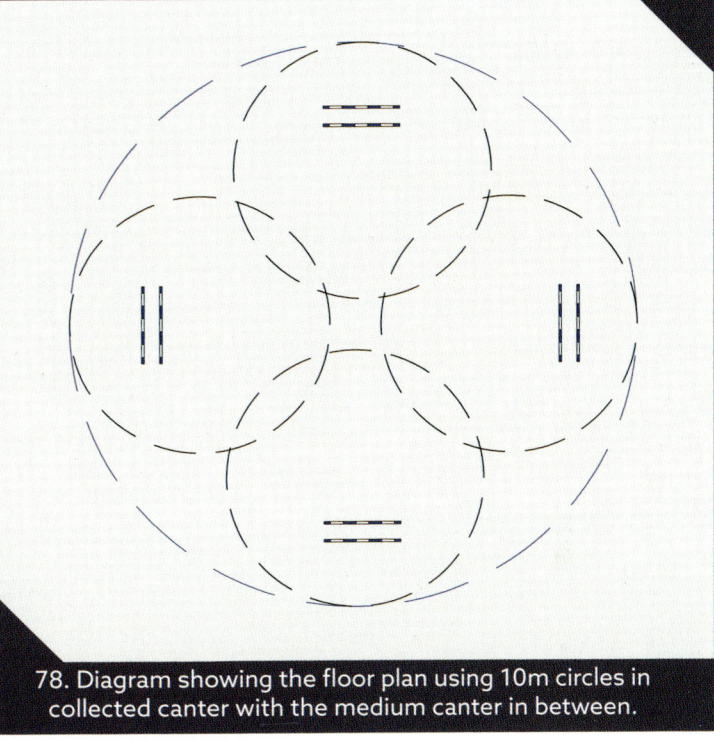

78. Diagram showing the floor plan using 10m circles in collected canter with the medium canter in between.

So, the exercise consists of twelve or thirteen strides on a 10m circle in the collected canter followed by four strides of medium canter to the next 10m circle and so on … Focus on the quality of the canter and your body position – in particular not collapsing your hips to the outside. Note the effort that your horse puts in and recognise it if he becomes fatigued. Move out of the exercise after each revolution of four 10m circles just to freshen the canter and allow the horse to slightly stretch his top line.

Relevance to competition

Having the ability to ride accurate, good-quality transitions will really increase the percentage of your dressage mark, but the exercise also enhances obedience to the gear-changing aids, which is essential for showjumping and cross-country riding.

8.1f Training the square halt

This is one of the most important areas of an event horse's training and it requires a lot of very valuable preparation. The need for awareness of connection, collection, obedience, positioning of hind limbs and rider posture will become apparent. The correct square halt is one of the easiest ways of securing a 7.5+ mark in the dressage if it has been well trained, purely because it comes down to muscle memory and, with practice, your horse should offer it every time he is asked to halt.

Set-up and equipment

Halts should be trained and ridden anywhere – whether it's in your training area, in a field, out hacking, on the gallops or just when you have finished your riding session and are dismounting. However, once the initial training has been established you can use the square exercise with the parallel poles to create more discipline, precision and straightness. This will give you a specific point at which to perform the transition with correct preparation.

Warming up

Riding a good-quality halt will really only be achieved when the horse is warmed up properly and working correctly through from behind. Use your routine warm-up period, which should include some basic lateral work to ensure that there is connection, engagement and a forward thought. The ingredient essential to a correct halt is the trot-

79. A super example of a square halt. Horse and rider symmetrical and completely balanced.

Training to Compete Exercises

walk-trot transition, which will encourage the forward stepping of the hind leg as the downward aid is applied. Spend as long as you need to produce quick-reacting transitions that coincide with a soft top line as the initial walk step occurs.

Working the exercise

Whilst riding the downward transition to walk, be aware of which hind leg is hitting the ground and pushing through. Use the words 'left', 'right', 'left', 'right', stating when each hind leg is coming through and use your related leg lightly as it happens. This will create an awareness of your leg connecting to the horse's hind leg and develop a rhythm to which the horse will respond by expand his step. Initially, use a mirror or feedback from someone on the ground to develop this awareness, and you will start to experience the horse's back muscles swinging correctly and understand how the horse puts his feet down in a 'hind limb' 'forelimb' four-time beat. Once you have established some correct transitions, start to ride the trot-walk-trot transitions with only two or three strides of walk to keep the horse alert. Use a tall upper body, soft-feeling arms that allow the 'front door to be slightly ajar' to allow a forward intention, and be quick to find the beat with your leg aids in the right order. Only then should you introduce a halt transition. Using positive leg and softening rein aids, ride forwards into walk then, riding as many walk strides as necessary, keep actively riding the hind leg into halt until the horse finishes off with a 'hind limb' 'forelimb' footfall. This will almost ensure that the halt will finish

80. This image shows a nearly square halt. Note this horse's poor conformation throughout his back. He dips away underneath and behind the saddle area and has fairly straight hocks, which makes it more difficult and uncomfortable to work round across his back and engage his hind limbs underneath him.

81. This image shows the horse resting a hind limb in the halt: he has clearly not finished the transition correctly. The rider has the curb rein too tight, which could be a contributing factor to the poor halt. The curb shank should be at an angle of no more than 45 degrees maximum when in use.

82. This image shows an incorrectly finished halt. When a horse leaves a leg out behind it is often a result of poor preparation and an unestablished trot-walk transition.

off squarely, with equal weight positioned behind and the horse still gently connected through to the bit. If one hind limb is left out at the back, move forward to correct this instantly so you train your horse that the halt is a forward-thinking transition. If the horse doesn't offer to bring his hind leg through correctly into halt more than twice, move out of the exercise, develop a good-quality trot again and redo the trot-walk-trot transitions, repeating until they are active and forward again. Then – and only then – should you revisit the trot-walk-halt transition.

As your horse starts to understand the concept you must make sure that you only ever ride the halt with good preparation. Think of how many times you halt in a training session, even if it is just to tighten your girth, and use every single halt as training. This way of training is what we know as having 'podium mentality' with huge discipline.

Relevance to competition

At least one halt, if not more, will have a bearing on your penalty mark at the end of the competition. A good halt will develop the horse's awareness and will have him on the aids throughout the competition, whereas a poorly ridden halt will allow the discipline to slip and boundaries to move.

8.1g Training the rein-back

The rein-back is a forward-thinking movement in which the horse takes steps backwards in diagonal pairs with no moment of suspension. Each diagonal pair is counted as one step and the horse should remain light in the contact with the poll at the highest point and each step being equal in length. The rein-back enters into competition at Novice level and is tested throughout up to 5* level, however it should start to be introduced in training fairly early on once your horse is going forward and understands the halt transition.

Set-up and equipment

A rein-back that is straight will come from a horse who is connected equally to the bridle on both sides and is straight, with no evasion. However, initially it is useful to have two poles laid out where you aim to do the rein-back to help with direction. An assistant on the ground would be useful when initially training the rein-back. Further poles may be handy for your warm-up.

Warming up

Use your normal warm-up routine, but introduce a series of trot-walk-trot transitions and a few halt transitions at specific points around your training area. Using raised poles, if available, will promote suppleness and forward-thinking and be advantageous to the training.

Working the exercise

When introducing the rein-back for the very first time it is important to revisit your pressure and reward aids prior to asking. Within the warm-up, ride forward into the contact in the trot and apply a small equal pressure aid with both reins then yield instantly as your horse responds with a softening jaw and rounder top line. Then ride some correct trot-walk-halt transitions at specific points around the training area, ensuring the forward impulse to the bridle. Once in halt ensure that you encourage immobility and maintain lower legs that sit in 'neutral' at the girth area. Then, have your assistant on the ground (if available) apply a small amount of pressure to the horse's chest area in between the forelegs, take both your legs off the horse and apply them lightly behind the girth area (so there is a clear difference between the neutral leg aid and the rein-back positioning leg aid) and feel the rein contact equally to apply the rein-back aid. Use a lighter seat by sitting taller through your seat as you apply the aids but, the instant that you receive a step back, release the rein aid, position the legs back to neutral, ask the horse to walk forward and praise. Repeat a few times in the first training session until the first step back is forthcoming and soft. Then revisit the exercise in the next few training sessions to establish an understanding (still with an assistant if needed) before you start asking for a specific number of steps. If at any point

83. The rider's aids being applied for the rein-back.

you come across any resistance, go back to the trot-walk-trot transitions to establish the preparation again. If you find that your horse is anticipating a rein-back it is because your leg aids aren't clear enough, or your horse isn't correctly forward into the halt. Both are easy to correct, but need recognition and thought.

Relevance to competition
As with any of the dressage movements, the quality of your rein-back will have an impact on your penalty score and therefore your competition result. The rein-back, like the halt transition, is a reflection on whether your horse is soft, supple and submissive through his connection. Correct training will be the gateway to him working correctly with understanding.

8.1h Short side training – square exercises with corners
Whether you are performing in a 20x40m arena or a 20x60m arena the short side, of 20m, is of crucial importance to produce an accurate test. Like any area of training, the work on the short side needs to be built up in small increments so that your horse feels confident and balanced. This short area should be used for preparation, refreshing the stride, and of course it will be involved in movements such as 10m, 15m and 20m circles, halts, rein-backs, true and counter-canter strike-offs and turning on and off the centre line. The frame and outline of the horse should remain consistent and correct throughout the whole test, but the short side is an ideal place to 'show off' the horse's

outline and rider's position as the judge at C can see the partnership side-on. The corners will become more established as the horse develops strength and balance and eventually you should be aiming for each corner to consist of three canter strides or six trot strides, which will look and feel like a quarter of a 10m circle. Once the set-up has been established, it can be used for several useful exercises.

Set-up and equipment

You will need twelve poles, preferably half-rounds, no shorter than 3m / 10ft, and four cones or upright posts that can be used as boundaries to establish the corners. Use eight of the poles to form four corners anywhere suitable in your training area. If your arena is 20m wide, set the poles just inside the fence line so that your square ends up being a little smaller than the maximum, but you are using poles rather than the fence line as your outside boundary. Then place another four poles exactly halfway between each corner so that the middle one sits on the 10m spot. Once your corners are set up, place the cone or jump stand approximately 3m / 10ft in from the corner as a boundary for your horse to go around.

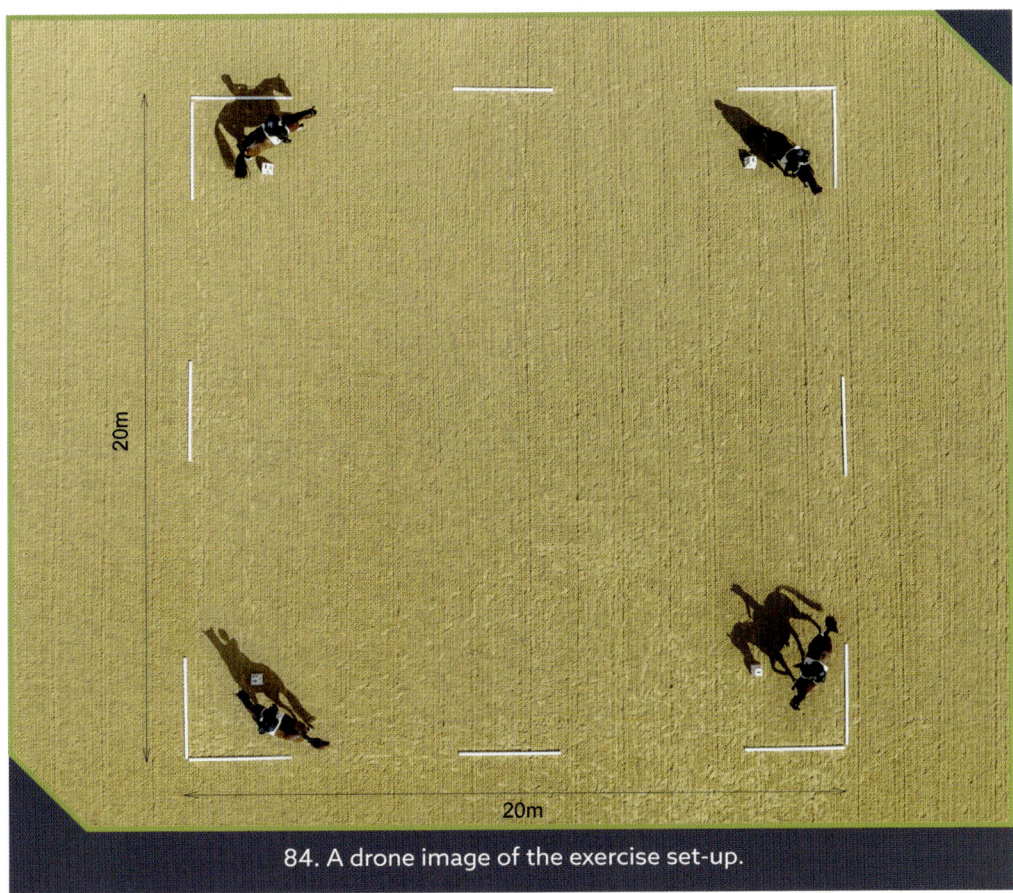

84. A drone image of the exercise set-up.

Warming up

Because this is quite intense work, requiring a lot of balance and engagement, it is absolutely essential that your horse is warmed up and loosened through all his big muscles before you start riding around the corners. Use your normal warm-up routine with lots of transitions and canter work to open the horse's lumbosacral region, positioned on the horse's back behind the saddle area.

Working the exercises

Once sufficiently warmed up, start by establishing a 20m circle within your square in trot. Make sure that you only touch the track at each pole on the centre line for one straight stride, then look to the next point denoted by a pole and stay just inside the cones that you have put out for the corners. This method of riding a circle should ensure a circle size that is absolutely correct, has an equal number of strides on each quarter and allows you to have an awareness of any weak areas in your horse's balance.

Next, start to develop the corner work. Ride in trot around the square, but use a trot-walk-trot transition at each corner for only three strides. This will feel as if it happens very quickly and will develop a quick thought process and a sharp focus from your horse. Using the walk in each corner is the basis of developing balance into a corner and a forward feeling out of the corner. Ride this exercise on both reins equally before missing out the walk transitions and continuing the whole square in trot with just the half-halt into the corner and the forward, fresh feeling out of the corner onto the straight. Imagine that there is a mirror in each corner that you sit up and focus on, as this will give you height in your posture and a correct focal point. Build this exercise up slowly within your training by having this floor plan laid out regularly in your training area so that you can use it as a routine, and soon your horse will be ready for the next training stages of this exercise.

Shoulder-in

Developing the shoulder-in within this floor plan is a fabulous way of training the transition into and out of the movement by repetition. Start by establishing a good-quality trot with a half-halt into the corner and a fresh, forward feeling out. Next, start to turn into the shoulder-in immediately out of the corner on the first stride. Turn the withers to the inside, maintaining the rhythm and direction with your aids before straightening up again after four or five strides to ride the next corner. Use a shoulder-in that has a small amount of angle and not too much bend, purely because the focus is on the transition in and out of the movement. Repeat initially down every other side before moving on to every side once your horse has settled into the exercise. It is a highly intense exercise, mentally and physically, so respond to your horse's needs if a break is required.

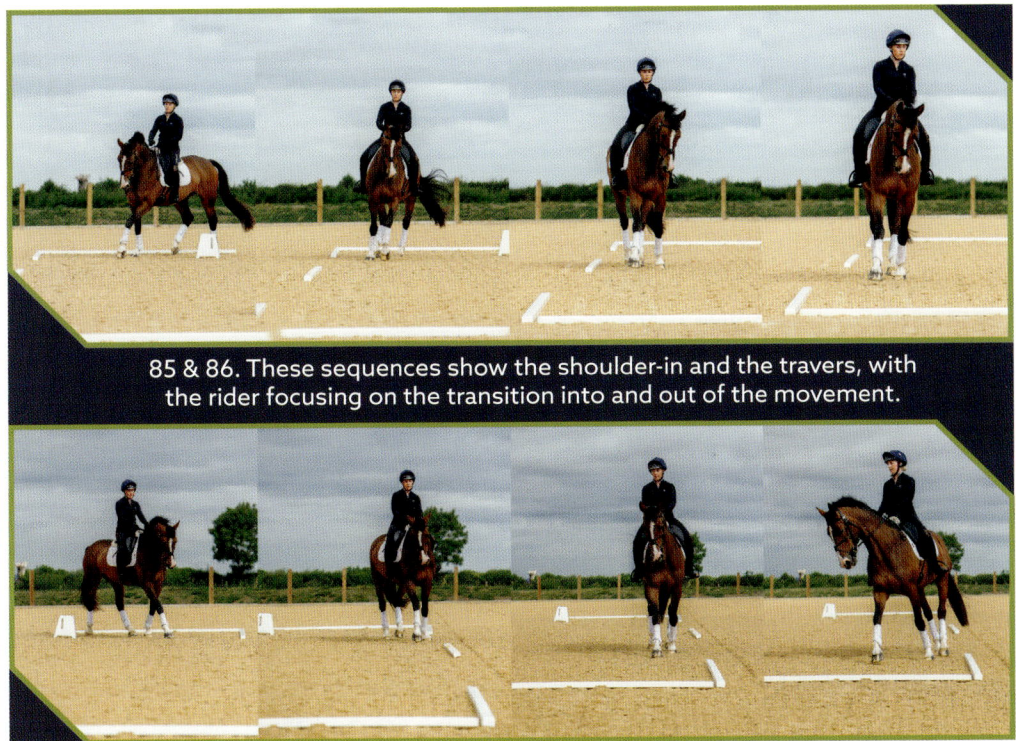

85 & 86. These sequences show the shoulder-in and the travers, with the rider focusing on the transition into and out of the movement.

Travers

Travers is a prerequisite for half-pass and an essential suppling exercise. As in the shoulder-in exercise, ride into a small angle of travers as you leave each corner for just four to five strides before taking the horse's shoulder back to the track and riding straight into the corner again. Focus on maintaining the rhythm and suppleness around your inside leg but, if you lose any quality within the trot, move out of the exercise by riding a circle and establish the energy and engagement again before rejoining the exercise. The forelegs should travel straight and stay parallel with the track.

Medium trot

The short side of the arena is potentially too short for a medium trot, however, using a small transition out of the corner to lengthen the stride and add some 'flair' to it, then riding a small transition into the following corner is very advantageous to the event horse's training.

Repetition of this exercise will create a training memory for the horse to balance going into the corner and push the hind limbs through when leaving the corner. This has the added effect of showing an 'uphill' outline across the short end of the arena, which will both develop that degree of forward thought in the horse and impress the judge in competition. Be careful to maintain the rhythm and not allow any change within the tempo, so as not to cause a loss of balance.

Turns across the centre

Turning onto a centre line or across the arena requires a certain degree of balance, which can be fairly difficult for the younger horse. Treating the centre line turns as a quarter of a 10m circle can help the balance coming onto the straight line and initially, when you do this exercise within the 20m square, you should allow the turns to have a curve that will only give you approximately five straight canter strides on the centre line or ten straight trot strides before needing to turn again. As your horse starts to develop his balance over time there needs to be a straight canter stride, or two straight trot strides, out of the corner before making the turn onto the centre or across the arena. This takes a high degree of balance, coordination and engagement, but it is your aim.

Simple changes across the arena

This is a training exercise that is essential for partnerships wanting to move up through the levels. The FEI Eventing dressage tests are considered very progressive and, if you study the movements, you will see each movement at 5* level has a lower building block at 4* and the same moving down to 3* and 2*. The progression from the canter-trot-canter at 2* to the simple change at 3* and to the flying change at 4 and 5* lies in the positioning of the movements, which are mainly done either on the long diagonal, short diagonal or the centre line with a straight line across the arena. Teaching the horse to do the simple change across the arena requires you to know how many strides to use to prepare, which then leads on to the single flying change in the same place (see diagram 87).

Start by cantering the centre line turn and staying on the same rein, using the three strides around the turn and then five or six straight strides on the line before the three strides again around the turn before the next corner. The nature of the exercise will develop the collection required for the simple changes. Then, after using some canter-walk-canter transitions on a circle, start the turns onto the centre line within the 20m square and, after the initial turn, count two strides before asking for the canter-walk. Ride forward into the walk for three to four steps before asking for the new canter then ride straight before the next turn. Repeat and repeat, but be aware of any anticipation by the horse, in which case refresh the work with some circles and go out of the square for some relaxation work and medium canters before repeating again.

10m circles

Riding a correct 10m circle requires initial balance and engagement from the horse, with spatial awareness and correct posture from the rider. Using the 20m square as a floor plan will help with the preparation and correct sizing. First, ride the four corners to produce a degree of collection and then, each time you leave a corner, ride a 10m circle exactly in the centre of your short side, starting and finishing it exactly at the pole that is positioned on the 10m mark. In the trot you should have approximately six strides on

Training to Compete Exercises

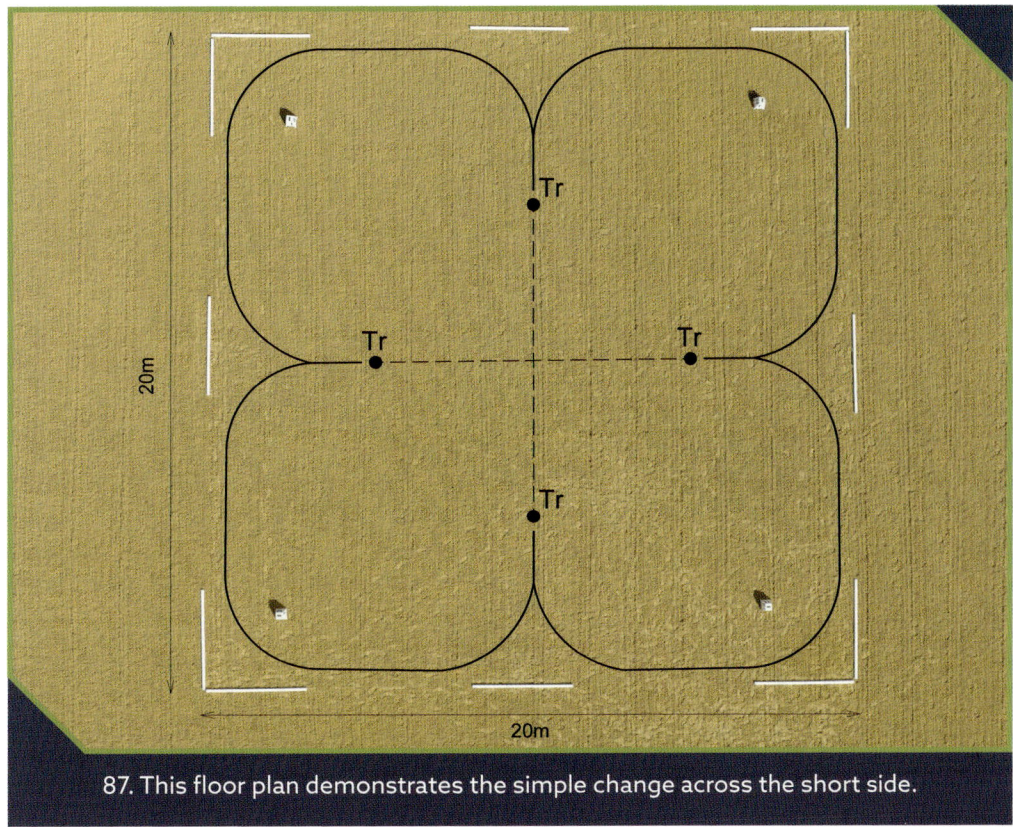

87. This floor plan demonstrates the simple change across the short side.

each quarter of the circle and in the collected canter three strides on each quarter of the circle. When the circle is finished, move on through the corner to the next centre line where you ride another 10m circle. Have an awareness of not going over the centre of the square at X. Repeat at all four 10m circles on both reins (see diagram 88).

Relevance to competition

Riding a dressage test accurately, with suitable power but with the relaxation required to perform an obedient test, takes much training. Using the square exercises to develop the balance around a corner and the straightness on a short side will give you more time to prepare a movement, especially as the horse moves up through the levels in his progression. This, in turn, will help maintain relaxation.

8.1i Centre line training

The centre line is the first movement that the judge will mark and, although it shouldn't, it can sometimes have an influence on the marks for a proportion of the test. A well-positioned and correct centre line can say 'I'm straight', 'I'm confident', 'I'm forward', 'I'm working through to the bit', 'I'm obedient' and 'I've been well trained'. It makes sense to put lots of time and effort into this movement so it is well practised.

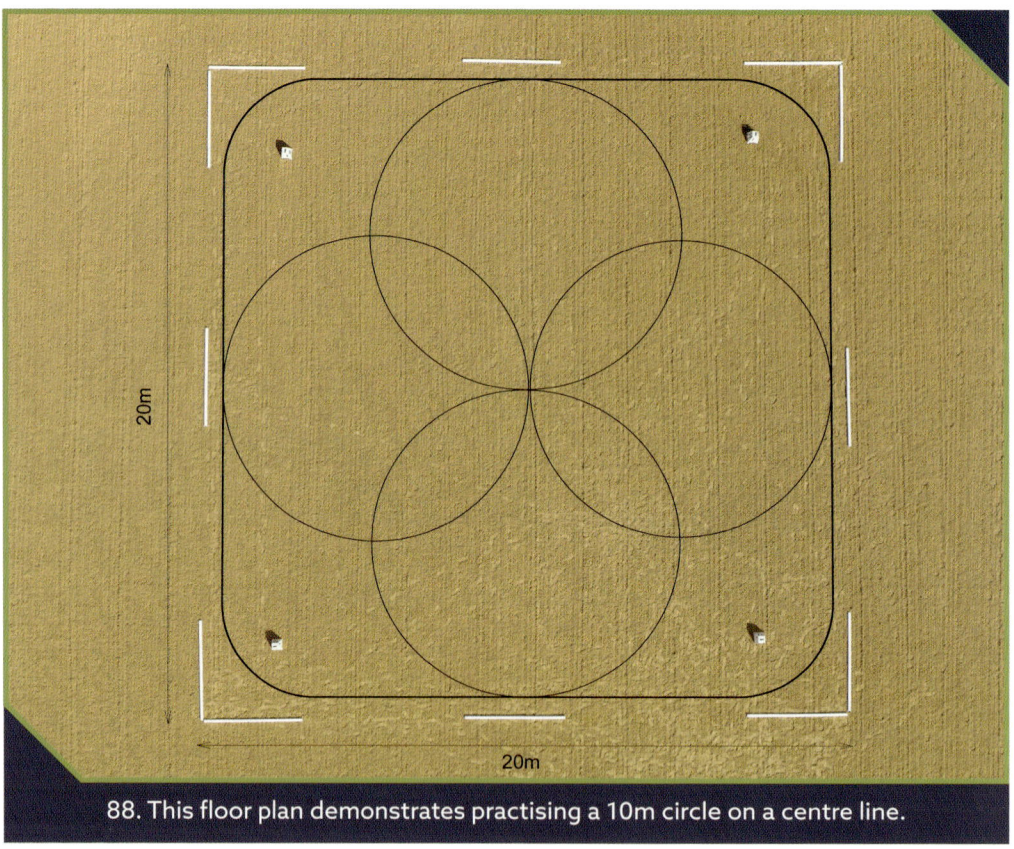

88. This floor plan demonstrates practising a 10m circle on a centre line.

Set-up and equipment

Using guiding poles into and out of the centre line will give you a focal point, so ideally set up three pairs of parallel poles, one pair 5m / 5.5yds off the track on the centre line at A, another pair at the corresponding place off the track at C and one pair at X. In addition to these poles use another eight poles, two in each corner to ride around.

Warming up

Use a routine warm-up with transitions and plenty of canter work on circles to get the outside of the horse stretching. Be precise in your warm-up by using specific markers and having an awareness of an equal number of strides either side of your circles.

Working the exercise

First, in the working trot, get familiar with the floor plan of riding a corner followed by the centre line, with a change of rein followed by the corner afterwards and repeating on the other rein. The essentials for this exercise are that the *preparation* is done before the corner by riding the horse up into the outside rein and testing the softness to the inside with a *breathing* inside rein aid. Then use your eyes to focus down the centre line, never taking them off the focal point at C, and ride forward to aid straightness.

Training to Compete Exercises

Correct any minor wobbles in the balance by recognising where the horse's weight is going and *prepare* the change of direction by riding up into the new outside rein and testing the softness to the new inside direction way in advance of the turn. Ride the turn with the feeling of a quarter of a 10m circle onto a straight short side then ride around the corner with a feeling of shoulder-fore.

Centre line training with shoulder-in

Keeping the same floor plan but riding some shoulder-in on the centre line is an extremely useful exercise. In a more collected trot, turn for example, onto the centre line on the right rein. When you have travelled through the first pair of poles, focus on keeping your body on the centre line and turn into a shoulder-in to the right. Before reaching the poles at X straighten up then ride a 10m circle to the right followed by a 10m circle to the left and back onto the centre line again. When you leave the poles at X use the engagement and bend produced from the 10m circle left to ride a shoulder-in to the left. Straighten up to ride through the poles at G (see diagram) before turning left and repeating off the left rein. The main aim of this training is to be able to keep your body on the centre line with the horse's hind limb also staying on the centre line. You are in charge of the angle and bend and should be able to dictate these with a slight movement of your body. Keeping the angle small, with a little softness around your inside leg without your horse stepping away from it will help maintain the quality of the trot.

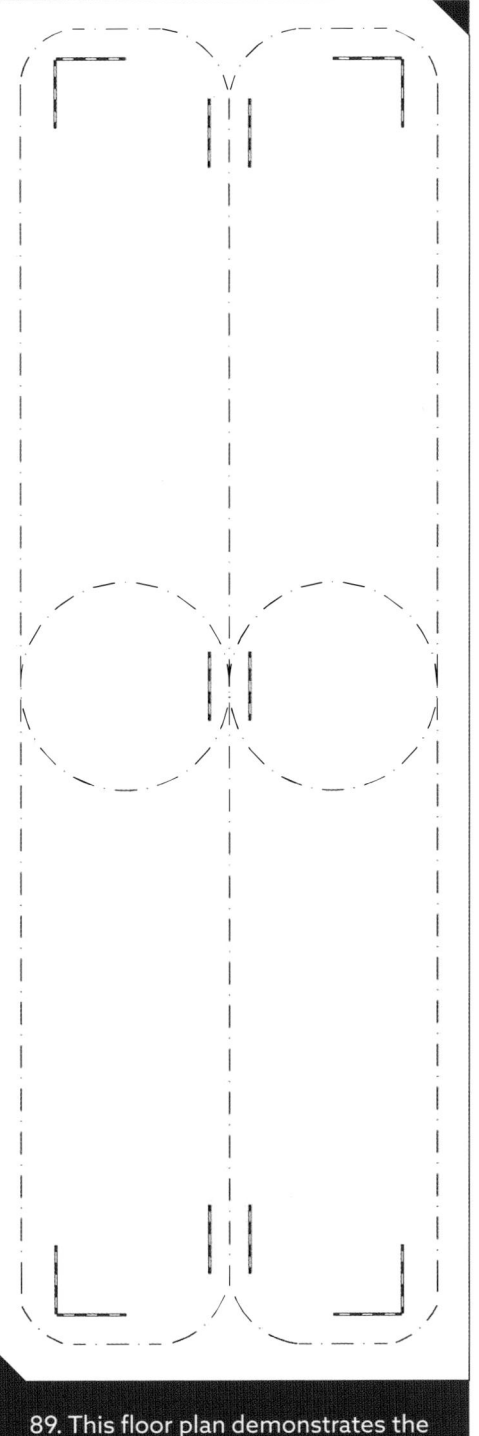

89. This floor plan demonstrates the use of poles in the centre line training.

Ride the same exercise in trot in travers but keep the horse's nose, ears and forefeet on the straight line and allow the angle of the hindquarters coming in to provide the degree of bend.

Then ride the same exercise in canter, initially just staying on one rein to work on straightness and turning on and off the centre line. Then you can add a 10m circle at X on the canter lead that you're on and either carry this on back to the centre line or ride a simple change and a second 10m circle to the other direction, then carry on to the centre line on the other lead. Riding a 10m circle at any point on the centre line and riding back onto it straight in a shoulder-fore position is really good spatial awareness training. Riding a medium canter on the centre line promotes a forward intention and practises straightness to the highest degree, especially through the transitions.

Relevance in competition

Training horses to hold their balance on the centre line through transitions will have a big impact on your dressage percentage, but will also help throughout all three phases of competition.

8.1j Training straightness – leg-yield into counter shoulder-in

This exercise is to train the horse to hold a line, stay straight and produce engagement and suppleness. It allows the rider to move the horse's withers and shoulders effortlessly, which is essential for all three phases. It is a very good warm-up exercise for all three disciplines.

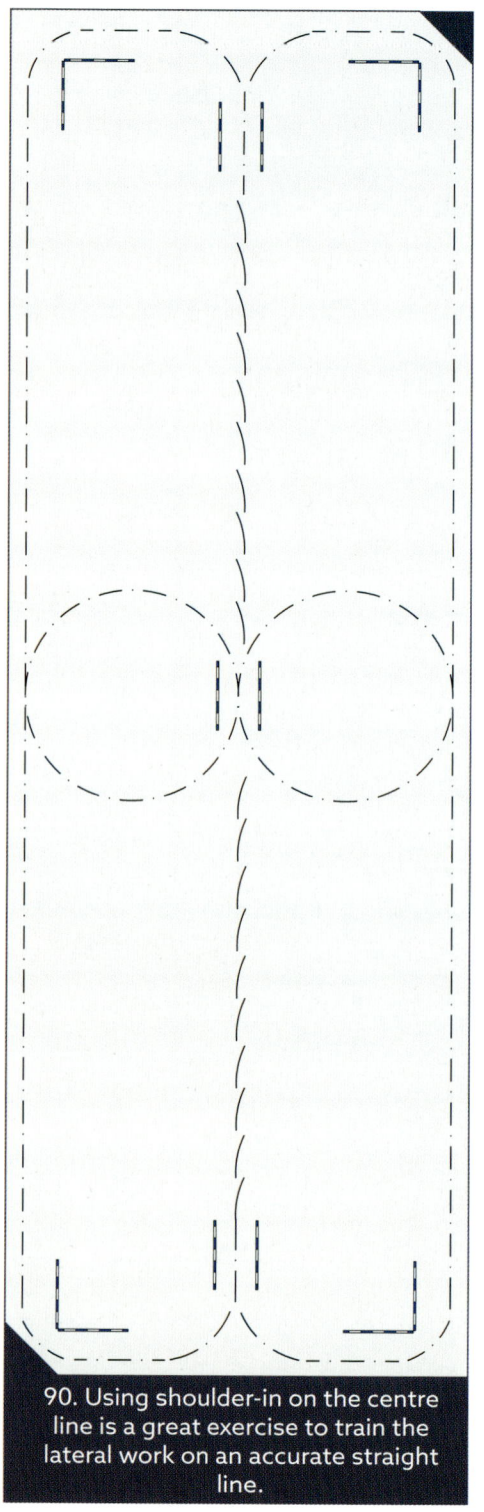

90. Using shoulder-in on the centre line is a great exercise to train the lateral work on an accurate straight line.

Training to Compete Exercises

Set-up and equipment
This exercise doesn't need any equipment and can be ridden in any training area.

Warming up
Use your regular warm-up routine, but this exercise can also be used to work the horse through in the warm-up procedure.

Working the exercise
Ride a good-quality working trot and, after a couple of half-halts, ride around the corner from the short side onto the long side and leg-yield away from the track to approximately 3m onto an inside track. Once on the 3m line, turn your body into a shoulder-in towards the outside, classed as counter shoulder-in. Your main important responsibility as the rider is to set your eyes on a focal point and maintain the line with an awareness of the horse's balance. At any point you can straighten up and finish the line off with a correct turn back onto the short side.

Using lateral work to develop the medium trot and create a 'job' for the hind limb in the downward transition
The exercise can be adapted to develop a medium trot with a young horse who is struggling with the concept of lift and suspension. First, make sure that the horse has warmed up with plenty of canter work, with some transitions within the canter, so that he is mentally and physically engaged. Then, in trot, ride an active and very parallel leg-yield away from the quarter marker off the corner onto a line approximately 3m in from the track. Once on that line, use a focal point to straighten your horse then immediately ask for some bigger strides of trot. The key areas are the maintenance of the horse's soft frame, the rhythm and the tempo staying the same, and that you aim to maintain the balance with an 'uphill' feeling. To ride the downward transition, as you are nearing the end of the arena start to ride a series of tiny half-halts by sitting taller and using your legs with an active, light touch at the girth and with little, 'talking' pressure aids down the reins, then ride the leg-yield back to the track and ride through the next corner.

91. This image shows the clear pathways through the leg-yield to the left followed by the right shoulder-in (counter shoulder-in). The horse is resisting the contact with a slightly open mouth and the presence of the tongue.

Relevance to competition
The exercises above are not used in competition. However, they are some of the biggest tools to allow the rider to take control of the horse's body, mainly the outside shoulder.

8.2 The developmental system to train flying changes

You will often see your horse galloping around his field throwing in clean flying changes every time he changes direction. Most horses will naturally have the ability to perform a flying change, but to train a horse to stay connected in the appropriate frame, soft throughout and produce a single flying change on the aids at a specific marker takes years of correct training. Like any of the skills that we are teaching our horses, the flying change needs strategic building blocks, as you will often find that you will take steps forwards and backwards. The learning of this skill can often be very fragile and your training system will get tested, so it's important to recognise signs of misunderstanding to keep the flying changes problem-free. It can take up to three years to teach a horse right through the *developmental stages* of flying changes from having no understanding to consistently producing a change worthy of scoring an 8 in a dressage test. The key stages are as follows.

The rider's understanding of what is required
The canter is a three-time gait with the outside hind leg stepping first, followed by the diagonal pair of the inside hind and outside fore together, then the inside fore completing the sequence as the leading foreleg. This is followed by a moment of suspension when all four legs are off the ground at the same time. The flying change is performed out of a collected canter, which should be of a certain quality before starting the stages of the training. The 'clean' flying change happens within one stride with the fore and hind legs changing at the same time during the moment of suspension and the change should be the same length as the canter that the horse is working in. Problems occur within training when the horse is allowed to change late behind. This is best explained by canter lead and balance with the forelegs changing first and the hind legs one or more strides later on. Once a horse has learned a behaviour through poor practice it takes a lot of restructuring to correct the method. To teach flying changes you need to have a high level of understanding and 'feel', so it is advisable to learn, read, watch and experience riding horses who have already been trained in this (or, indeed, other movements).

The canter
Developing the quality of the canter is the most important ongoing training that is required for the flying change. Ultimately the canter needs to have height, elasticity, be

truly connected, straight, equal to both directions, with lightness as the forelegs touch the ground, and the horse should show a willingness to go forwards whilst staying in good balance. This is where you have to be very patient, as this sort of canter only comes with correct training and lots of time. It involves using the '*power button*' to activate and feel as if you are quickening the hind legs, followed immediately by the '*balance button*' to produce height and ultimately feel as if you are slowing the forelegs, followed by the '*soften button*' to allow the horse to breathe through his body and soften to the aids. This power, balance and soften sequence should be repeated as many times as necessary to help produce the 'uphill', light canter.

Lateral work in the canter

Using small angles with your lateral work can help the balance and ultimately the set-up for the single flying change. Initially start with leg-yielding by working away from the track towards the leading leg. Create a balance within the canter then, after riding through the corner and keeping the straightness onto the long side, use your outside leg very slightly behind the girth and, with no bend in the horse's body, use your weight intention to leg-yield in by 3–5m. Once on the inside track or quarter line, work for a straightness using your focal point and ask for a very slight flexion, just at the poll, away from the inside canter lead. This is called counter-flexion and can help develop the straightness within the canter but, more importantly, it is a prerequisite for the flying change in training. Also using small angles of shoulder-fore and travers can help produce the degree of straightness and suppleness required for the flying change. The shoulder-fore is useful to practise placing the withers to an inner line, which connects the inside hind and outside fore and develops 'functional straightness'. The travers is useful for producing a larger, more engaged inside hind leg step which, in turn, lightens the forehand.

The counter-canter

This is very important to secure in the horse's training, mentally and physically, before training the flying change. Practise going from true canter to counter-canter and back to true canter to secure the mental aspect of accepting the movement and the aids. Ensure that you work hard on the functional straightness of positioning a slight shoulder-fore, especially on the return to true canter, as this is often a time when rider and horse will go crooked. Once working in the counter-canter, practise the counter-flexion to aid suppleness and balance management. This will allow you to put the withers wherever you want them to aid the balance and straightness. Initially your counter-canter work needs to be in a larger area to promote confidence, but slowly reduce the size of the area until ultimately you can ride 10–12m circles in the counter-canter.

Understanding the 'pressure knob'

As you train your horse with energy, balance and softening you will start to have a control mechanism to add and reduce power. Ultimately the aim is to be able to produce lots of power but reduce the tension, and this takes lots of practice. Work on putting more power in when riding the true canter and slightly reducing the power when moving into the counter-canter, making sure that you don't allow the canter beat to alter at all. Then, whilst in the counter-canter, ride with more power in safer areas, such as straighter lines, and reduce the power very slightly when moving to a more fragile area such as a corner or smaller circle. By doing this you give yourself a tool to use when training the flying change by managing the mental anticipation when the horse wants to please. You will be able to reduce the power very slightly to reassure your horse that he is staying in the counter-canter and not doing a flying change when not asked to.

Direct transitions from canter to walk to canter

These transitions are essential for the clarity of the aids and timing. Once the good-quality downward transitions are established from canter to trot to walk and the horse understands the forward intention, you are ready to train the direct canter transitions. Whilst in the canter, use a smaller circle to collect the strides, keeping your thighs closed to the saddle and your lower leg loose and active, with a seat that sits deep but not slumped. The timing of the aid is important. When the horse canters, we know it's a three-time beat, but there are two areas to it, the '*upbeat*', which is the hind leg hitting the ground and the '*downbeat*' which is the forelegs hitting the ground still with the same three-time of the canter. Ultimately the aim is to ask for the walk transition so your horse lands into the walk light on his forelegs and maintains his balance. So, counting the beat of the movement, just when you're about to walk, ask for one more stride with the hind leg before the downward transition, and this should prevent the withers lowering. Initially this takes much thought and preparation from the rider but, as you become well-practised, it becomes second nature. The walk-canter transitions need to be active and instantaneous but with softness so that the top line stays round. Ask for canter when the inside hind is on the ground so the next step is the outside hind leg and the first step of the canter. Practise lots of walk to counter-canter to develop the horse's awareness of the aids.

Canter leg-yield to walk

This is a building block that is really useful to return to when your horse gets muddled and you need to recalibrate the aids. It sets up the balance and positioning that would occur just before a flying change but you ride into a walk rather than a flying change. Use a very slight leg-yield towards the leading leg and count three strides into the walk. The three strides should have a collecting effect and produce lightness in the shoulders and, most importantly, your horse should move his bodyweight into the new outside rein, which is the last positioning aid before releasing a flying change of leg. Repeat as often as needed to keep your horse confident in his balance. Whilst on an outside track, do this exercise in counter-canter.

Asking for the flying change for the first time

Go through your set-up system of collecting the canter, walk to counter-canter, leg-yield to walk, then freshen the canter with some transitions from collected to working to medium and back down again and do some work to engage the hind leg with some travers. Then give your horse a small walk to rest before striking off in the counter-canter. Have a schooling whip in your outside hand and ride on a slight inside track. When you're ready, as you are nearing a corner, leg-yield slightly back to the track and apply extra pressure with the leg-yield leg to collect the step. When the time is right, release the leg that's applying the pressure by slipping it forwards and, at the same time, whilst keeping the frame of your horse the same, just touch him with the stick

92. Producing a canter with lift and 'air-time' is essential. This mare is quite croup-high in her conformation and finds engagement in the canter quite difficult. The second image demonstrates transferring the balance from the left into the right rein as the new outside rein, directly before the change stride.

93. The clean change showing a little resistance, as this is still a new skill for this young horse. Producing a good-quality stride immediately after the change is essential for the straightness and the balance.

on the top of his rump on the outside to encourage the outside hind to react and come through for a clean flying change. If the change is correct, walk and give your horse a long rein to relax and think about what he has just done. If your horse has just changed in front and is disunited, pop back into the counter-canter and repeat the same aids but with a touch more pressure.

Because the training of this movement can get a little heated at times it's important to keep allowing the horse time to breathe and absorb the aids. If you get a clean change on each rein leave the training for that day and revisit again on a different training day. Sometimes leaving the training of this movement for a week or two allows time for the horse to think and absorb. If it isn't happening the way you would like, go back a couple of stages and revisit later.

Once the aids are semi-established it's time to put the changes in across a diagonal. Start with some small engaging circles then ride across the short diagonal, keeping your eyes and body on a focal point. Before going through the process of energising the step off the new inside leg, position the horse's balance into the new outside rein. Then ensure good quality in the movement and, at the right time, release the new inside leg and give a quiet leg aid with your new outside leg just behind the girth a stride after releasing the new inside leg. You will often go through good and not so good training sessions with the changes, but the most important thing is to be consistent in your set-up, positioning, aids and timing so the horse has clarity and understanding.

8.3 Jumping exercises

If the basics are firmly in place, as you move up through the levels you should be able to start adding skills to the horse's toolbox. There are some systematic rules to follow to ensure that the partnership will build in confidence and perform well in competition.

- Remember that your horse does not know anything until you have taught him the skill.
- Keep using a building block system and add skills in small increments.
- Start very small so that any problems won't dent confidence.
- Repeat the skill as often as possible to cement the knowledge and understanding.
- Start in a familiar training area then take the skill to an unfamiliar ground before competition.
- Regularly check your own *rules* to ensure that you are riding at your best when training your horse.

Training to Compete Exercises

If you have worked through some of the exercises in Chapter 6 *Training to Learn*, you will have developed a canter that is manageable with different gears. The training of the jumping canter should always be ongoing, either in regard to building strength, establishing balance, developing power or just running through routine gear changes. The three main areas to consider whilst you are jumping are:

- The relevant **stride length**
- The relevant gear and speed, which is your **power**
- The correct **balance**

These three areas will be interchanging throughout your showjumping or cross-country round and will need monitoring regularly to keep the relationship correct for the job in hand. This will depend on distances, terrain, design questions, topography and what your horse's state of mind is at that time. A highly skilled rider will be able to monitor and adjust these areas easily without any obvious aids, whereas an unskilled rider may deliver incorrect messages to the horse. This can result in an incorrect stride length, too much speed in relationship to balance, too little power for the jump or too much power for the question. Having the skills to *calibrate your eye* and '*feel*' is one of the most important ongoing skills to develop as a rider.

8.3a Training the turn to a fence

This is a crucial part of the developmental stage for both horse and rider. Everything that is done in training relates to the skill of coming around a turn and going straight. Imagine driving a car around a corner in a gear that is too high with too much speed and you would get the feeling of losing control of the balance, especially on slippery grass. The turn to a fence is the horse's 'reading time', so if you turn in with five straight strides he has 20m / 22yds to absorb the question; with four strides he will have approximately 17m /18.5yds, whilst three straight strides will give him only around 13m / 14yds before take-off to read the height, distance and width of the question. This is where the clever course designer will allow five strides plus at 2* and below, four strides at 3* and sometimes only three strides at 4* and 5* levels in both the showjumping and cross-country phases.

Set-up and equipment

Use the same square of parallel poles as you did with the flatwork exercises at the start of this chapter, with a 17m / 18.5yds span from the outside of the poles. If your arena or schooling area is more than 50m long, build it in the centre of the arena; if it is less than 50m long build it at one end. In addition to the square, build two small fences, both verticals initially, 10m / 11yds away from the exits of the square on a straight line (see diagram 94).

Warming up

Use your regular warm-up routine for approximately 20 minutes to encourage your horse to be obedient and working through with connection. Start to work the square in canter to develop the three active turning strides before the three straight strides to the next turn. Focus on how straight your horse is between the parallel poles without too much help from you.

Working the exercise

Move out of the square and produce a jumping canter by riding bigger strides with lots of transitions and variations before rejoining the square. Then, start the jumping exercise by riding one square and then come out to jump the fence in a straight line. Your aids need to be clear.

- Eyes looking in advance towards the direction you are travelling.
- Inside rein aid acts as a gateway to open the horse's eyes to the direction by coming away from the neck rather than pulling back towards the body.
- The inside leg staying at the girth area helps support the balance and maintain energy.
- The outside leg asks the horse to maintain a forward intention.
- The outside hand acts as a wall to prevent the energy from popping out of the shoulder. It should be elastic, sit close to the neck and be ready to direct the horse's eyes to the fence.
- The bodyweight should be slightly to the inside through the inside heel, with the inside shoulder taller and supporting.

Stay straight on landing, maybe using some poles to tunnel the straight line before turning and jumping the other fence and rejoining the square. When your horse is balanced enough, introduce a larger fence and add a back rail to make a spread fence, as added height will challenge straightness and balance. If you land on an incorrect canter lead, embrace the counter-canter by working your horse, maybe riding a large circle before changing the lead either through walk, trot or a flying change.

Relevance to competition

This is a very important skill to learn and is relevant to every fence you approach in competition. This exercise, ridden regularly with the parallel poles at first, then without the parallel poles when established, will help teach both you and your horse to have economical and balanced turns to a fence, which is the key to success.

8.3b The angled fence

Jumping a fence on an angle will generally be a question found only on the cross-country. However, training a horse to read and jump a showjump on an angle is essential as it may easily be needed at the higher levels. Using showjumping poles in training is advantageous as you can move the fence easily to increase confidence.

As you learned earlier, the direction in which the horse lands is governed by the balance on take-off and is indicated by the rider on the approach to the fence. With an angle, as the horse leaves the ground he will read that one side of the fence protrudes out more than the other and will have the intention of moving away from that side. This will change the mechanics of the jump and will encourage the leg that he veers towards to be put down first and therefore he will end up on the opposite leading leg. Within the initial training it is important to instil straightness in the air across the fence as this will have an impact on the line that you will land on. Jumping angles in training is essential to your regular training as it reminds your horse that it is safe.

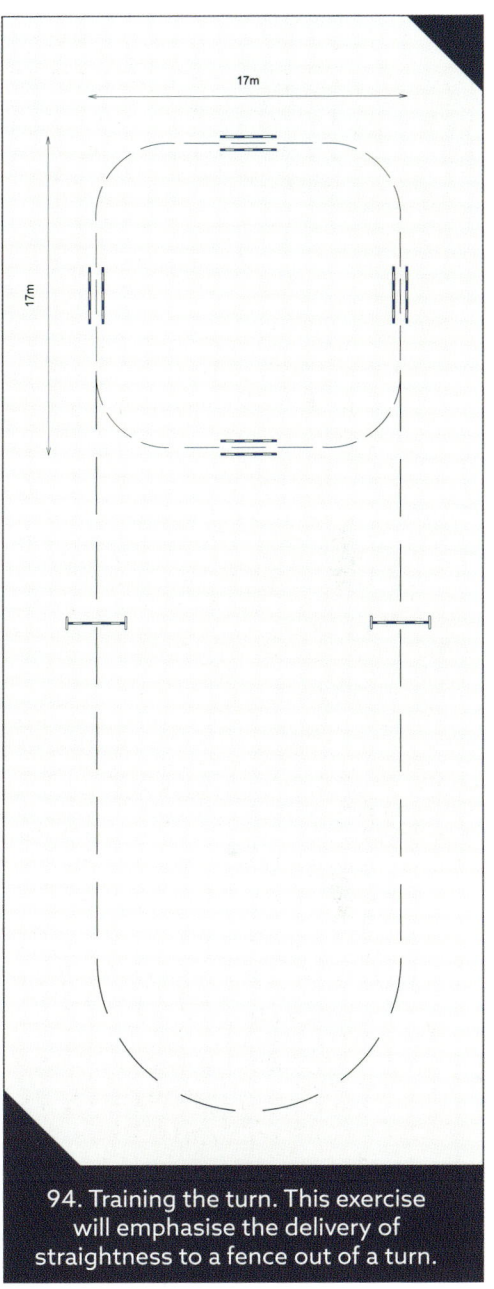

94. Training the turn. This exercise will emphasise the delivery of straightness to a fence out of a turn.

Set-up and equipment

You will need two vertical fences, no bigger than 1m / 3.3ft in height, set up in a straight line on a distance of either 14.6m / 16yds or 18.2m / 20yds. Use ground-poles either side of the two fences as they are a key part to the exercise later on. Use two parallel poles as tramlines leading into the first fence, approximately 9m / 10yds away and the same after the second fence to channel your horse in a perfectly straight line on landing (see diagram 96).

95. The 2018 World Champion dissecting an angled fence out of the water at Badminton 2022. Note how the line of the jump is straight mid-flight.

Warming up

Use your regular warm-up routine to get ready for jumping, with lots of transitions and leg-yielding work for engagement, obedience and suppleness. Where the two vertical fences are, place three or four trotting poles out approximately 1.10m / 3.5ft apart. It is essential to use trotting poles initially for this exercise before you move on to the two fences as this will install the need to travel through the tramlines, which is the key to the success of this exercise.

Working the exercise

Start by riding the straight line through the first set of parallel poles, over the two sets of trotting poles and through the second of parallel poles, finishing your turn correctly at the end. Do this on both reins, noticing if your horse wants to deviate off the line at all and being quick to correct, with light pressure aids as a prevention. Your eyes on the focal point are the key to riding this exercise well and will help you notice any deviation instantly. Once you are happy with your horse's balance, set the two fences up and canter through the exercise, ensuring that your horse takes off and lands on the corresponding spot and goes confidently through the parallel poles on the landing

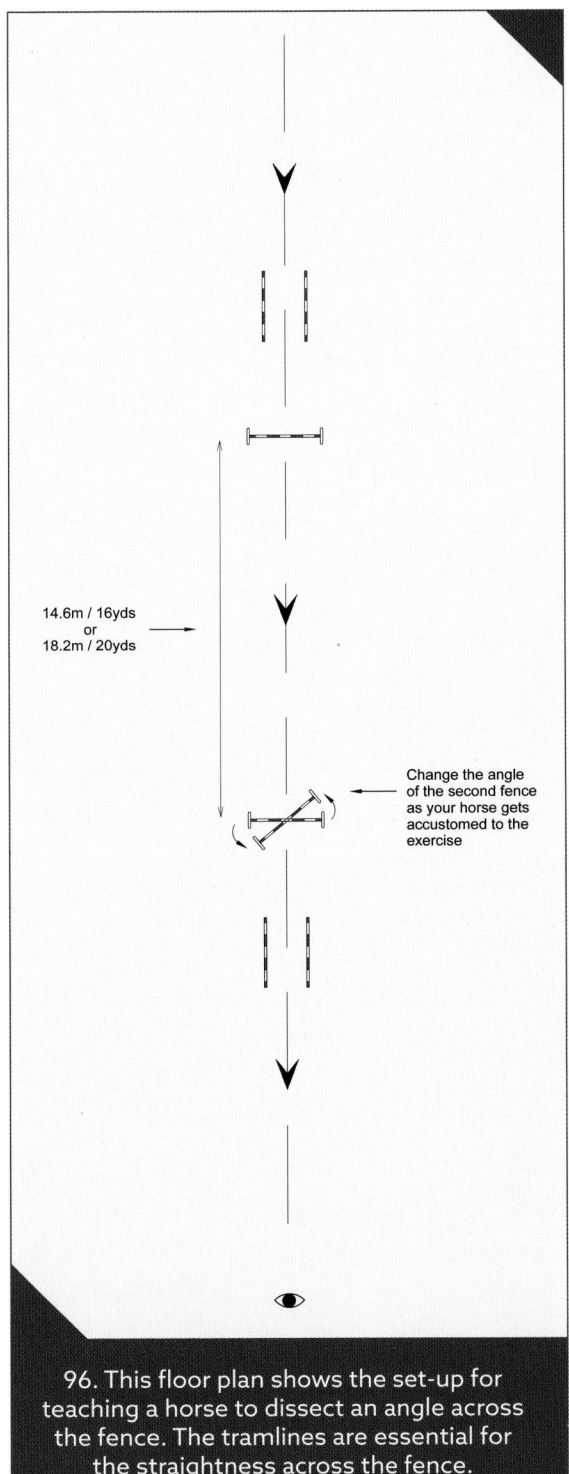

96. This floor plan shows the set-up for teaching a horse to dissect an angle across the fence. The tramlines are essential for the straightness across the fence.

side. Next, still using the same two fences, move the second one to a small angle, ensuring that the centre of the fence doesn't move, so that the distance between the fences remains the same. Now canter down the line of the two fences maintaining the straight line so that the second fence is jumped across the angle. On landing, be insistent on staying on the line through the parallel poles. Build up the exercise by applying more angle each time until you are dissecting the fence at 50 to 70 degrees before moving the angle to the other direction. The aids remain the same as when you rode the line in trot; a light 'wall' either side until your horse starts to deviate, at which point you can apply a stronger steering pressure until he moves back onto the true straight line. It is important to note that the horse will move away from the part of the fence that is protruding more. If the fence is angled so that the left side is closer to you and the right side is further away, this will invite a run-out to the right. However, as the horse jumps the fence the angle will encourage a natural drift to the left in the air. The tramlines on the landing side play a huge part in the exercise as they encourage both the horse and rider to jump the angle straight. Repeat equally with the opposite angle.

97. Establishing the straight jump using the tramlines.

98. Finishing off the jump through the landing stride is crucial to long-term success.

99. Turning the second element to achieve the angle required. Note how the horse would like to follow the angle with the right shoulder but will be encouraged to remain on the line with the landing tramlines.

Relevance to competition

As you move up through the levels of competition the angled questions, often called slices, will become more difficult and success will be reliant on whether you and your horse can hold a straight line across the fence. If your horse loses confidence you will have to go completely back to the basics to reinforce the idea that the fence is safe to jump. This exercise is that basic building block and will often be revisited by horses at all levels.

100. An angled hedge at Avenches in the 2021 Senior Europeans.

101. An angled house at Strezgom in the 2018 Senior Europeans.

8.3c The corner fence

Corner fences, whether situated by themselves on the flat, within a combination, linked to the water complex or on undulating ground, will be responsible for a larger percentage of the cross-country penalties. This is because there are three questions to a corner fence: the first is the angle of the front rail; the second is the fact that the width between the flags can be fairly narrow; the third is that the breadth from front to back is often quite wide. Corner fences come in different forms.

Open corners. A corner fence made of poles such as tree trunks or telegraph poles, which will often have frangible front and back rails.

Box corners. A fully filled-in solid fence, which often cannot be collapsible in any way. The front face will vary in profile depending on the level.

High-sided brush corners. A corner fence that often has a narrow area to jump through, which can be very imposing to a horse if the angle is approached incorrectly. This fence is rarely collapsible.

102. An open corner in a 3* competition. Note the frangible safety device on both top rails. The bottom rail sits without binding in case a horse stops and puts a foreleg over the rail. The rail can be pulled free instantly without causing injury.

103. The MIMclip being activated when a horse jumps into the middle of the corner.

104. A good example of the MIMclip preventing a horse falling and the bottom rail being dislodged.

Training to Compete Exercises

Consequently, whatever the level of the horse, confidence needs replenishing regularly. At the lower levels the angle of the front rail will generally be quite inviting and the fence will be positioned where your horse has lots of time to assess it. Moving towards more advanced levels, the angle of the front rail can become very sliced, often offering only a 1.10m / 3.5ft gap to jump between the flags, and it may be positioned off a curving line, or in a place where you need to be extremely accurate in the approach. When training your horse to jump corners you should build up slowly before adding questions of height or technicality. Make sure that you always build security and confidence in training by using relevant distances that offer a safe feeling for the horse so that he never questions his belief.

The following exercise of introducing a corner through a curving line is highly advantageous as it addresses the forward intention, the width of an open corner and the steering away from the apex (point). Adding a fence after a corner is considered very

105. The box corner. This particular fence is used for training, note the slightly sloping profile and large brush on top to allow for mistakes when a combination is learning a skill.

106. A high-sided brush corner, which will challenge the straight mid-flight stride as a horse will naturally want to lean towards the point and away from the tall brush. This question was complicated because it challenged a tight right turn after a drop into water.

Training to Win

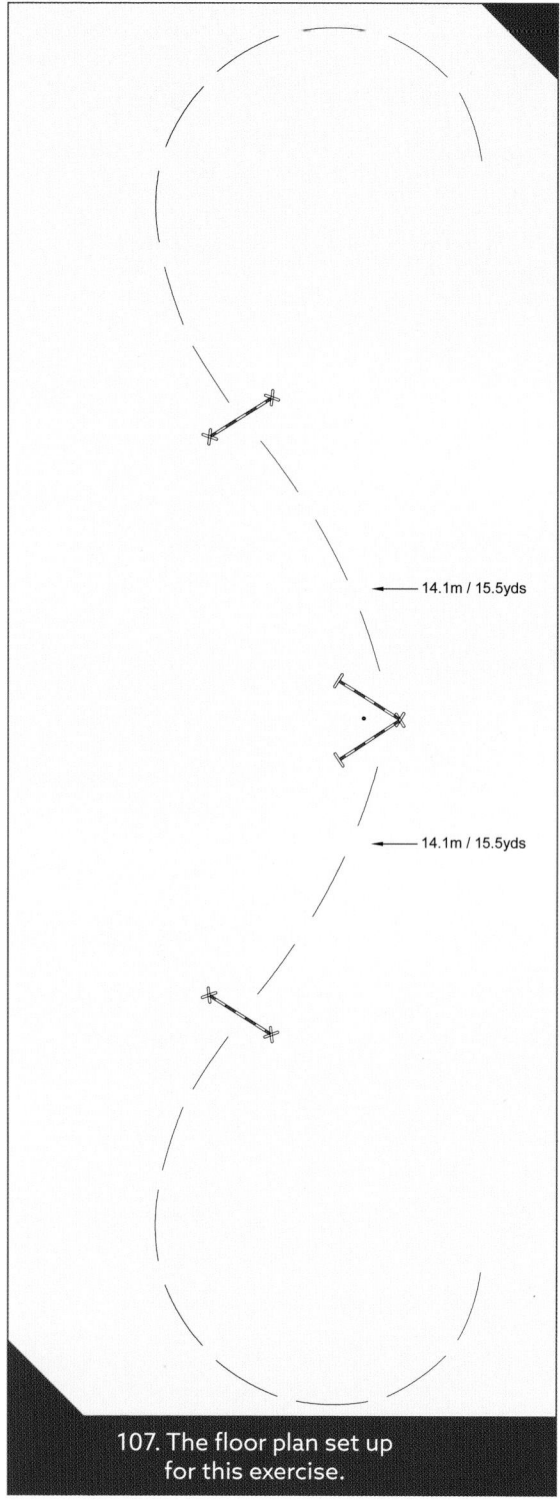

107. The floor plan set up for this exercise.

useful in training as it will focus your eye and train you to ride the corner within a combination. In addition to teaching the horse the basic concepts, this training will be of continual benefit to building skill and confidence in both horse and rider, in preparation for increasing challenges when progressing up the levels.

Initial set-up and equipment

Initially build an open corner fence midway along your training area, siting it at least 5m / 5.5yds away from the track. If you have a chance to use this training exercise on grass this would have an advantage in terms of space and would be more relevant to competition. The corner should have a short wing at the point with some form of flag, post or boundary. The other ends can sit on wings with a ground-line either side. The corner angle needs to be set depending on the level of the horse, starting initially at 45 degrees moving towards 90 degrees eventually. Placing a solid wing in the centre of the corner fence will prevent you from jumping the area that is considered too wide to jump, plus it will be more like the sort of fence that you will see in competition. Then place two fences or cavalletti either side of the corner fence on a curving line measuring 14.1m / 15.5yds to the part of the corner fence that you intend to jump.

Warming up

Use a routine warm-up in preparation for jumping but focus on the following exercises:

- Leg-yielding in the working canter both towards and away from the leading leg.
- Variations of stride in the canter, using all the range from collected to extended.
- 10m circles starting in a collected canter but moving up to a medium canter on the last two strides coming out of the circle.
- Zigzag trotting poles that are placed on angles with one end touching another pole so that as the horse trots through the centre he dissects the centre on an angle similar to a corner. This familiarises your horse with holding a line across an angle.

Working the exercise

Use the two cavalletti to do some directional changes away from the corner fence focusing on your position, focal point and directional aids. Then, choosing the rein that you would like to jump the corner off to start the exercise, remove the back rail and ground rail so that the front rail is the only part of the corner fence that you intend to jump. Practise jumping all three fences as a combination, riding from the first cavalletto to the front rail of the corner and, whilst in the air over the corner, turn your body and the horse's withers to the third element of the combination. Ideally your horse should jump this combination happily, with a confident three strides between each

108. A confident jump over the corner, with the rider looking to the third element, encouraging a line away from the point.

element – although initially the second distance will feel long. Insist on directional aids being correctly interpreted over each element. Keep your aids quite light, apart from a slight increase in an outside pressure aid on the approach to the corner to confirm to your horse that he is not allowed to drift his body towards the flag. Once confident, replace the back rail along with the ground-line at the back. Continue jumping the combination on the curving line, but with more emphasis on the third element as sometimes a wider corner will encourage the horse to move towards the point. You can develop a bigger and wider middle element as your horse gains in the belief that it is safe and fun, and also practise using the cavalletti as a directional change to add an extra dimension to the training.

Relevance to competition

Corner fences will appear in almost every cross-country course at every level and regular training for a confident partnership is the key to these fences being within the comfort zone.

Further development

As you move up through the levels of competition the course designer will question the partnership's ability to dissect the angle of the front rail of a corner, so it is essential for your horse to have the belief that it is safe to do so by bringing it into your training prior to competition.

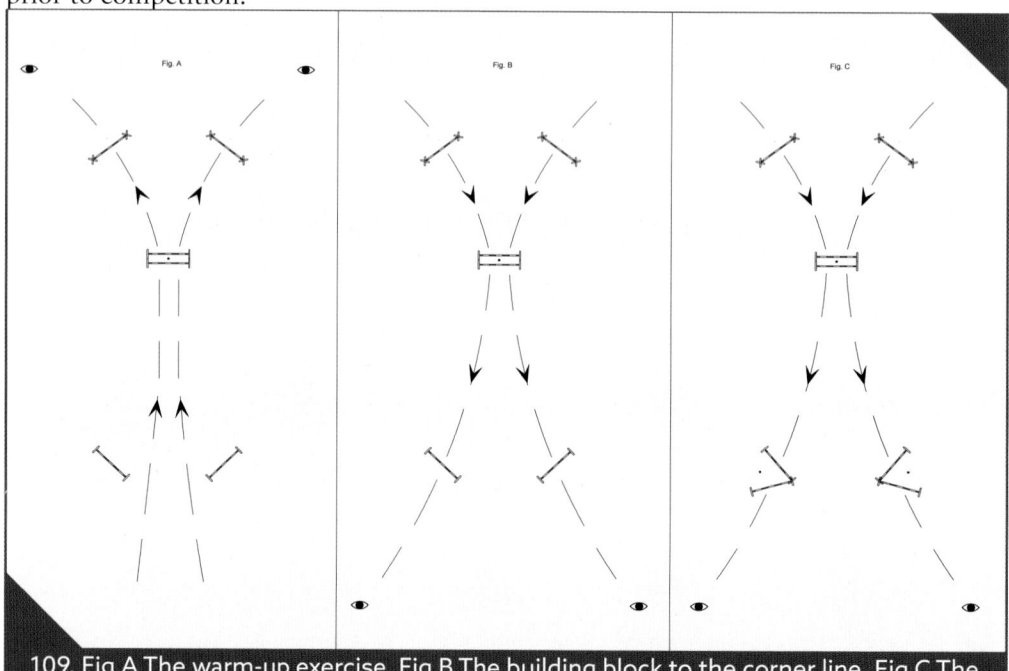

109. Fig A The warm-up exercise. Fig B The building block to the corner line. Fig C The exercise set up to include the corner fence. Note the positioning of the flag in the centre of the spread, which emphasises the need to hold an accurate line.

Training to Compete Exercises

The set-up and equipment for developing more confidence
Start by building a small spread fence in the middle of your training area, a grass field being preferable if the ground surface is suitable. Then, from the back of the spread, build two angled rails on a slight curve from the spread – a distance of 14.6m / 16yds is ideal. One angle needs to be built from the right side of the spread and one from the left. Use a short wing on the furthest point and have a spare wing and back pole ready to use for each angle. Use two small fences or cavalletti on the approach to the spread, again on a gentle curve, one leading from each rein on a two-stride distance, building on 10.5m / 11.5yds. Finally, have a spare plastic flag or upright post to use in the middle of the spread to make the exercise more technical.

Warming up
After your initial routine warm-up for jumping, use the following exercise to lead your horse into the main exercise.

Turn the spread into a small vertical to jump towards the cavalletti and place the spare plastic flag at the back of the fence directly in the centre. Then, approaching off the right rein in a positive working canter, jump to the right side of the flag and then jump the right cavalletto on a slight curve. Make a directional change over the cavalletti. Repeat on the left rein.

Working the exercise
After warming up, build the vertical back into the original small spread fence, placing the spare plastic flag in the centre of the spread with the point of the flag pointing away from the direction of approach. Start by jumping on the right rein, using a canter with a forward intention, jumping the cavalletto on the right to lead into the line. Then ride the two-stride distance to the right-hand side of the spread followed by three strides to the right side angle. Repeat from the left, riding from the left cavalletto to the left side of the spread to the left-angled fence. Building up your horse's confidence by repeating these curving lines, which question the outside shoulder over every fence, is an important prerequisite before adding the back rail.

Once confident with repetition from both directions add a back rail to the angle, this turns the fences into corners. Initially keep the width quite narrow, then once confident you can move the front rail to increase the width which, in turn, challenges the degree of angle on the front rail.

Relevance to competition
This is a crucial training exercise to create belief for the rider when walking the course and for the horse's association of safety when reading the question in competition.

110. Jumping the spread on the left curve, holding the correct line left of the middle flag.

111. Jumping the right-handed corner on a left-curving line.

112. Jumping the left-handed corner on a right-bending line.

> **Points to consider**
>
> - Head up and eyes looking through to the third element.
> - Supporting body position with secure lower legs.
> - An opening inside rein aid offering direction (gateway).
> - A supporting outside rein and leg aid to secure the direction and forward intention (wall).
> - Weight pressed firmly down the inside heel.
> - Application of an extra outside pressure aid on approach to the angle.
> - Ride away from the third element with purpose of direction.

8.3d Reaction training for horse and rider: bounce-24yards-bounce

Everything that we do when training the event horse should relate to quick reactions, good footwork and reading height and distance. When in competition, our horse should be able to take a fair amount of responsibility in terms of being able to read a question and work out where he needs to put his feet to stay upright and in balance. However, this ability is only available to a horse if the rider allows him to use his own natural reactions, rhythm and balance.

This is an extremely useful exercise for all levels to help develop the horse's eye to read a distance and react accordingly. Done often enough in training, it will develop skills such that, when allowed to have freedom of the reins, the horse can look after his own limbs and balance.

Set-up and equipment

Set up two bounce fences in a straight line, using just single poles with no ground-lines. The distance within the bounces should initially be 3.65m / 12ft, and between the two bounces 22m / 24yds. The height of the fences should initially be set at approximately 70cm / 2.3ft.

Warming up

Use a routine warm-up for preparing to jump, but focus on using the full range of stride lengths in the canter. A useful exercise in canter is four strides of collection followed by four working, four in medium followed back down the gears into working and then collection, and repeating. This will keep your horse thinking quickly, reacting to your aids, engaging his hind legs but also sufficiently warming up the muscles he will use

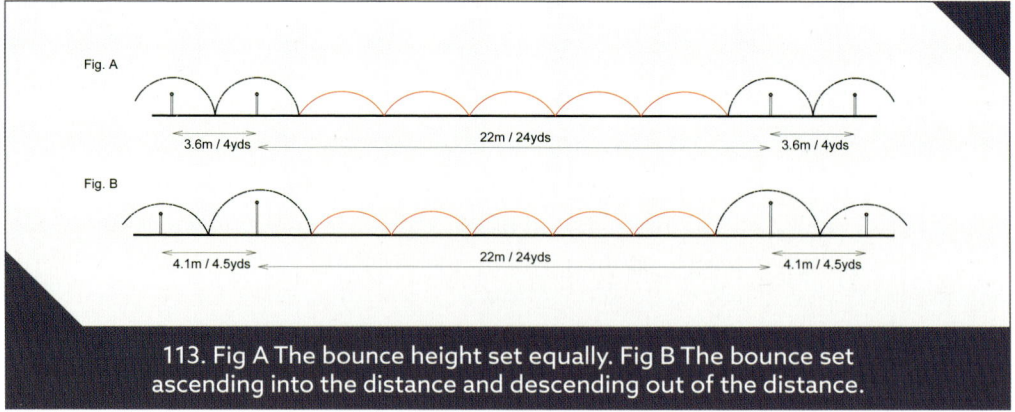

113. Fig A The bounce height set equally. Fig B The bounce set ascending into the distance and descending out of the distance.

in the jumping exercise. Using some small single fences allows the jumping muscles to warm up.

Working the exercise

Start by producing a good working canter and initially jump the bounces individually, away from each other from both directions and on both reins. Ensure that you hold your line with a clear focal point and ride straight on from the landing in a good rhythm. Then, link the two bounces together in a straight line and allow your horse to read his own distance in the middle and react accordingly by staying in balance. The nature of the two bounces on this distance will lead your horse to a longer five strides or short six strides. Allow your horse to make his own choice by relaxing your rein aids and allowing the horse's neck either to go out to expand on the distance, or shorten himself up.

Next, raise the height of the two verticals that are on the inner of the related distance to 95cm –1m (about 3ft 2in) so the 'in' bounce is ascending, with a smaller first element and larger second element and the 'out' bounce is descending, with a larger first element and smaller second element. Also, lengthen the bounce distance to 4.1m / 4.5yds by moving the lower part of each bounce out. Now that the fences are slightly larger, encourage your horse to move away from the first bounce in a positive fashion so he jumps the line on five strides. This will have him going forward into the second bounce, where you can practise slightly lengthening the reins to allow the horse's neck out and, yourself, practise a more upright shoulder position. This exercise can allow you to practise the position required for a drop fence.

Relevance to competition

This exercise offers the horse the opportunity to practise reaction and responsibility skills. It offers the rider the opportunity to practise being passive and allowing the horse to make decisions. These skills are needed regularly in competition and, if applied in training, you will have an idea as to how your horse will react when allowed to take responsibility.

Training to Compete Exercises

8.3e Developing the skills to jump narrow fences

As you develop your competition experience and go up through the levels you will discover more complex questions involving narrow fences.

- On a straight line in a related distance. This will question the ability to take off and land on the corresponding spot.
- On a curving line through a related distance. This will question the ability to hold a straight line around a bend without losing balance.
- On an uphill mound. This will question the horse's belief in his own ability as he will be taking off on ground lower than the fence, which makes the dimensions larger than the actual fence. This also questions the ability to move up to a fence.
- On a downhill gradient. This will question the balance and frame riding downhill and the ability to jump off any pattern and stride, as this often alters when jumping downhill.

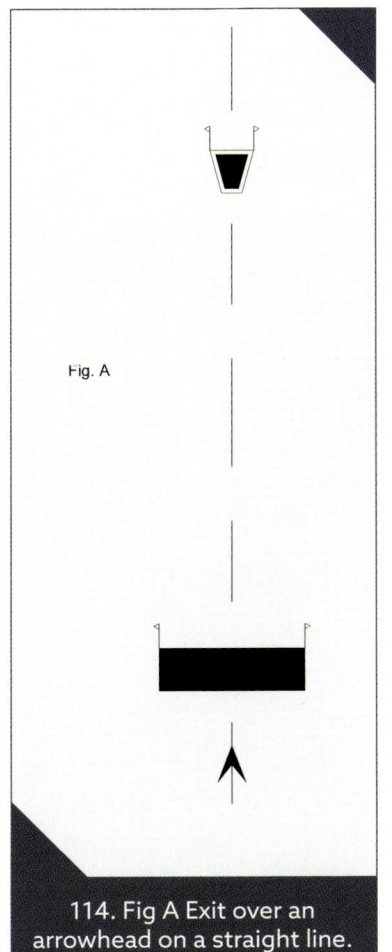

114. Fig A Exit over an arrowhead on a straight line.

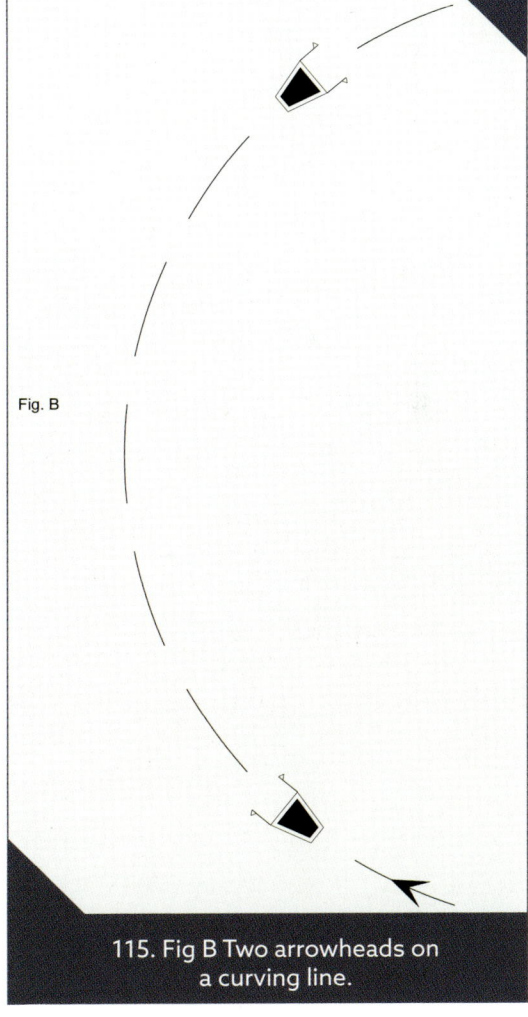

115. Fig B Two arrowheads on a curving line.

Training to Win

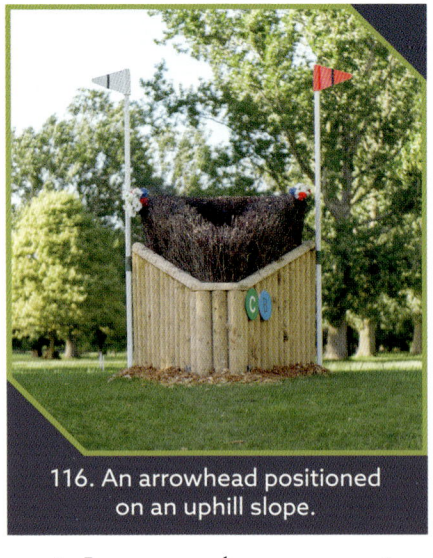

116. An arrowhead positioned on an uphill slope.

117. An arrowhead positioned on a downhill slope.

- In or around a water question. This will question whether the horse is completely confident with both the water and the narrow fence aspect.
- Over a ditch. This will question whether the horse is comfortable with both aspects of the ditch and narrow fence and can jump straight over a ditch.
- Off a sharp turn after a big soft-profile fence, such as a large table. This will

118. An arrowhead positioned before water.

119. An arrowhead in water.

Training to Compete Exercises

question whether the rider can ride forward to the table in a controlling stride so as to be able to land in control and on the desired line.
- Off a sharp turn of three strides. This will question the rider's ability to control the canter stride length, power and balance, and the horse's ability to read and react instantly.
- From a step down. This will question whether the horse is reading the narrow fence from the top of the step and whether he can jump down a step in a straight line.
- Up a step. This will question the power of the canter to jump up the step and the desire to jump a fence at the top.

All of these scenarios will be encountered at some point as the partnership moves up through the grades and it is essential that they are emulated in training at some point.

To begin this process, choose a suitable mobile narrow fence that questions the accuracy but perhaps not the height initially. A plastic brush with cross-country flags at the sides is ideal as you can move it and put it in all the above situations on a cross-country training area.

Main training rules for narrow fences

- Ensure that your horse is completely comfortable with travelling through a narrow area, such as upright flags, without trying to avoid them. Practise your three straight strides before and after the flags to discipline the mental straightness. Use small fences to test your horse's

120. An arrowhead positioned over a ditch in training.

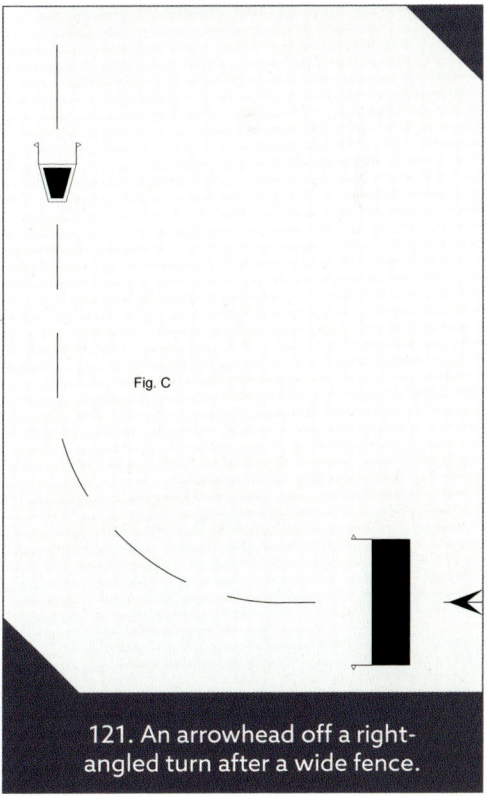
121. An arrowhead off a right-angled turn after a wide fence.

desire to jump narrow fences with softer, non-pressurising rein aids, then you can use either praise for jumping or reinforcement if he makes the decision to go around the fence, also checking the fairness of your approach.

- When training in conjunction with another question such as water, steps, mounds, etc., ensure that your horse is comfortable and familiar with the situation before confronting him with the two aspects put together.

123. Using extra flags at the side to help with initial confidence.

122. A narrow training fence after a step up.

124. A happy and confident partnership in training.

Training to Compete Exercises

- Repeat regularly before adding more technicality or extra height to ensure that the horse has a belief in the safety of the question.
- If you encounter any straightness problems, improve the basics by going back to the exercises in Chapter 6 *Training to Learn*.
- Keep the distances quite open, or on the slightly longer side, as this will encourage forward riding which, in turn, develops the desire to take an obstacle on. The repetition of riding with a forward intention trains your horse to read a question early and whilst he is travelling towards it.

8.3f Training the shoulder brush fence

Shoulder brushes, as their name suggests, will have two heights with a sloping area between them. The lower part of the brush is the area of the fence that is designed to be jumped and will be on the competing line, whereas the higher part is often built so big that it will discourage your horse from jumping that part of the fence. Consequently these fences require a huge amount of accuracy, belief and the ability to stay on the line when they are used as part of a combination. The training needs to be methodical and very progressive to ensure long-term confidence with these types of fences.

The crucial ingredient for successful training of this particular fence is the straightness of the approach. If you are on the correct line and allow your horse's nose out on the approach he will read the fence in a way that gives him a full view of the exit from the fence. If you are riding with a stronger rein contact on either one side or the other, your horse's sight will be adjusted to read either the larger part of the fence or the incorrect side of the flag. This will undoubtedly cause concern and result in your horse running out. If this happens, you can establish the training basics and develop your correct approach with a smaller fence before revisiting the shoulder brush question with better skills.

Once you have trained your horse to enjoy jumping shoulder brushes confidently, you can develop his skills by changing the angle of the fence so that you question the ability to take off on a straight line and land in the corresponding spot.

Developing the confidence to jump a shoulder brush on an angle

This question will generally be asked at 3* upwards and will often be responsible for a certain proportion of penalties. As

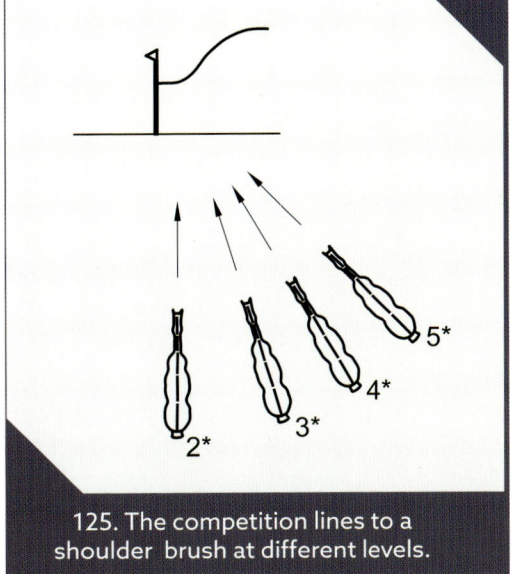

125. The competition lines to a shoulder brush at different levels.

your horse approaches a shoulder brush on an angle he will see the higher side of the shoulder on the take-off stride. If he is being ridden forward in a connection this shouldn't be a concern, but if you are either riding with a rein contact that is restricting, or the partnership is out of balance, this will encourage a run-out.

You will need to spend time training the skill of holding the line with a chance to sight the exit away from the fence. This is a fence that truly tests the partnership's confidence and skill levels.

Set-up and equipment

One way to train your horse with a small shoulder brush is by going to a cross-country training course that offers fences of varying heights to give you a chance to build up step by step and go back to a smaller fence if there is a problem.

The other, very effective, training method is to use a shoulder brush training fence that you can set at any height and build up to quite an advanced question. Start by building two fences in a straight line, preferably in the centre of your training area on a distance of 14.6m / 16yds. The first fence should be a small vertical and the second, a shoulder brush training fence with a ground-line set away at 0.5m / 20in and a tall flag to create a boundary. The shoulder brush should be set on the line so that the centre of the vertical is directly on the line to the small area of the shoulder brush that you intend to jump. If you have just the one shoulder brush training fence you will need to choose either the left- or right-hand side to start with before moving it completely. If you have two shoulder brush training fences you would use two identical lines sitting either side of the centre line, both jumped to the same direction. The left-hand side shoulder brush would sit on the left side of the centre line with an approach off the right rein and the reverse for the right-hand side shoulder brush. Ideally you will need a helper on the ground to change the shoulder brush(es) to a different angle in small increments.

Warming up

Use a routine warm-up in preparation for jumping, to include variations of stride length and lots of leg-yielding work in canter. These warm-up tools will be used throughout the jumping exercise when you apply a supporting aid as a boundary when jumping the angle. Use the small vertical away from the replica shoulder brush to warm up the jumping muscles, ensuring that you practise your focal point and line-holding skills.

Working the exercise

Start by using the related distance of the vertical to the shoulder brush (set quite low) so that you can refresh the basics of stride length, power and balance. Use the first few jumps to check your own personal rules of eyes up, focal point, longer rein, lower leg security and finish off after the jump by working on the immediate balance and softness. It is crucial that on the landing of this type of fence, which questions a drift

Training to Compete Exercises

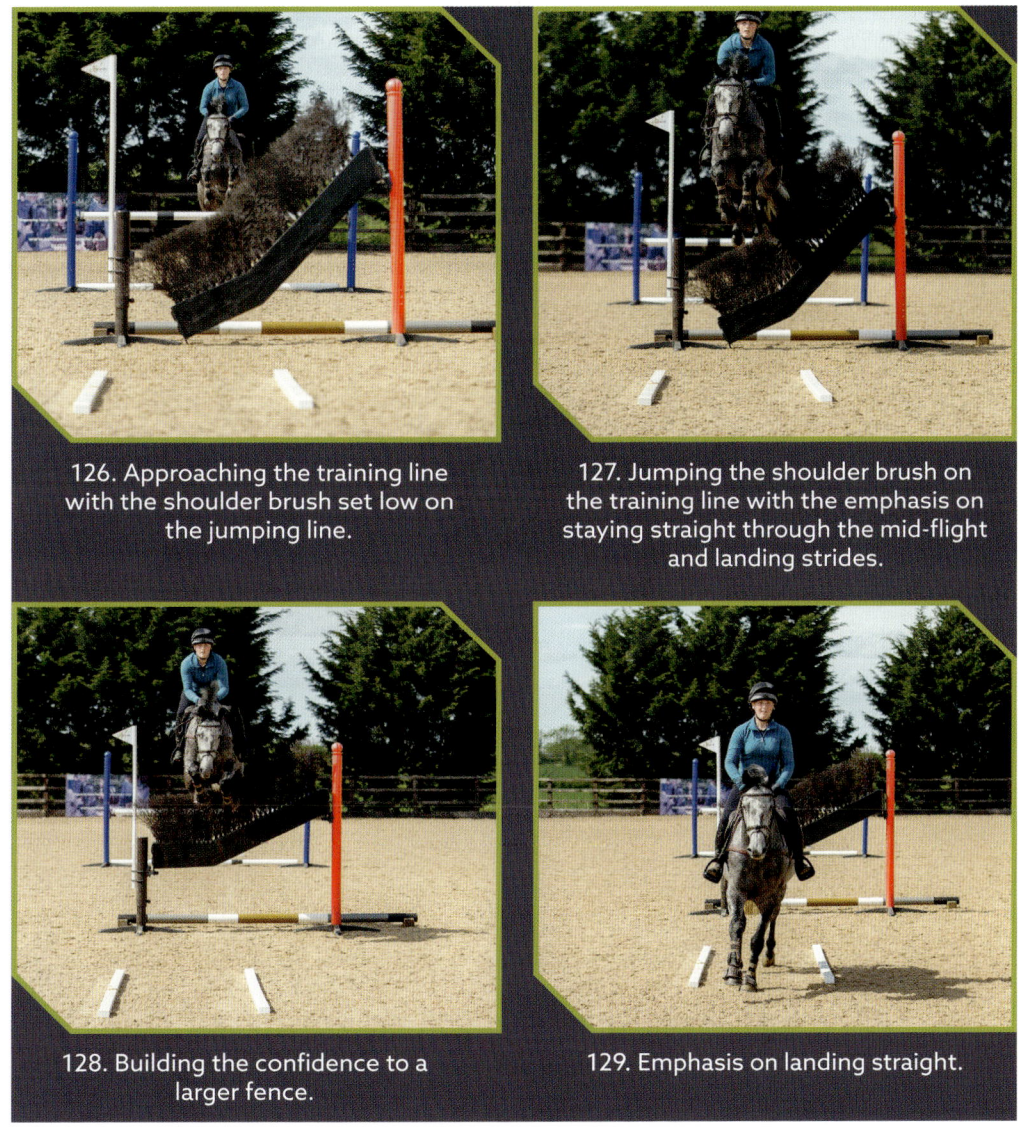

126. Approaching the training line with the shoulder brush set low on the jumping line.

127. Jumping the shoulder brush on the training line with the emphasis on staying straight through the mid-flight and landing strides.

128. Building the confidence to a larger fence.

129. Emphasis on landing straight.

out through the shoulder whilst in the air, you must immediately leg-yield back away from the flag and onto your original line to reinforce the straightness. This will lead to your horse wanting to stay straight in the air.

Once your horse is completely confident and enjoying the jumping line it is time to add some angle to the shoulder brush. Ask your helper to move the smallest part of the shoulder brush away from the approaching line. Start with a very small angle and build up according to your horse's desire to keep jumping straight. As the angle increases you will need to reinforce the straight line on the approach, mid-flight and again on the landing. If you have two lines working at the same time, repeat them equally unless

130. A happy and confident 5-year-old horse. The following training sessions would include more movement on the angle.

you find a weakness, in which case go back to the smaller, original exercise. If you have only the one shoulder brush, work on the more confident and straighter line first before changing the fence around to work on the weaker side.

Relevance to competition

These fences are an advanced question, especially when they are linked to a related distance line of more than one shoulder brush. However, they are also beginning to be brought in at the lower levels at the relevant height. Jumping them is the ultimate straightness skill that a horse needs to own, and the training needs to be very regular to consider this type of fence within a comfort zone in competition. The shoulder brush fences are also used as corner fences, but the confidence levels need to be high before these are considered in training.

8.3g Training steps up and uphill fences

Steps up and down, although a question in themselves, are generally found in competition only with the addition of other fences related to them. In such cases, there need to be high levels of understanding, confidence and skill so that, when another question such as water, a narrow fence, or a corner fence is added you can use the steps productively to land in the correct canter and on the right line.

Training to Compete Exercises

131. A shoulder brush in training for the more advanced horse.

132. Putting two shoulder brushes together on a straight line with a small angle is a typical cross-country question at 3* and above.

Training to Win

> ### Rider Rules for a step-up
>
> - Adjusting the canter early enough so that the frame, balance and power are ideal for the question at hand.
> - The freedom of the reins is enough to allow the horse to use his neck and bring the hind limbs through without any restriction.
> - The rider's body balance stays over the point of gravity lining up with a perpendicular line over the withers as the horse pushes off the ground.
> - The hands stay independent of the body balance and shouldn't be used to lever the upper body forwards.
> - A focal point will help keep the rider's eyes up and form the landing line.
> - It is important to ride positively forwards on the landing stride to ensure momentum away from the step.

To jump up a step the horse requires good balance and a canter that is shaped in the frame needed to push off with power, not speed. It is physically impossible for a horse to be in a frame that equates to a top-speed gallop and alter it instantly on take-off to compress the body in a frame to jump up a step. The canter needs sufficient preparation. The forelimbs, on take-off, will push off the ground in a lifting motion, with the hind limbs adding the power to complete the jump. The landing is important to understand as it will affect how you ride. Because the forelimbs are landing on a slight angle the first stride won't have as much momentum and stride length as it would be the case when landing from a fence on the flat, so it's crucial that you give support with the leg aids on the landing stride.

8.3h Training fences on a mound

133. Riding uphill to a bounce combination on a mound.

A fence with a steep uphill approach requires positive power and a relevant stride length, but not necessarily speed. Horses tend to read fences earlier and easier with a downhill approach than an uphill approach, so more thinking time is often required for the latter. With any fence on a gradient it is important to support the horse's belief and confidence that there is a safe place to put his feet on the landing side.

> ### Rider Rules for a fence on a mound
> - A correct line of approach, with at least one extra stride more than a normal approach.
> - Ride up and forward to the fence so it is met with a forward intention on a slightly expanding stride.
> - Eyes kept up and beyond the fence, never to the base, as this may result in running out of room.
> - Slightly lengthen the reins on take-off so that the horse can stretch across and use his eyes to read the landing.
> - Upper body kept over the withers so as to go with the movement without unbalancing or restricting the horse.
> - It is unlikely that the horse will want to take off on a stride pattern that is far away from the fence, so the rider should keep a good connection between leg and rein aids throughout the whole approach, mid-flight and landing.

8.3i Training steps down and downhill fences

Building up confidence and technique for jumping down a step or a fence with a drop is fundamental in an event horse's training. If you have done your initial training correctly your horse will understand that a drop is safe and fun and now you can add the training that is required for competition.

To understand how a horse jumps down is crucial, as this affects the way you ride the approach.

As you are nearing a drop fence the horse will need instructions from you to reduce the speed and shorten the frame in preparation for reading the question.

As the horse comes to the edge, he will lower his head and neck to see where he is putting his feet, consequently you need to lengthen the reins to allow this to happen. The horse will crouch his hind legs underneath his body, taking them to the edge of the drop, leaving them there as long as possible to support the lowering of the forelimbs. At this point, you should use a supporting forward intention with your legs and allow your upper body to go with the movement of the jump by staying over the withers in a soft manner. As the horse lands, you should allow him to raise his neck again by offering freedom through the contact, then resume the canter away from the step or drop as early as possible to train the horse not to dwell on the landing.

Typical questions in competition

- Drop down to a narrow fence.
- Drop down to a corner on a curving line.
- Drop down into water.
- Drop down to a sliced angle.

> ### Rider Rules for a drop down
>
> - The rider's eyes must stay up on a focal point to manage the upper body balance.
> - Stride length, power and balance should be prepared well in advance.
> - The horse must always have a forward intention.
> - The rider must go with the movement so as not impede the horse's balance.
> - Ride away from the drop immediately to train the horse to focus on the next fence.

Approaching a downhill fence – the rule of 15 per cent

A car travelling down a hill will increase in momentum and a horse will do the same. When you're in your car going down a hill towards a bend in the road you will probably change to a lower gear and keep checking the brakes. When riding a horse down a hill, especially towards a fence, you will need to do the same. Keep your reins down at the withers, with your upper body tall and supporting, and make little pressure aids on the reins that refresh the contact rather than pulling or holding. The gradient of the slope will have quite an impact on the horse's natural stride length.

A gentle downhill slope that is less than 15 per cent in gradient will encourage the horse to gain in speed and stride length. His weight will naturally load onto the forehand because of the gradient, which will encourage him to lean into the rein contact and can often be interpreted as him pulling. He will need a lot of help to rebalance, especially if there is a question at the bottom that requires a shorter frame and correct balance.

A downhill slope that is more than 15 per cent gradient (around 10 degrees) will often have the opposite effect and the horse will start to take more weight onto his hind limbs of his own accord to maintain his balance. If the angle is considerably higher, such as 40

Training to Compete Exercises

per cent gradient (around 22 degrees) the horse will undoubtedly try to take short steps and naturally slow himself down as an act of self-preservation.

Course designers love to use gradients and the overall topography to question the balance and accuracy skills, so it is essential that you take your training away from flat areas and use training combinations on uphill and downhill slopes. All the following combinations require control of stride length, power and balance to negotiate successfully and are typical questions in competition:

Rider Rules to consider with a fence on a downhill slope

- Eyes up to the new direction, never to the base of the fence.
- Prepare well in advance so that the horse is in good balance, with a forward intention.
- Support the horse's stride pattern rather than trying to alter it.
- Lower legs kept supporting rider's balance at the girth area, with heels pushed low.
- Upper body unfolds early by allowing the reins to slip longer.
- If the downhill fence is part of a combination, always set up the next fence in the horse's eye-line in order to land on the new line rather than landing then having to reposition on the new line.

134. Riding down a slope towards a fence. Note how the rider is giving support to the horse's balance with his upper body and lower leg position.

Training to Win

- Downhill approach to a soft-profile fence followed by a turn to a narrow fence or corner.
- Downhill approach to an upright rail before a ditch.
- Downhill approach to a fence into water.
- Downhill approach to an angled slice combination.

8.3j Training confidence at water questions

Jumping confidently into water requires that the horse believes that it is safe to put his feet in, knowing that there is a solid base underneath, even though he may not see it. This is built up from lots of positive experiences within the horse's training, and also the skills and experience that he has gained in previous competitions.

These two forms of experience can be viewed as training to learn and training to compete.

135. Walking in the water, allowing time to look and observe the footing.

136. Trotting through water to gain confidence in the footing.

Training to Compete Exercises

Training to learn – confidence growth step by step
- The first steps into water should be a positive experience with a shallow depth and a good secure footing.
- Build in small steps up and down.
- Canter through an expanse of water.
- Use small showjumps on the edge to introduce the first small jump into water.

Training to compete – confidence growth step by step
- Start to introduce small showjumps and cross-country fences into and out of a water complex to build confidence.
- Moving on from a showjump, start jumping directly into water over a small log or roll top, building up the height over a period of time.
- Building in a narrow fence. First on the exit from a water complex then adding a small narrow fence on the approach to the water, eventually adding a narrow fence to be jumped directly into the water.

137. Using a small showjump to introduce the first jump into water.

138. Building up the height and confidence in unison.

139. Jumping a small log pile into water. It is advantageous for a horse to be able to see the water through the jump rather than it being solid.

140. Training the narrow fence into water with flags as the first building block.

Training to Compete Exercises

141. Confidence-building with a small narrow brush jumping out of water.

142. Confidence-building with a small narrow brush jumping into water.

143. Confidence-building with a larger plastic fence not directly into water.

144. Confidence-building with the plastic brush fence now directly into water.

145. Confidence-building with the plastic brush now in the water.

- Jumping a fence in water. Initially using a small solid log pile that meets the water level before using a hanging log, which ultimately doesn't have a ground-line. Eventually, when the confidence levels are increased, you need to train with a narrow fence in the water. Make sure that you use a fence that is on a good distance if the question is related to a jump into the water. If it is a fence unrelated to another fence, ensure that it is positioned far enough into the water that the horse's stride pattern isn't affected by the water's edge, in case there is any hesitation or a large leap from dry land to water. In competition the length of the water expanse mustn't be less than 6m / 6.5yds unless there is a step out, in which case it must be no less than 9m / 10yds. After a drop into water there mustn't be a fence on a distance less than three strides away and, when jumping a fence out of water, there mustn't be a distance of less than two strides after a jump within the water. These rules are designed to give a horse a fair distance in which to read a fence and stay in balance, so they must be adhered to in training.
- Have an awareness of the water's depth. This will depend on weather conditions and human interventions with depth control by having the facility either to add water via a hosepipe or remove it via a pump. The competition depth must not exceed 35cm / 14in at any part of the water complex.

8.3k Ditch training with additional questions

Training the horse to compete involves ensuring that he experiences everything he might face in competition in his training. You will get to know how much repetition is required depending on his weaker areas. With all fences involving a ditch, it is important that the ditch is never a question, so by building all the different scenarios into your training your horse will not be phased by it in competition.

Using the ditch in the middle of a related distance is your horse's first introduction to a coffin fence. The following is a step-by-step way of increasing confidence.

- Ditch in and fence out on the flat.
- Fence in, followed by a ditch and fence out. Initially on the flat, then using a scoop or gradient.
- Rail over ditch (trakehner).
- Flags on the landing side of the ditch to denote a narrow area.
- Narrow fence behind ditch.
- Ditch in the middle of a curving line combination.
- Ditch in the bottom of a scoop.
- Ditch in the middle of a combination on an angle.

146a & b. An inviting rail over a ditch with a good obvious ground-line at 4* and a less inviting angled rail over a ditch at 5*.

8.4 Riding to a cross-country fence at the correct speed

Riding to the time on the cross-country is a skill that is developed over time and comes with experience and practice. The optimum time is set across the course on a route that the technical delegate measures starting from the start box and finishing at the finish flags. The time will vary depending on the level of competition. Depending on topography, course layout and ground conditions, the time will either be relatively easy to gain (often called a fast time) or very difficult, classed as a slow time. The speed at which you should approach each fence will depend on a variety of considerations.

Profile of the fence

The actual jump is an extension of the canter and, if the fence requires a long, wide flight profile (for example, a sloping wide table) then the canter needs to have some length and speed so that the fence is taken easily within the stride. If, on the other hand, the fence is fairly vertical the canter needs to be in a shorter, more high-powered frame to provide a rounder profile of jump.

Within a related distance

If there are two or more fences related to each other by a set distance it would be advantageous to jump into that distance in the canter that is required in the middle. You can make the decision whether it is a long, open distance or a shorter, closed distance for your horse.

What is on the landing side of the fence?

A surprise, such as a ditch, can cause a last-moment hesitation, so the canter for approaching such a fence needs to be reasonably short and adaptable.

A drop fence that has a leaf pit profile

This is usually quite an imposing type of drop fence with a landing on sloping ground that runs away fairly steeply. This fence would require a very slow, short-striding approach in the canter or maybe even an approach in trot so that the horse has time to see and assess the question.

Into water

Jumping into water, especially from high ground to low ground, will have a profound slowing-down effect as your horse hits the water. Consequently the approach needs to be positive, with a forward intention, but with balance and connection. The water depth will have an impact on your speed and will need to be checked when walking the course.

Fence type	Pace
1st gear. Trot. Young horse to ditch, through water. Leaf pit type of drop fence.	Make sure that when dropping down to trot it is highly connected and straight.
2nd gear. High-powered, short-stepping canter. For anything with a surprise on the landing side, when the horse may hesitate and need an extra stride. Jumping down a drop fence.	This canter should feel like a coiled spring with the hind legs underneath the body in an energetic way. The forehand should be light and high, with the neck ready to expand to the fence.
3rd gear. A medium showjumping canter that is engaged with a stride length relative to the question. Used for narrow fences with an upright profile, jumping into water, related distances or combination fences with an upright profile.	This canter should feel that you can easily control direction and balance.
3.5 gear. More stride length and speed than the 3rd gear. This gear would be used for corners and narrow fences with width, but with a technical aspect.	This canter should feel as if you are travelling and moving up through the approach and turn to a fence. Meeting a wide but technical fence in a big stride will give your horse the confidence to move through distances with ease and is a prerequisite for moving up to top level.
4th gear. This is a gallop and is used on the approach of soft-profile fences such as sloping brush fences, wide tables and any fence that has been dressed in such a way as to offer a ground rail that prevents the horse going too close to the base.	This speed is not top speed, but is ground-covering and should have just a minor gear change on the approach when you go from your 'top speed position' to the 'shoulders up' preparation position (see riding to a soft-profile fence).
5th gear. This is your top speed, which is used in between fences and shouldn't be jumped out of without some form of gear change and preparation.	

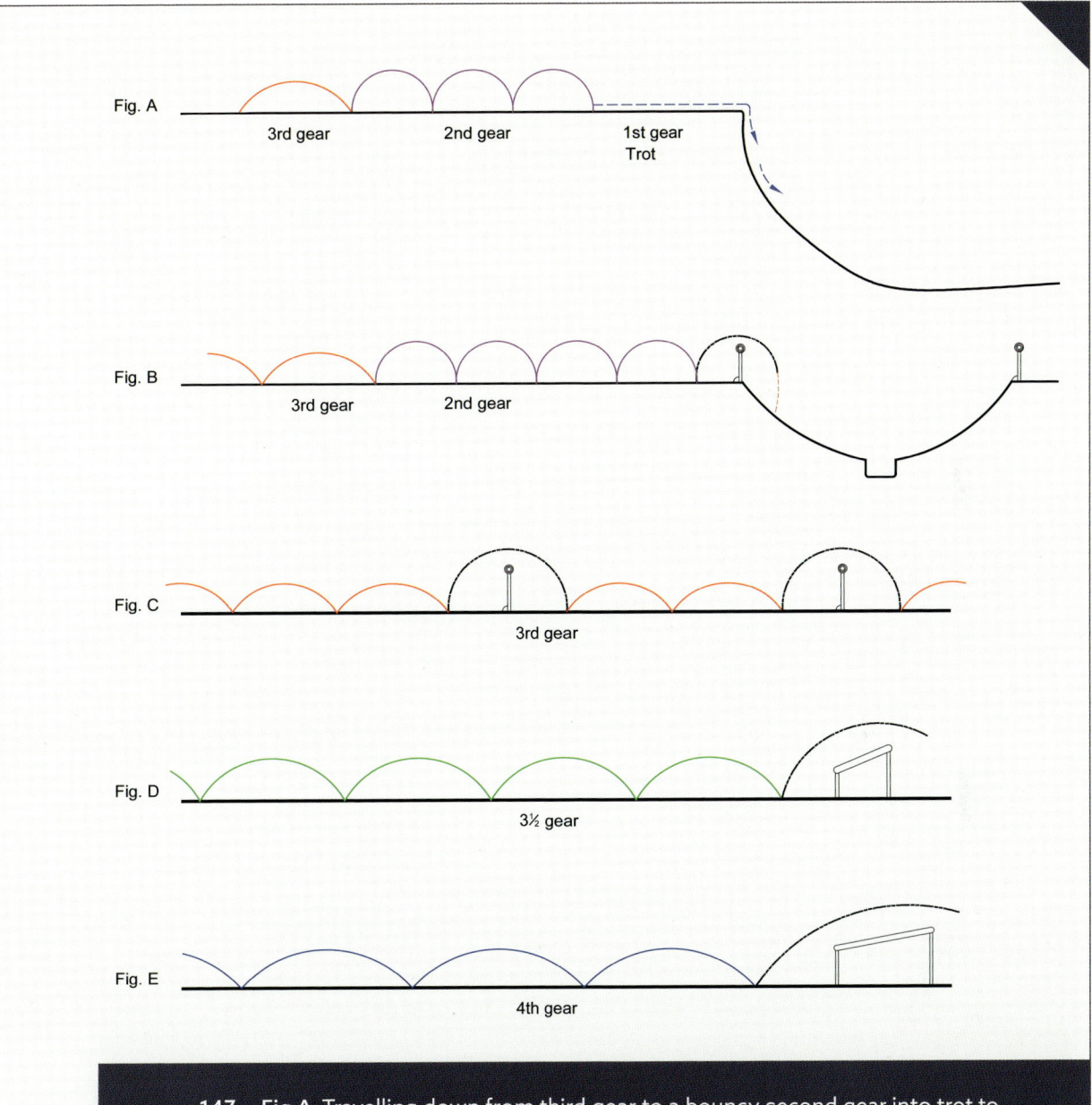

147. **Fig A** Travelling down from third gear to a bouncy second gear into trot to give the horse the correct amount of time to read the drop with a slope away.

Fig B Travelling down from third gear to second gear to produce a high-powered, short-stepping canter to accommodate any last-minute questions from the horse.

Fig C Canter stride relative to the related distance.

Fig D A bigger stride required for an accurate but soft-profile fence.

Fig E Not quite top speed, but a gallop relating to a soft-profile fence.

Topography

Recognising how the horse is finding his balance whilst moving up and down the gradients will give you an idea of the speed at which you can safely move up to a fence. The younger, less experienced horse will need to be ridden with more time to assess the situations arising than the older, more experienced horse, who has learned to read and assess questions at speed.

Practising riding to a soft-profile fence

Riding to such a fence (for example, a sloping table or a steeplechase brush fence) at the required speed should be included in your cross-country training and speed training as often as possible.

- Set your speed at an appropriate gallop depending on ground conditions and topography. Have your position in the 'top speed' galloping position, which is a close contact, forward seat.
- On approach to the single, soft-profile fence, draw your shoulders up so they are just in front of the vertical and lower your hands whilst tucking your seat underneath you to secure your position. This positional change should have the effect of taking your horse from top speed to down a gear into a speed that is still a gallop but in a balance, with the hind legs coming more under.
- Take your focal point and look beyond the fence to the new direction to prevent your head and eyes being drawn to the base of the fence.
- Read what pattern your horse is on and support him with the connection between your legs, reins and upper body. Never try to alter the pattern, only offer support.
- If you are moving towards the base of the fence, allow the reins to become softer with a little length so your horse can use his eyes to look and his neck to balance.
- This is a time-saving fence so keep your legs in contact in the air and aim to land moving straight back into the same speed by adopting the 'top speed' position immediately on landing.

The straightforward galloping fences have a lot of uses. At any point around the course where you feel your horse needs some education – for example, if he is starting to drift across the fences to a certain direction – use these rhythm fences to correct the straightness and hold a specific line to ensure that the horse is responding to the aids in the air. If your horse is becoming too overwhelmed and is starting to run through the bridle you can use these rhythm fences to shape the jump by forfeiting some time penalties and using a slower speed. If you feel that your horse is losing confidence in his jump and is starting to draw back in front of a fence you could ride more forwards to encourage him to jump better out of his rhythm again. *Every fence on the course should have a use.*

Training to Compete Exercises

8.5 First-minute training and riding to the time

Going from the warm-up area to the end of the first minute is a crucial part to your cross-country round. Keeping yourself and your horse in the right frame of mind, relaxed but ready to burst into top speed, is not easy and needs some thought and practise. The first minute on most courses will involve going from a standing start to three straightforward galloping fences to get you into a rhythm and to jump the maximum height. Out of the start box the ideal is to get into a positive, forward canter touching 400–500mpm depending on how close the first fence is, then moving straight into your top speed immediately. With an experienced horse, if competing at 2* level your top speed in between fences is likely to be 540mpm, at 3* 570–600mpm, and top speed at 4* and 5* could be 600mpm upward. At the 2022 World Equestrian Games in Pratoni, Lordships Graffalo recorded 844mpm. If you don't take advantage of the soft-profile galloping fences, especially in the first minute, you will find that you are sitting behind the clock with the inability to make up the time. To do this effectively, walk the tightest lines and put into practice the rider rules for jumping fences at speed. At home or at your cross-country training venue choose three or four rhythm fences with soft profiles that are spaced out at approximately 150m on a distance of 520m. Start from the halt, go into walk then straight into a 450mpm canter to the first fence around 30m away then, on landing, practise getting up to your top speed and, using subtle gear changes, ride to the fences of choice. Time yourself to see if you are under or over the minute across the 520m. This will give you a feeling of your first minute at 2* level.

148. Confidently out of the start box.

Making the optimum time on the cross-country is an important part of the competition but needs to be carefully planned. It may be that you use some events to educate your horse at a slower speed and others to run quicker. The practice of going at top speed early on in a young horse's career can have an impact later on as he moves up through the levels and may also cause an injury early in his career. The early stages should be educational, with the focus on developing rhythm and accepting gear changes so that different profiles can be jumped safely. It takes time to build up the required muscles and stamina to be able to gallop in balance around the whole cross-country course.

8.6 Riding the last minute on the cross-country

The last minute is the time when mistakes can easily happen and most course designers will want to check that the rider has control of both the balancing and the steering aids. Usually the penultimate fence will be a turning or accuracy question, often in a combination where a gear change will need to be made. If your horse is tired there is more likelihood of a run-out, in which case you will have to work really hard to re-create the momentum on the return approach.

Rider Rules for the last minute on the cross-country

- Maintain the same rhythm throughout.
- Ride what is underneath you regarding how your horse feels. It is essential to recognise if a tired horse is losing balance.
- If you are down on the clock, maintain a sensible speed but don't chase the time and risk any loss of balance or an approach that lacks preparation.
- Keep your own balance and position right the way through to the finish and beyond.
- Maintain a good rein contact as you ride through the finish, moving down to a slow canter, a trot and, after 15 seconds, return to walk with a good transition before dismounting. Often you will be in a state of euphoria and will want to praise your horse, but save that until you have supported him through the transitions so that all of his weight doesn't fall onto his forehand when he's fatigued.

Training to Compete Exercises

149. The importance of maintaining a good balance through the finish is paramount.

8.7 Effective use of the showjumping warm-up

Developing a personal warm-up routine for the jumping phases is crucial to having a successful round in the ring or on course. It is the time when you put the horse into the right frame of mind, keep him alert and ready to perform. Ideally, you need to perfect your routine warm-up at home and be as consistent with it as possible in competition. This allows your horse to be comfortable with the warm-up jumps, since he will know what to expect and hopefully put plenty of effort into his work.

Because most warm-up facilities are on grass or a well-used artificial surface, the ground conditions may be far from perfect. The ground could easily be very firm mid-season or, if the weather has been poor, it could be muddy and deep on the take-offs and landings. Consequently keeping the jumps to a minimum wherever possible will keep your horse fresh and hopefully confident. Everyone will have a different routine, but it is very common to see riders jumping two cross-poles, then five or six verticals before moving on to the spread fence. There, they will often start quite small and build up with five or six spreads or parallels until they are satisfied and ready to jump one last vertical before going into the ring. This routine has given the horse approximately fifteen jumps which, on poor ground or if they are weary at a long format, is way too many. I have perfected a warm-up routine with riders I help that limits the jumps to seven to nine fences, which means that the horse still has plenty of energy and 'jump' left in him before he goes into the ring. I would normally do the following:

1. Small square parallel.
2. Repeat or up two holes.
3. Widen the back rail.
4. Put the back up four holes to encourage the horse to reach and keep his eyes up.
5. Put the front up to match, with a good ground-line pulled out.
6. Raise the square parallel, with or without the ground-line, depending on what the horse requires.
7. Tall vertical with a good ground-line.
8. Tall vertical with ground-line pushed in.

This routine is practised regularly at home so both horse and rider are confident with the changes made. The timing of the last few fences will vary from horse to horse. Some horses respond to a break after the warm-up routine whereas others need a last jump immediately before they go into the ring. This will depend on anxiety levels. The anxious horse will need some time to allow his heart rate to reduce and maybe a walk on a long, relaxing rein, whereas other horses will need to keep a high mental alertness to perform well and may need a reminder jump immediately before the round. The responsibility should fall on your helper to arrange this timing as you will have your thoughts on the performance of the round. Going from the last practice showjump to the first fence in the arena can be the deciding factor of whether you jump a clear round or not. Nerves and the rider's aids play a huge part in the way the horse performs so it is essential that you develop a system that allows you to stay focused. Being undeterred by outside interferences and learning to breathe correctly

150. Small parallel.

Training to Compete Exercises

can maintain clear thoughts. This will be covered later on in the book (see *Chapter 10.5a*). Your helper in the collecting ring should have full knowledge of the collecting ring rules and regulations at National and International competitions, as they vary. For example, at a National competition a ground rail is compulsory whereas at an International competition there are no requirements for a ground rail underneath any type of warm-up fence. At National competitions the maximum height of the lower rail is 1m, whereas at an International competition the lower rail has no restrictions if you want it to sit directly underneath the top rail.

151. Small parallel but a little wider.

152. Back rail higher to make an ascending spread.

153. Front rail up to meet the back rail and the ground-line pulled out a little.

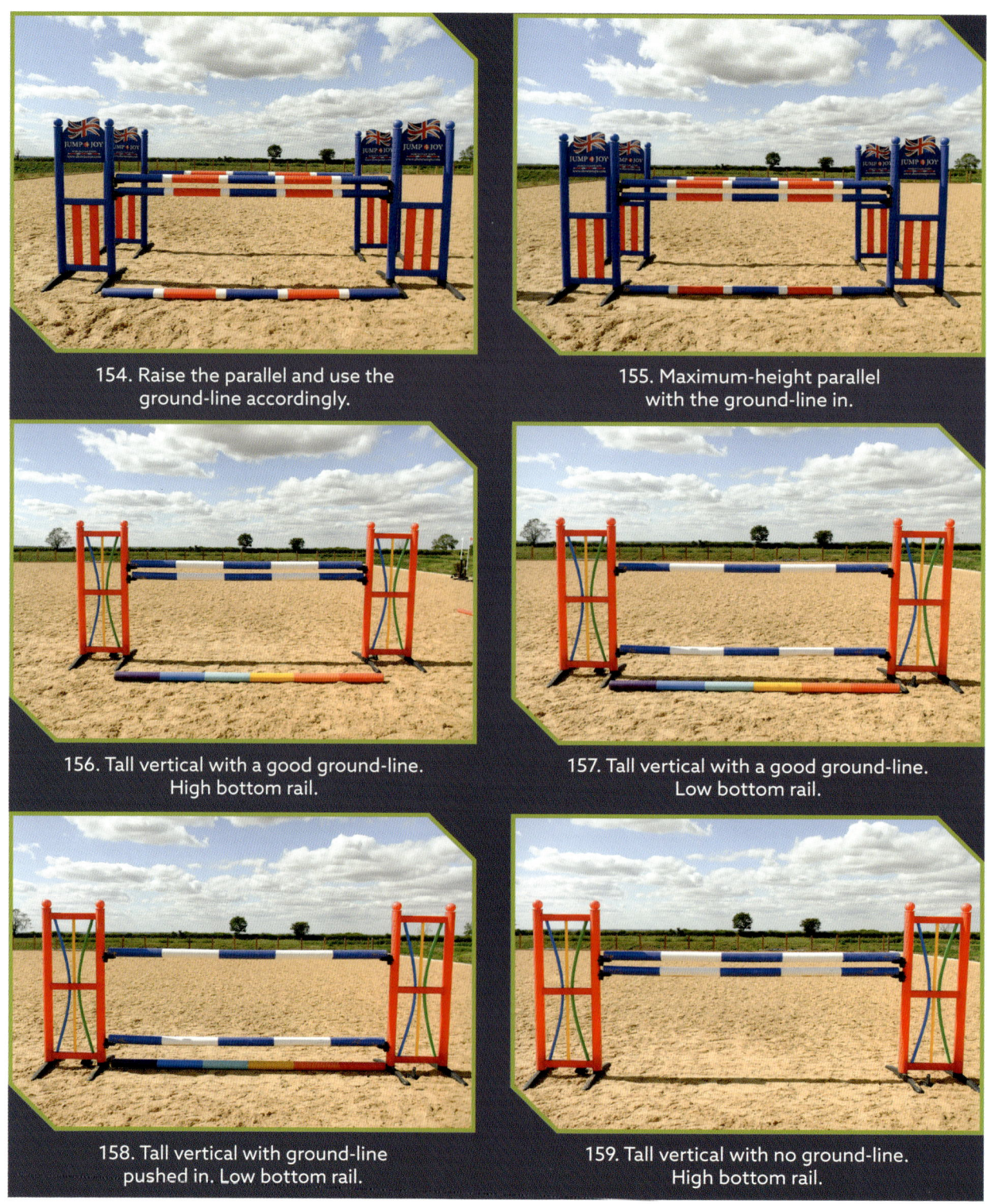

154. Raise the parallel and use the ground-line accordingly.

155. Maximum-height parallel with the ground-line in.

156. Tall vertical with a good ground-line. High bottom rail.

157. Tall vertical with a good ground-line. Low bottom rail.

158. Tall vertical with ground-line pushed in. Low bottom rail.

159. Tall vertical with no ground-line. High bottom rail.

Chapter 9

Training to Win – the Making of a Champion

All the way through this book I have emphasised performance over outcome and now, although that mantra should be still ingrained, we are also concerned with winning. If you have followed the system in this book, it will have given you and your horse clarity in developing correct basics, a building block system to add skills to, a desire to train with total focus and enjoyment in training your horse to be the best.

Now it is time to strive beyond just good performance to become a rider who has skills above and beyond those of your competitors.

9.1 Marginal gains

Isn't it funny how day by day nothing changes but when you look back, everything is different?

C.S. Lewis

Performance profiling is a way of looking at your performance objectively in order to recognise weaker areas and look at improvements.

When we think about being the best, we sometimes think that we need to do something revolutionary to make vast improvements to win. Actually, it's the opposite where training horses is concerned. Horses are creatures of habit and learn from their last experience. They need routine, continuity and belief that something is safe to perform. If we tried to change their training drastically in large increments it would most likely have a negative effect and throw the horse into disarray. If our performance goals are small but achievable this promotes a motivational mindset, which is the key to making improvements.

In 2003 David Brailsford (now Sir David Brailsford CBE) was brought into a poorly performing British Cycling Team to improve their performance. Sir David's approach was to focus on very small changes and seeking constant improvements of 1 per cent until these small changes compounded into vast improvements and, from 2007 for the next ten years, the British Cycling Team dominated the sport until other countries caught up on the training and management techniques.

So using this format of making minor improvements in the horse's performance, the simple formula is *recognition*, *goal-setting* and *action*.

9.2 Performance profiling

Performance profiling is a way of looking at your performance objectively in order to recognise weaker areas and look at improvements. It can be most frustrating to know that you are underperforming and have a weaker area, but not know how to change it for the better. Often a rider will repetitively practise the skill at which they are underperforming, but without making any changes so, in effect, they are practising 'bad practice'. A more effective way of making improvements is by taking that particular skill and breaking it down into different component parts, then making small improvements in each area before putting the skill back together again.

How do you do this?
- Make a list of all the attributes that you recognise in a role model of your choice.
- Make a list of different categories that are crucial to top performance in the sport of eventing.
- Break these categories down into smaller areas of skills.
- Break the skills down into component parts.
- Look objectively at each area and note or score yourself on where you are now and where you need to be. It would be useful to do this with a coach who can look from the outside.
- Make a list of the small areas that you need to improve on (performance goals).
- Create an action plan.
- You will need feedback on the performance of these skills, so work with a coach or mentor to keep revisiting areas until the skills are well within your comfort zone and can be performed without mistakes in training.
- Developing new rules for yourself is essential for success. Creating little process goals such as 'eyes beyond the fence' or 'posture correction before half-pass left' will help secure your new system.

Example Case Study 1

A rider has recognised that she regularly gets a mark of 6 or 6.5 for the left shoulder-in. This had previously gone unnoticed as it felt okay.

- Along with her coach, the rider then dissected the shoulder-in down into smaller areas such as:
- Quality of the rhythm in the trot.
- Roundness and submission into the outside rein.
- Engagement of the inside hind.
- Bend around the rider's inside leg.
- The outside shoulder staying on a line.
- Moving into the shoulder-in movement.
- Finishing the movement off correctly.

After videoing the left shoulder-in from different angles, looking at competition videos and having feedback from the coach the rider has recognised that the horse would like to offer too much bend in the neck. This leads to stepping out onto the right shoulder and losing the correct angle and consequently the rhythm alters after the third step of the movement. The rider recognises that she is unclear about starting the movement at a specific point and finishing off the shoulder-in correctly.

The coach and rider put a plan of action together to make small improvements, as follows:

- Working some 10m circles around the arena to produce a uniform bend in the horse's body.
- Noticing her own position and using memory points around the arena regularly to make minor adjustments to sit correctly.
- Riding some shoulder-fore work (10–15 degree angle) in the trot and canter to develop balance and the correct support of the inside hind leg.
- Riding some shoulder-in away from the track with a good focal point.

Case Study 1 continued

- Practising riding in and out of a shoulder-fore position regularly around the arena so that the horse gets used to making the transition in and out of the shoulder-in smoothly and without any change within the quality of the trot.
- When all of these areas have improved in ease and quality of performance, the left shoulder-in will have become a successful skill.
- If at any point performance is lost, the rider will have the ability to go back to any one of those components to up-skill again.

Example Case Study 2

A rider is starting to become frustrated because she regularly has the last fence down in the showjumping phase. The rider knows that her showjumping skills are her weakest link, but up to now has been happy with the one fence down because she has managed to jump around the rest of the course successfully and she will normally get a top ten finish because her dressage is normally at 75 per cent and the cross-country is always clear within the optimum time.

The rider then spends some time watching back videos of her showjumping rounds and asks her coach to sit and analyse them with her. This reveals a change in balance as the rider jumps around the track, which causes the horse to start rushing at the end of the course, often tapping the last few fences and regularly getting flat in the jump by the last fence. Also, when questioned, the rider happily reveals that by the time she is coming towards the last fence she stops riding the same quality of canter and lets her guard down. The showjumping phase needs to be broken down into these larger areas before breaking the important issues into smaller components:

- The quality of the canter. Stride length *versus* power *versus* balance.
- The warm-up procedure.
- Preparation immediately prior to the competition.

- Riding the lines. Related distances, dogleg distances, curving lines, straight lines, roll back turns.
- Course-walking and 'chunking' the track.
- Riding within the time allowed.
- Understanding course design.
- Mental approach to staying focused and not allowing outside interferences to distract.

After considering these points, the rider and coach decide to focus on the canter quality throughout the track, chunking the track into three sections and looking at course design.

The following action plan is agreed upon:

- The three cavalletti exercise, which focuses on stride length and balance.
- Working through the four-stride exercise in canter of four strides collected, four strides working, four strides medium, four working and four collected to perfect transitions and balance in the canter.
- Doing some faster work at 400mpm and then returning immediately to a showjumping canter at 350mpm to jump some showjumps. This will challenge the sensation of nearing the end of a showjumping round.
- Walking a course and chunking it into three sections. The first section will include up to the first distance and double. The middle chunk will include more related distances, which are often open distances before the final chunk, which will normally include a treble combination, and an open distance to a final closed line. The rider will need to practise the rebalancing work after the open distances to work on the problem of losing balance at the end of the track.
- The rider will look at different showjumping tracks at different International competitions and study different rounds on YouTube, recognising the strengths and weaknesses of different rounds.

> *Case Study 2 continued*
>
> - The rider will develop some *personal rules*, which will involve always imagining that there is another fence after the last so that the quality of the canter is maintained, and also monitoring the stride length, balance and power throughout.
>
> **Working through the above produced a training system that looked at the small areas and delivered improvements throughout, including clear rounds.**
>
> **Profiling your own performance is only successful if it includes regular reviews to refresh the strategy. If you build in feedback and planning sessions they will cause you to keep looking at tiny areas of improvement. This is smart training and will maintain your personal motivation to succeed.**

Don't decrease the goal. Increase the effort.

Tom Coleman

9.3 Training in the pressure zone

Being subjected to stress in competition can reduce a good performance, preventing clear thoughts and leading to areas of weaknesses, causing mistakes to happen. This is mainly because the skills that are learned in training are within a familiar environment, often without any realms of pressure. It is essential that the partnership is subjected to performing in the pressure zone within a training environment as well as in competition. Stretching the mind and body to provide challenges can often be difficult in training, so it requires planning and ingenuity.

The following are two examples of exercises in the pressure zone within a training environment.

9.3a Stride reduction around a track of showjumps

Whatever level you are competing at, the optimum time in the showjumping phase can have a bearing on the outcome. It is essential that you train yourself and your horse to be economical within a good balance so that time penalties in the showjumping never occur.

Set up a track of fences in your training area, or use an unaffiliated competition where you have the opportunity to jump the round twice to replicate this training exercise. The track needs to mirror the height, width, technicality and length that you

Training to Win – the Making of a Champion

would find in competition. Ideally, be working alongside another rider, or preferably a small group of riders all at the same level.

Warm up using a routine competition warm-up programme before jumping around the course. Have a coach or adjudicator time the round from taking off at the first fence to landing after the last fence. Alongside the timing, have the adjudicator count every non-jumping stride around the whole track. After that, reflect on any areas that you feel could be improved and, after choosing no more than two, decide on a plan to make small adjustments with that intention. As well as the planned improvements, think about the track as a whole and look to see where you can potentially remove ten strides around the track. This needs to be performed only by riding tighter lines and without any change in stride length, power or balance.

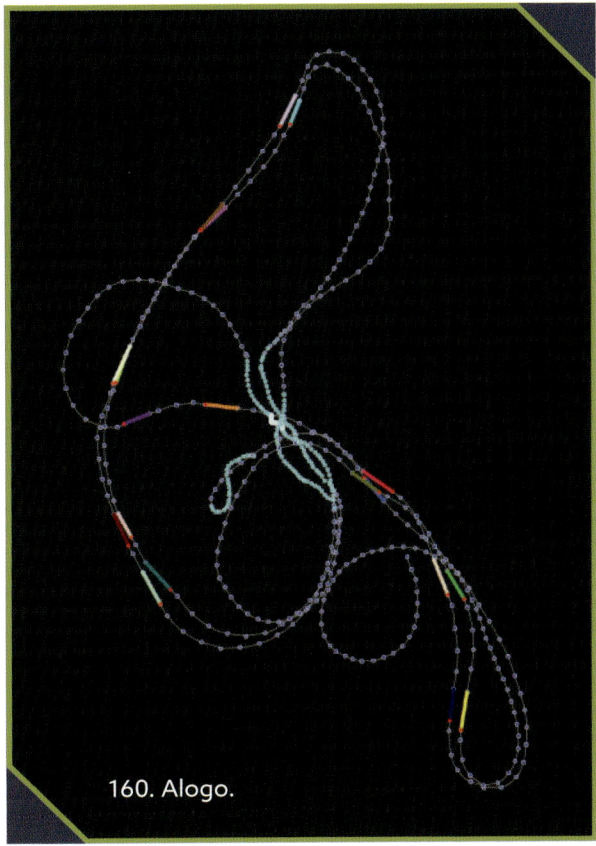

160. Alogo.

If other riders are taking part in this exercise, each is then to jump the same track whilst the other riders monitor the two planned improvements and the coach/adjudicator counts the strides and times the round.

This is a safe and productive way of taking a rider out of the comfort zone and into a pressure zone. The competitors amongst the riders will want to be the best and will look to reduce the strides by more than ten, whilst the riders who are more concerned about performance may be more cautious. Both categories of riders can potentially come out on top as winners – however they may need to look at their peers to learn how to be the best in all respects. The Alogo Move Pro unit is a useful addition to your equipment as it will record and document stride length, height of jump, speed and heart rate but the key element here is GPS path mapping. It will show you the lines that you rode and overlap your second course to show the reduction in strides.

9.3b Exercise to develop ability to task-load

Using the same scenario as above, on the second round of jumping create a task-loading situation. Each rider is to swap their jumping whip over four times around the track and they are to choose one fence (not the last fence) at which to completely remove their feet out of their stirrups and regain them on landing. In addition to this, one of the other riders will throw a question at them at some point during the round, to be answered immediately by the rider jumping. This changes a relatively easy task into one that contains a certain amount of pressure to mimic what could be experienced in competition. Unexpected problems could be a possible upset in rhythm when the horse feels the whip being swapped over, or when the rider jumps a fence without stirrups, which has the potential to change the pressure aids. These will have an impact on the rhythm and balance within the canter, which the rider will need to monitor and correct. Finally, taking the rider's concentration away by having to listen to, comprehend and answer a question can have an impact on the performance and it requires regular practise for the rider to be competent in dealing with such issues.

9.4 Training high degrees of accuracy
9.4a Turning tight into a line and exiting straight

This exercise is highly technical as it requires balance, obedience and total straightness around a ninety-degree turn to jump a fence with no deviation from the line in the air, whilst being challenged with a narrow fence on landing. It is also a useful exercise to improve jumping technique and to refresh the directional aids.

Set-up and equipment
Build two small square parallels with an inviting ground-line on the approach. Then, 14.1m / 15yds in front of the fences, lay down a line of poles to denote the edge of the arena. On the landing side of each of the parallels put a small narrow fence on a one-stride distance of 7.3m / 8yds.

Warming up
Use your regular warm-up routine to prepare for jumping, to include lots of 10m circles in the canter. The circles should be ridden accurately with a start and finish marker and three strides on each quarter of the circle. Use some canter poles to work on your accuracy and a small parallel or vertical with a regular, long approach to warm up the horse's jumping muscles.

Working the exercise
Choose a starting rein, create a good-quality jumping canter and make a turn from the inside of the edge of the arena poles to jump the small parallel exactly in the centre. Maintain the straightness mid-flight to land on the line to the narrow fence. Build up

Training to Win – the Making of a Champion

this exercise using both parallels on each rein. Practise looking around the turn with your eyes and then beyond the narrow fence as you jump the parallel.

Relevance to competition

This exercise teaches the horse to stay on the rider's line around a turn and exit after a jump straight without any deviation, which is crucial in competition as the lines become more challenging.

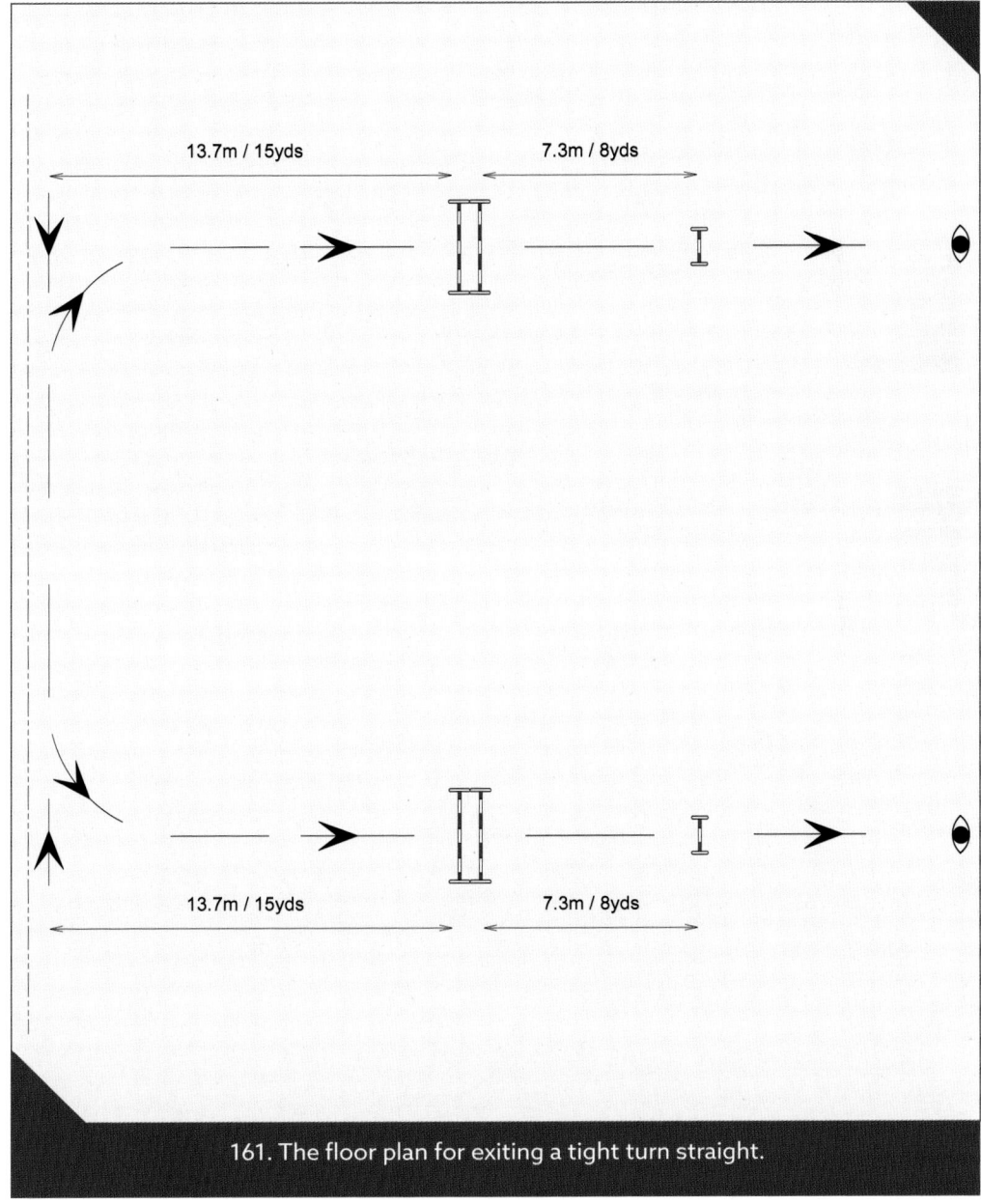

161. The floor plan for exiting a tight turn straight.

162. The turn to the fence. Note the inside hind engaged underneath the body and the nose being pulled out onto the line of approach.

Training to Win – the Making of a Champion

163. A straight jump with horse and rider looking on to the third element.

164. A small but very significant jump, which emphasises straightness throughout.

9.4b Jumping into a line on a curve and exiting straight

This exercise is an ideal challenge for a horse who tends to drift one way or another over a fence through poor balance or habit. The pressure is applied from the approach where the horse enters the exercise on a curve so is likely to want to keep that curve through the air. However, the training is about using the fence to straighten up over and react to the rider's positive pressure.

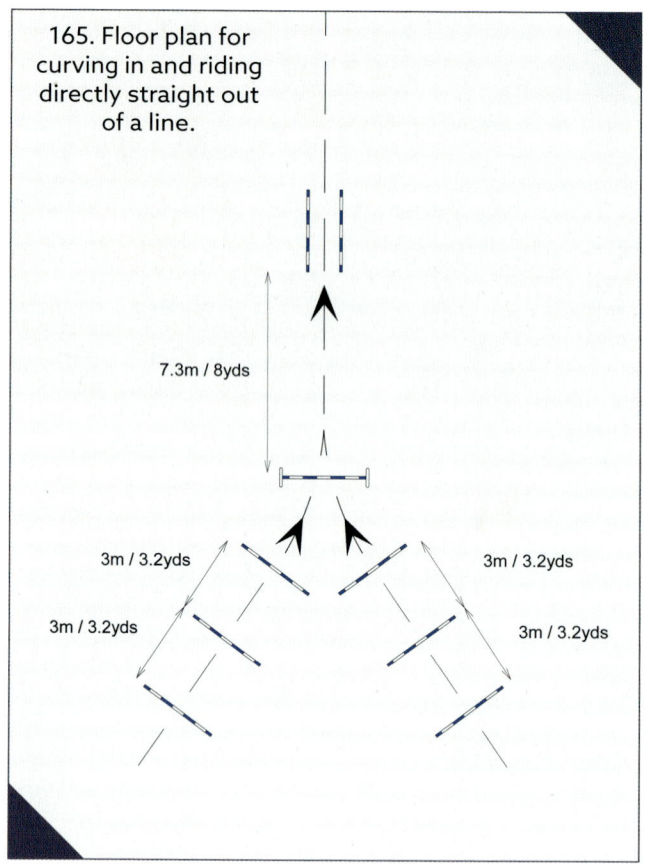

165. Floor plan for curving in and riding directly straight out of a line.

Set-up and equipment
Set up one vertical in the centre of your training area with a good ground-line and two poles at the top close together. Then place three canter poles with a distance of 3m / 10ft between them on the approach, but on a curve from each rein. On the landing side place two parallel poles as a guiding line away from the fence on a straight, central line.

Warming up
Use your routine warm-up to prepare for jumping. The exercise is going to challenge the horse's suppleness, bend and engagement of the hind limbs and the rider's control of the withers to go straight, so all of these challenges need bringing into the warm-up. Use exercises such as 10m circles in the collected canter followed by riding into a medium stride then a transition to return to the collected canter into a square or straight line.

Working the exercise
Start on your preferred rein and approach the vertical in a positive working canter. Ride to the centre of each pole with a little bit of added pressure on the take-off stride to keep straight in the air and continue the straight line through the parallel poles on the landing side. Once your horse has accepted the straight line away from the fence he will start to put effort into his own balance. Repeat on both reins, changing the rein

Training to Win – the Making of a Champion

166. Drone image of the exercise in use.

each time. When your horse is finding the exercise suitably easy, add more challenge by adding height to the vertical. Adding a narrow training fence one stride from the vertical is another question and should be well practised at a more advanced level.

Relevance to competition

Cross-country course designers are forever pushing the boundaries of testing skill levels. This exercise is a typical question at top level when it tests where momentum and centrifugal force should move through an outside shoulder, but the skill is straightening up mid-flight. When you are course-walking and see this sort of question you will often have a choice of testing this skill and going direct or taking a slightly longer route, which will be time-consuming but safer.

9.4c Precision training with three cavalletti

The cross-country course designer is constantly asking riders to open up to a big table and then land with total control to turn to a corner or jump a narrow fence. This requires a learned technique where you provide power and stride length on the approach to the wide table but, on the take-off stride, have the skill to reduce the expansion of the stride in order to land in balance and full control on the new line.

Set-up and equipment

This is a very simple exercise to set up. Using three cavalletti on their highest setting, place them in a straight line with 14.6m / 16yds between each one.

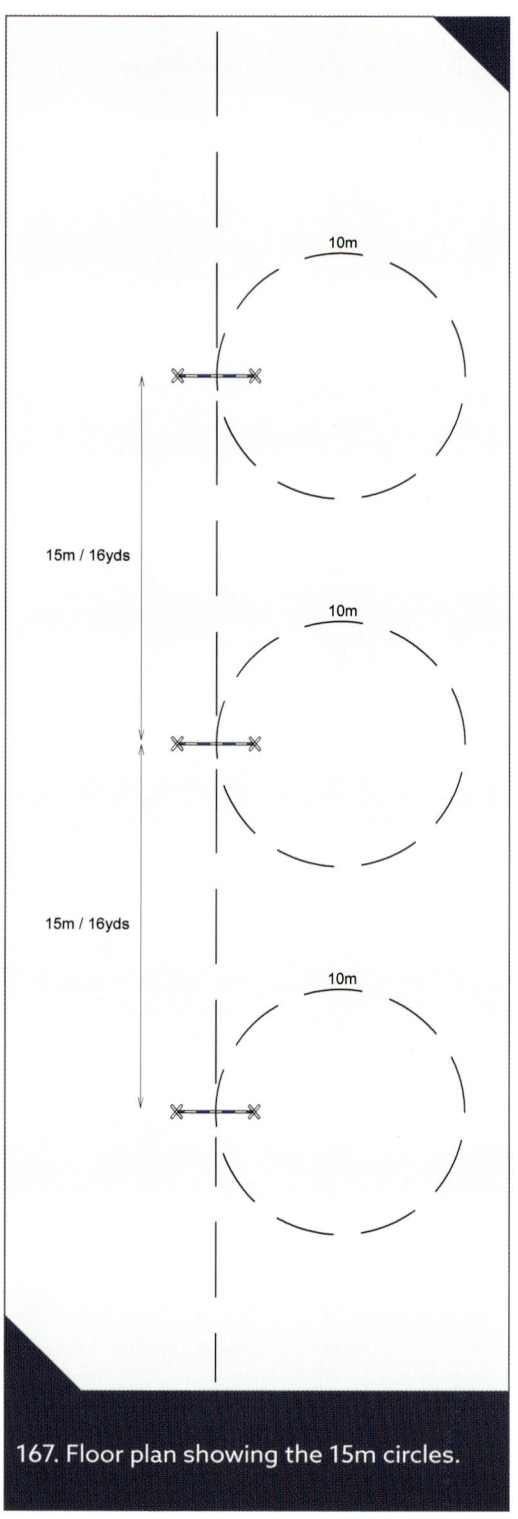

167. Floor plan showing the 15m circles.

Warming up

Use your routine warm-up in preparation for jumping to include a 10–15m circle with a collected canter into the circle and a medium canter on the last quarter of the circle as you move onto the straight line. Use the cavalletti individually to do some directional changes and practise both landing in an onward-bound canter and a more collected canter.

Working the exercise

Start by just jumping along the line of the three cavalletti using three non-jumping strides between each one. Focus on staying level, straight and being non-restrictive with your position. Then start an exercise of jumping the first one and landing straight onto a circle of about 15m before jumping the first one again. Then ride four short, active strides between the first two cavalletti and repeat at the middle one, jumping, circling and jumping again, before riding on four short, active strides to the last cavalletto, jumping, circling and jumping to finish the exercise. The four strides will come easily because you are in a more collected canter from the circle.

Once you have done this on both reins you are ready to start the more advanced stage. Start by jumping the first cavalletto again and riding a circle but, on the second part of the circle, start to expand the canter so you jump into the first distance in a big, ground-covering stride. Ride positively on three strides but, on the third stride just before take-off for the second cavalletto, bring your body more upright and close the stride so you are able to land on a short stride moving into the second circle. Repeat again with an expansion on the second half of the circle giving you a forward, big stride in the distance and close up just before take-off of the third cavalletto to once more land in a controlled closed stride. Repeat on both reins.

Relevance to competition

This exercise trains your horse to read your body position and teaches him to land in a controlled stride so that he lands with obedience, balance and on the new line to the next fence. As well as on the cross-country, this is really useful in the showjumping phase when you have an expanding distance to a spread or triple bar and a closing distance down to a vertical.

9.5 Improving the horse's jumping technique

All horses will have a different technique over a fence, often relative to their conformation, their canter and movement. Some horses are really loose in their movement and will throw a big jump, often giving more height than required, but could dangle their lower legs below the knee a bit. Some are neat but end up being a little flat and tight through their jump. Some like to be supported with a clear rein contact whereas others like a very relaxed rein. I've worked with horses who've initially had a very poor technique, but developed to be mentally very careful, whereas others who jump with a super, eye-catching technique have no desire to leave the fences untouched.

Developing the will to be careful over a fence is something that grows the more the horse doesn't touch a fence. The secret is the quality of canter and staying level with enough energy on the approach and between fences.

To encourage 'effort' I like to teach a horse to learn to jump from a spot close to a small parallel so that he has to use all of his body in the air to be neat at the front rail and reach for the back rail. Alternatively, I train 'effort' to a vertical from a long distance in a lower-powered canter so the effort has to come from a greater lift of the forehand.

9.5a Improving bascule

This exercise is a favourite to use as a warm-up before jumping a course of showjumps at home or on the Sunday morning at a long format competition when you want to

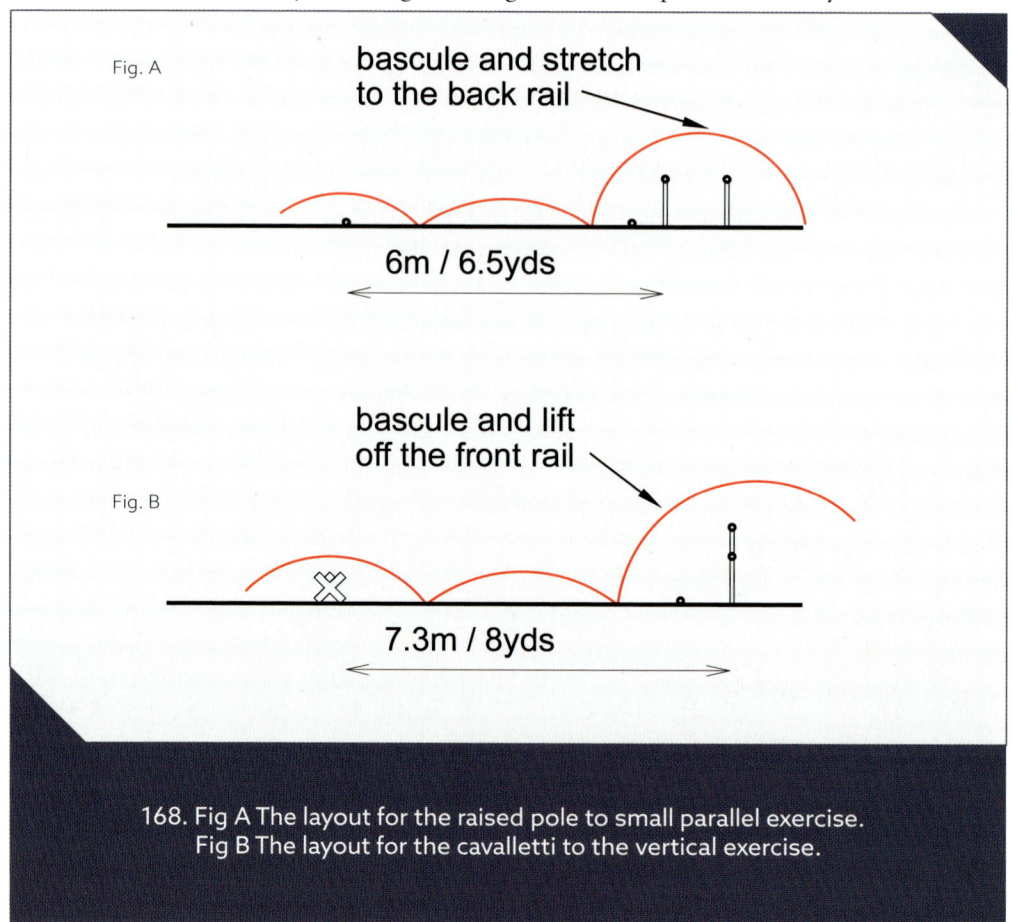

168. Fig A The layout for the raised pole to small parallel exercise.
Fig B The layout for the cavalletti to the vertical exercise.

Training to Win – the Making of a Champion

shape the jump up again after going cross-country the day before. At an International competition the FEI allows you to use a 6m / 6.5yds pole (on the floor) in front of a spread fence, but at home I will slightly raise the pole off the ground by 5cm / 2in to give clarity to the stride.

Start with a very small square parallel with a ground-line out 10cm / 4in and a raised wooden pole 6m / 6.5yds in front of the fence. Using a round, working canter, jump

Rider Rules for this exercise

- Maintain a level stride and try to focus beyond the fence, not on the pole.
- Keep your arms soft and allowing through the contact so as to offer the reins in mid-flight.
- Concentrate on power rather than speed and work on the ratios of stride length, power and balance.
- Keep the jump central and on a line by using a focal point into the distance.
- Let your arms drop either side of the withers to allow an unrestricted follow-through to the back rail.
- Praise your horse when he puts in maximum effort.

169. Approach over the raised pole. Note the rider allowing the horse's nose to go out.

Training to Win

170. A good bascule from a close take-off point.

the pole followed by one short stride that will take you to the base of the fence, but the ground-line will help the shape. Widen the fence and put it up in height equally front rail and back rail, but keep the height well within the limits as this is quite a testing exercise.

9.5b Developing lift

This is another useful exercise prior to track jumping. It develops lift from the shoulders and teaches the horse to use a rounded profile of jump on the take-off. Build a vertical with two poles close to the top and two ground-lines set at 45cm / 18in in front of and behind the fence. This offers an inviting take-off point with a big gap underneath the poles which, in turn, encourages the horse to look at the top rail and focus on reading the height. Use a cavalletto or similar on a distance of 7.3m / 8yds away from the vertical as a placing fence set at a longer distance than normal. Warm up using lots of variations within the canter and pop a few small fences to switch on the jumping muscles and the horse's eye. Use the combination to change the rein each time you jump the fence by holding a line left of centre off the left rein and right of centre off the right rein. Use a canter that is low in power, relaxed and non-expanding. This will produce a 'pop' over the cavalletto, putting the horse quite a long way off the vertical so, in order to clear the fence he has to put quite a lot of effort into his lift and follow-through. It is a very simple exercise with minimal equipment but, if ridden in the correct tempo, can really improve the jump profile in front of the fence.

Training to Win – the Making of a Champion

> **Rider Rules for this exercise**
>
> - Make sure that the canter stays level and relaxed.
> - Allow freedom with the rein contact by keeping the hands low and following the horse's nose.
> - Keep a disciplined line of approach by using a focal point and correcting any minor deviation off the line.
> - Use a slight pressure with your new inside leg to denote the leading leg.
> - Keep your head up to prevent the fold becoming too low over the withers which, in turn, will have a knock-on effect of collapsing on landing.
> - Praise your horse when he puts in maximum effort.

171. The cavalletto provides both lift and precision if ridden correctly.

172. Creating lift from a longer take-off point.

9.5c Jumping out of counter-canter

I think that this is a good training exercise for many reasons.

- ★ It places the focus on balance and away from fixating on a stride pattern.
- ★ If you have a horse who tends to rush towards the fence on the last couple of strides because of previous poor training, it will encourage him to stay level and in a good-quality stride.
- ★ Sometimes your horse will land on the incorrect leading leg in the ring and there isn't the time (or you may not have the balance) to do a correct flying change. In which case, if your horse is well-practised at jumping out of the counter-canter, there is a good chance that you and he will be able to cope with it in the ring.
- ★ In training, if your horse lands on the incorrect leading leg it is a great time to embrace the counter-canter and work hard on it. This will improve the counter-canter, but also encourage the horse to land correctly next time. It gives him a choice with a consequence.

Chapter 10

Competitions

10.1 Competition planning

For effective planning it is essential to look at a four-year plan rather than just the oncoming season. This will help you plan your horse's career alongside his training, fitness, growth and development and will allow you to look at the big picture and the main goal. This book essentially focuses on how you can take a horse through his training career over that four-year period, and the competitions should be the end result of you giving your horse all the necessary skills.

When deciding which competitions to enter there are a lot of potential considerations. With poor weather conditions and other factors it is important to have a contingency plan so as not to be caught out by not entering an alternative event in time. Deciding which events you are going to use for fitness, education, a qualification, as a competitive event, a trial, moving up to the next level or even dropping down to regain a loss of confidence will have a big impact on your seasonal planning. Here are some main considerations.

Main aim

This is very important as it will set your horse's path of training and competitions. It needs to be realistic for both you and your horse so that it is achievable within the realms of your horse's age, type and basic scope. Setting a goal that is unrealistic can lead to you becoming demoralised or potentially pushing your horse beyond his capabilities, which could lead to lameness and poor performance. At all levels there are competitions that hold some form of championship in which you can potentially be the highest performer and become a champion. This might be the Pony Club Championship, the Junior European Championship or the World Championship – they all require a training system that allows you to be better than anyone else at that level. Once you have decided on your main aim you will need to add in some mid-

Every horse is an individual and will have different needs leading up to a competition.

Season planning considerations.

term competition aims, which will often include the qualifications or MERs (Minimum Eligibility Requirements) that are in place to produce a safe standard before moving up a level. It is important within your training of your horse over the years that you give him a rounded competition plan and treat the MERs as 'minimum' and, if time allows, use different events at that level to give extra education. Moving up through the levels quickly will often not cover all of your horse's training needs and competitive experience and you will most likely find yourself moving back to the basic building blocks to regroup when problems arise because areas of training aren't consolidated.

Choice of events

Where you reside will have an effect on the amount of choice that is available to you. In the UK there is an abundance of National events at all levels, all in fairly close proximity, whereas in some other European countries there are often more International FEI events, with only a small number of competitions within organised by their National Federation. In the USA there is a fairly good selection of events in the East, with a season that runs from March to October, whereas the West Coast temperate conditions will allow the season to extend into November and start early in the year.

Course design

As a trainer of a potential champion horse it should be important to you that the competitions you enter give your horse a broad education of cross-country design. Although course design comes under a certain standard for each level, different designers will create unique types of questions that are essential for both you and your horse to experience if you are to be the best in your field. To give you some examples, if you were competing in France you would find questions that reward forward but very accurate riding, often with shallow water complexes that allow you to keep the speed up. In the UK you will experience a variety of different designs, some of which use lots of ground-lines and dressing to allow more open riding, others of which will encourage riders to take more care and give consideration to the balance in the lower gears. Also, some designers will ask questions that relate to the top end of the level involved, whereas others may design a more lenient track, which is often labelled a 'first time' competition. Riders who are inclined to stick to the easier competitions will not be challenging themselves or educating their horses in a way that is safe to move to the next level.

Ground conditions

Over time in the sport you will find out which events offer ground conditions that will suit your horse. Often at the beginning of the season in the UK the ground will be softer and moving into the summer we will all be challenged with the firmer ground. In the USA the West Coast will tend to have prepared ground that is ploughed, watered and rolled, which gives very consistent going, whereas the East will have grass, which will be organiser-dependent. Some horse will prefer to gallop and jump out of a bog, whereas others are happy galloping on hard ground and it won't ever affect them. That said, it is important to know your own horse and his preference, as running on unsuitable ground can affect his longevity in the sport.

Topography

Cross-country courses that have a lot of gradients or man-made mounds will offer more challenging questions just through the nature of balance and fitness. When choosing events it would be fairly crucial to aim for an event with fewer variations of gradient as your first competition when fitness may be an issue, whereas using a competition with big hills would be ideal when starting to increase fitness heading towards a long format competition. Young horses will gain a lot of experience at the lower levels when choosing competitions with topography that has a lot of gradient. It will teach them to think about their own balance and experience fences that are positioned up and down a hill.

Age and level of horse

This has a big bearing on how many competitions you plan to do, as the younger horse will require more runs as part of his education whereas the older, more experienced horse will only require the runs for either fitness or as a warm-up for the main aim. Leading up to winning the World Championships, Allstar B had only five competitions prior to the World Equestrian Games in September 2018.

Budget

If you have a limited budget it is important to take all of the above into consideration so that you don't 'waste' competitions by competing just for the sake of doing so. Try to find more local events, or share a lift if the event requires a long journey, and plan monthly competitions to allow yourself to get the most out of your training in between events.

10.2 Developing the working system leading up to an event

Every horse is an individual and will have different needs leading up to a competition. Some horses will need to feel well rested so that they can give a maximum energy output when the timing is right. This sort of system requires some good work periods the week before and then the work can be tapered slightly two to three days leading up to the event, with maybe just a jump the day before to get the jumping muscles warmed up and the eye in for some height. The advantage of this routine will be that you are taking a horse whose muscles aren't overworked or sore, but this is only really successful if you are riding a horse who performs well when he is fresh. This really does work well for a lot of horses, but it takes some time to work out the individual's programme. To the other extreme, there are lots of horses who only perform well if they get to a competition in a relaxed state of mind through working quite hard on the lead-up. Getting the stable management, feeding, turnout and work ratio correct is often crucial to a high performance and, again, requires trial and error methods to find the right ingredients. With horses who need the extra work it would be advisable if this was more along the lines of slow and monotonous rather than exciting and sprint-like, so the frame of mind always has to be taken into consideration. I have worked with horses who have needed a gallop before their dressage to reduce the tension, and also a horse who provided his best result to date at a 5* after spending a week on box rest prior to the event with an abscess in the foot!

Some horses thrive on being competed from the field. Working out a feeding regime to make sure that energy levels are suitable so that your horse stays in peak condition can be tricky and may need constant small adjustments so there isn't any weight gain. The only disadvantage to this system is when you are staying away at a competition and it will be a big change for your horse to be confined to a stable. With such a horse, leading up to the event it would be advantageous to have longer periods of time in the stable so as to avoid any metabolic disorders occurring, such as azoturia, lymphangitis or other similar conditions that are caused by sudden change.

The last jumping session before a competition is important and it needs to be specific to what the individual horse requires. Getting the height up in a confident manner, such as when coming out of a distance, can produce the right sort of belief just before a horse performs. If you have a horse who requires a lot of balancing work between the fences, or is a little over-keen, it would be advantageous to refresh the basics and improve the rideability with small fences and disciplined work. A horse who isn't always as careful as he could be may want some grid work with fences to make him think about his hoof-brain coordination. A line such as a wide parallel followed by a tall parallel followed by a wide parallel again (11yds or 10m) will work the horse's mind and body. Some horses love routine and will benefit from the last jump prior to the competition being the same system as in the practice area. I have a mare I work with regularly and she jumps her best if she's not jumped for a week before the competition.

10.3 Effective course-walking

Course-walking is something that you gain experience in after riding around a few different tracks, as you will be able to relate the challenges the designer has set to how something will ride. There are a lot of aspects to take into consideration when making a plan on what lines to take.

The weather
In competition you will experience all sorts of weather conditions from hot, dry weather to sleet and heavy rain storms. The most important aspect is giving your horse time to read fences and cope with different conditions, especially where poor visibility comes into the equation.

Light conditions and the time of day
Dark shadows and low sunlight are often a factor in the spring and autumn and cause the horse to need a little more time to fully read the question. At a long format, try to get a chance to walk the course at the same time as you will be riding the cross-country to give you an idea of what the horse will be seeing and how the light affects the look of the fence or combination.

174. A jump going from dark to bright sunlight.

The ground conditions
Different ground conditions pose different potential problems. Generally horses will run quickly on dry, firm ground but some horses will become more tentative, especially if they are thin-soled and predisposed to bruising of the feet. This latter issue may cause the horse to take shorter strides and the distances between fences may ride longer. If there has been a lot of rain, the ground can quickly become soft and slow the horse down in his movements. In such cases, look for fresh ground and give lots of support through your rein contact. Soft ground will also often affect the stride pattern and can cause it to become shorter.

When you get a lot of rain on top of firm ground it can make the ground slippery on top. In this case care must be taken round corners and turning lines, where you will need to focus on balance and turns that aren't too abrupt. It is important to use suitable studs in relation to ground conditions.

The topography
This is the gradient of the ground. As mentioned earlier, the gradient of the land will have a big effect on stride length and balance. The designer will site the fences to maximise education. Walk such areas with care and imagine what frame your horse is likely to be on during the approach.

Any outside interference such as crowds or sponsors' banners

When your horse is fairly young or new to the sport he may not be used to fence judges positioned near the fence or, at larger competitions, crowds of people near and around the fences. Most horses won't be affected by this, but some can get very spooked and lose concentration on the job in hand, so they need confident and positive support by the rider, especially around water obstacles where lots of people tend to congregate. Whilst walking the course take note of colourful banners and anything else that may take the horse's eye away from the fence.

The flow of the course

Most course designers have their own style of design which, although governed by rules and standards will have their own stamp, whether it is more geared towards bigger and bolder or more technical with risks on angles and narrow fences. They will also be influenced by the topography, so are often more able to test the control and balance of a combination when there are slopes and mounds, whilst having to rely on turns and very technical lines when the ground is predominantly flat. The course will often follow a pattern of fences that will encourage forward riding early on, with a combination test at fence 3 or 4 to check control of speed, balance and direction, then a variety of combinations and rhythm fences depending on the level, finishing with a testing penultimate fence and a forward finish. When you walk the course you need to plan your lines with the understanding that you might have to change to a longer route if you have a problem and need to rebuild confidence levels.

Tips on how to walk the course effectively

* Always leave enough time so that you don't have to rush. Some of the lines might need careful consideration, which can be time-consuming.
* Make sure that you are wearing appropriate clothing and footwear to prevent getting wet, cold or dehydrated before you start the competition.
* Try to walk the course more than once. The first time certainly to get the overall 'feel' of the course, the second time to scrutinise and measure the distances and if possible, especially for long format, walk once again on the same day to make a final plan.
* Walk with your horse in mind and with the horse's eyes. Imagine the first thing that your horse will see at speed, especially when he has a blind turn to a fence. What is in the foreground? What is behind the fence that might take his eye? Is there a clear exit away or is there another fence directly behind the one in question that he may assume that he's jumping? When will he see what's on the landing and how will that affect his approach and take-off? If he naturally moves to one direction over a fence expect him to do that in competition and walk your lines accordingly. If you know he gets longer and flatter as he travels around the

175. A cross-country obstacle with a tree on the landing side, which offers the rider choices of routes to take.

176. Creating a focal point when there is no natural landmark.

course, pick a point where you can use a piece of land or a fence to shape him back together before a significant combination fence.

* Whilst walking the course decide on an area for your preparation point and turning point for each obstacle and look to find a suitable focal point. Take notice of how the fence has been dressed. If the fence has high trees at the side with a good ground-line this will allow you to arrive at the fence slightly faster, because the trees will act like a high-sided cross-pole and encourage the horse to get a bit more height, whilst the good ground-line will encourage a round-profile jump. On the other hand, fences that have a big gap with a surprise on the landing side will cause a horse to draw back in front of the fence, so will require a slower approach and a rounder, more balanced canter. Note also whether the top of the fence is painted a different colour so the horse can differentiate between the front and the top. With a wide fence, note where the flags are. Flags at the front and back will help the horse get a sense of the width.
* Note the depth of water, as that will have a profound effect on your speed. At the lower levels the water tends to be slightly shallower – 20–25cm / 8–10in, but this can

177. A gate made easier for a horse with a different-coloured top rail and trees at the side.

178. Note how the trees are brought forward to create a take-off area for the horse that is further away.

179. A spread dressed to create a good jump. The flags at the front and back will denote the width, and the two colours of the top rails will encourage the horse to be more observant.

go up to 35cm / 14in at Advanced level, and this depth often needs careful but bold riding. If there is a fence in the water, note whether there is a suitable approach that allows you to get at least one stride, preferably more, before the jump to allow the horse to keep the momentum going.

* Try to walk with someone such an experienced coach or rider who will offer positive advice and engage in constructive discussion about the various questions that may arise.
* Know your rules on taking an alternative line without incurring any penalties for crossing your track.
* Walk the combination lines for every eventuality. For example, if you have a run-out at an obstacle you should know immediately where to go to take an easier alternative if that's the plan.
* Make notes of everything that is relevant: fence numbers, preparation areas, turning points, focal points, distances between fences and minute markers. This is easily done by making notes on your mobile device and having it to hand before you do your final visualisation before mounting.
* When walking combination fences it is clearly ideal to have an idea of what the distance is between two obstacles. This can give you an appropriate speed at which to approach and what to expect if the horse jumps into the distance without an issue. However, it is crucial as a skilled cross-country rider that you learn to develop an eye for a distance and be able to react instantly to what balance and

180. Walking an uphill distance.

stride length your horse has landed in to help give him good support to the next obstacle. Consequently it's important that you don't over-analyse the distance between two elements as this can start to become counterproductive. When walking the distance, start the measurement from an approximate landing site, which will depend on the topography, ground conditions, profile of the fence and speed of approach. Often the landing site can be up to 3m /10ft away from a slightly downhill soft-profiled fence, whereas if the fence is a pig-arch shape jumped off a turn the landing site could be within 1m / 3.3ft.

181. A MIMclip.

182. A MIMclip more sensitive to pressure for use with an angled front rail.

★ Note which fences have frangible safety devices. Some fences will have a pin that will activate with a downward force and others will have a clip called a MIMclip that will activate with a forward and upward pressure.

★ Try to think very methodically about the cross-country course design and work out how each fence can be a 'set-up' fence for the next. For example, if you have a corner fence with the point to the right, if possible, jump the previous fence to the left of centre and be clear that the horse doesn't drift across to the right. This will ensure that he is attentive to your aids and will hopefully stay focused and straight at the corner. If you are less disciplined in your approach it can lead to your horse not always staying straight – and flags will fly!

Measuring the length of the cross-country course is important as you move up the levels, especially in a long format competition. Have a prior knowledge of the lines that you plan to take and then, starting from the edge of the start box, measure the distance all the way around the course, making sure you take tight, racing lines wherever the ground conditions allow. If, for example, you are competing at 2* level the distance will be calculated at 520mpm, so when measuring the distance note every time you reach 520m and that should be your approximate minute marker. After you have all the minute markers you will need to think more about how the course is set out. Some minutes will be 'fast minutes', which may only consist of perhaps three soft-profile fences that can be jumped out of 550mpm plus, whereas another minute may consist of two combination fences, a hill and a water complex and would thus be a 'slow' minute, as these obstacles would take much more setting up at a slower speed.

There are various different ways in which you can obtain the minute markers. First, you can rely on someone else's calculations by using a mobile phone app, or sometimes the organiser will post the minute markers around the track. Alternatively, you can measure the course yourself with either a measuring wheel that physically measures the ground or a GPS watch that measures the distance from a satellite, both which are reasonably accurate. Measuring the distance yourself whilst walking the course gives you more in the way of landmarks, which will help you when you're riding round.

At various places around a course there should be stopping points marked out. These are areas which, in the unfortunate circumstance you get held on course, are strategically positioned so when you are restarted it is at a fence that is fairly straightforward rather than a difficult combination fence. These are often marked at an International competition by a white post.

183. A Garmin GPS watch used for measuring the length of the course and to calculate the minute markers.

* Note where the warm-up fences and cooling-down facilities are and whether they are appropriate for your horse. Some horses will get too excited before the start, so if the warm-up area is very close to the start you may need to do some warming up in a different place to prevent your horse's heart rate getting too high before the start.

- ★ Finally, before mounting to go cross-country it is always a good idea to take time and visualise yourself riding around the track in 'real time'. This involves finding a quiet area where you can be alone and take as long as the course will take to ride. Close your eyes and think about every fence and what it would feel like to approach, jump and get away from, reminding yourself about preparation, turning and focal points. Think what you might do if you have a problem and think positive thoughts about what you expect to happen.

10.4 Clean sport

Whether competing under National Federation rules or International (FEI) rules it is essential that you follow the Clean Sport Regulations. The FEI Anti-Doping rules for human athletes are set under the World Anti-Doping Agency (WADA) regulations, whereas the Equine Anti-Doping Programme is placed under the FEI Equine Anti-Doping and Controlled Medication Regulations. The Equine Prohibited Substances List is split into two sections. Banned substances are those that should never be used in a sports horse. Controlled medications are those that are deemed by the FEI to have therapeutic value and are commonly used in equine medicine, but are not permitted to be evident in the system of a horse at the time of competition, because they have the potential to affect performance and/or be a welfare risk to the horse.

Always be aware of what and when you give to or feed your horse. Controlled medical substances shouldn't be given without first consulting a vet and must be entered in the horse's medication logbook. Dating the entry and remaining aware of it is essential. Any horse at a National or International event can be randomly tested. FEI testing is standardised, so the procedure will always be the same at all International competitions. If your horse needs a controlled medication at and during an event this will need to be authorised by the FEI official veterinarian and administered in the designated treatment box.

When your horse is selected for random testing it is your responsibility as the rider to make sure that the samples are correctly taken and labelled as being from that horse, and packaged with seals. If the test is positive the rider will be sanctioned, along with possible members of the support team. This may also lead to ineligibility and a fine with a disqualification from the event, which may lead to a loss of individual medals and affect the placing of the team.

The feeding of supplements is also at the rider's own risk and extreme caution is recommended. Ideally select your support team wisely and carefully and make sure that everyone is familiar with the Clean Sport Regulations.

Training to Win

Notes on feeding

- Don't feed your horse human food or drinks – in addition to not being good for him it can result in a positive test.
- Ensure that feed bins are kept clean. Old feed can turn mouldy and certain types of mould can produce naturally occurring prohibited substances.
- Use clean bowls or buckets for feeding. It's not advisable to feed your horse from stable fittings such as troughs or mangers, since these are difficult to keep clean.
- Only use products from reputable feed and supplement companies.
- Always check the label. Some supplements contain prohibited substances that aren't listed on the product label. Choose a supplement it's competition-legal.
- Record batch numbers. Keep samples of hay, feed and supplements and any corresponding batch numbers to enable a thorough investigation should contamination be suspected.
- Store feed and medications carefully. Medications can easily be dropped into open feed bags or storage containers. When not in use, medication should be kept in a secure cupboard.
- Use a separate feed bucket when feeding medication. Medication traces can remain, even after washing. Stirrers used to mix feeds containing medication should be labelled and stored separately.
- Once your horse has finished any medical treatment, rest

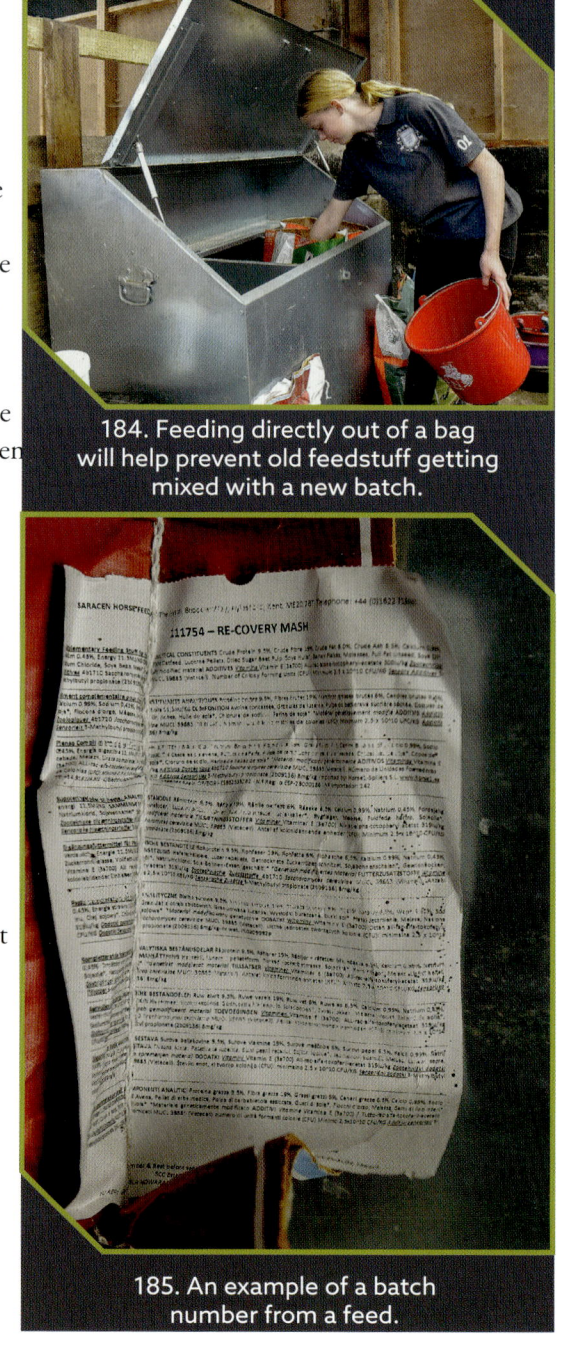

184. Feeding directly out of a bag will help prevent old feedstuff getting mixed with a new batch.

185. An example of a batch number from a feed.

your paddock for several days before it's grazed again and pick up the droppings straight away.
- Check your grazing. Fields and surrounding land may contain plants that could lead to a positive dope test, such as poppies, crocuses, nightshade and lupins.
- When it comes to using a stable at a competition or staying overnight whilst travelling to an event, make sure the stable you use is clean and disinfected. Do not use the bedding that is already down because of the risk of cross contamination.

10.5 'In the zone'

10.5a Nerves and how to combat them – creating a strategy

Dealing with the nerves of competition can often be one of the most important areas of a competitor's training. The symptoms of being nervous can have a huge and debilitating impact on your performance. When you feel stressed or anxious, your body releases a rush of hormones which, in effect, has the brain sending messages to the rest of your body. The heart will pump faster, the breathing rate increases and the muscles will tense, so it is essential to create a strategy that allows you to understand, manage and embrace your physical state.

Understanding *why* we get nervous is an important step towards the management of how the symptoms can be lessened. The most common cause in most athletes would be the fear of underperforming and the impact that might have. They may fear that they will let down themselves alongside all of the other support staff and owners, causing a worry about the implications after the event. This becomes magnified when riding in a squad for your country and, at the time, it will feel that nothing else matters. The fear of embarrassment can also add to the pressure of performance, with social media playing a large part in most people's world. The third main cause of being nervous is the fear of being hurt, mainly from the point of being incapacitated with an injury and the implications that has.

Turning such thoughts around is the first part of creating a strategy to combat nerves. When the fear of underperforming causes you to become nervous it is essential that you understand where you are in relation to the level of the competition. Are you moving up to a higher level? If so, is it okay to slightly underperform? Are you expected to do well in the competition because you are the favourite? Does that add more pressure on you than going out of your comfort zone to a new level? Of course it does. When the expectations are high this is more likely to increase the pressure on not making a mistake. If you focus on winning rather than producing a high performance this is likely to be a debilitating factor.

Good preparation is the way to alter these thoughts. If you convince yourself that you have prepared to the best of your ability, then you are likely to perform with confidence and belief. You must also understand that someone else may perform to a higher level than you on the day, which will clearly affect the outcome of the competition. Your main aim should be to produce the best performance that you and your horse are trained to. Focusing on the process rather than the outcome will allow you to be competitive with yourself and make improvements. This productive and positive thinking strategy will help you combat the fear of underperforming and allow you to compete in a happy, healthy manner.

If the fear of embarrassment affects your performance you must minimise your attention to social media whilst in the competition period. Although it might be a very powerful platform when trying to attract sponsors and owners, being concerned about what others are doing can have a profoundly negative effect on you.

If the fear of getting injured concerns you and has an effect on your performance, it would be important to work out a plan. If, for example, you are about to ride for your country in a championship, but prior to the event you have another competition, you might be nervous about getting an injury and consequently have the reserve take your place on the squad. Convincing yourself to be cautious or to ride slower across country could actually have a negative effect, as you won't ride with the same pressure and could cause your horse to second-guess the aids you use. A good way of combating these types of nerves is to imagine that the event prior to the championship is a dress rehearsal and this will help you in two ways; producing a positive thought process and making you focus on your own riding.

Breathing

Understanding the physical effect of being nervous is important when trying to overcome nerves. Your breathing pattern will often change and, without realising it, you may hold your breath. Oxygen is an important component of the metabolism that releases energy. Oxygen intake helps to relax muscles and clear the mind. When you hold your breath you create a pressure and nervous feeling. When you realise what state that puts you in it is possible to get nervous about getting nervous, or anxious about getting anxious. The pattern of your breathing will affect the pattern of your performance, and managing your own breathing is the key to thinking clearly and keeping yourself in a coherent state. A brilliant way of controlling your nerves is to use a breathing exercise that helps you focus on your body. Take a long, slow, deep breath in through your nose then, after holding for a count of five, exhale out through your mouth, again slowly holding for the count of five. Repeat this exercise for a full minute and you will immediately notice the difference in your relaxation, state of mind and pressure aids on your horse. A good time to do this is when you are alone before mounting or when you have finished your warm-up procedure in any of the three phases and are waiting to go into the field of play, such as after the last practice showjump before waiting to go in the ring. I remember watching the great sports mind coach, Charlie Unwin, use this technique with some nervous riders when they were linked up to a computer that measured their heart rate and state. The breathing exercise had a remarkable effect on the riders and it was shown on a graph with their statistics being measured so you could watch the positive effect on a screen.

Nausea and energy levels

Another physical symptom of nerves is nausea, which is a response to stress. During a moment of high anxiety you may just feel a little queasy, also known as 'butterflies in your stomach', and this kind of nausea will pass shortly. But sometimes, anxiety-related nausea can make you totally sick to the stomach, which churns so badly that you need to make a dash to the nearest toilet and in some cases be physically sick. This can often have a debilitating factor on your performance if you don't manage the effects. If you are aware that you won't be able to eat during the competition you need to find a way of getting the calories needed for your performance earlier. This may be with carb-loading leading up to the competition. Avoid a large carbohydrate meal the night before as this may leave you feeling full, sluggish and may cause more digestive problems on the competition day. Instead, start loading up two to three days prior to the competition, especially if you are riding a few horses and expect to be task-loading. For the competition day, find foods that will give you some instant energy that don't automatically make you feel sick, such as granola bars or even a Mars bar if you are in need of a short-term energy boost. Calories can also be in liquid form and, of course, electrolytes will help prevent the onset of dehydration when you are working hard in hot weather.

186. Milk shakes, electrolyte drinks, nuts, chocolate and bananas will help you get through a competition day.

Routine

When nerves hit and you get into an incoherent state it will greatly affect the way you think and apply pressure aids. This, in turn, will affect your horse's performance by causing tension and, in most cases, misunderstanding. The way to combat this problem, along with the breathing exercise, is to have an impeccable routine. Try to develop a warm-up routine at home for all three phases, which you repeat as often as possible. This will give you and your horse a comfortable feeling and something to rely on when the stress levels start to rise. You can't control the uncontrollable, such as the weather, other competitors around you, or a timetable that changes, but if you have a routine strategy in place you know that you will be prepared whatever the circumstances. Your horse will thrive on routine, your support staff will know what to expect and, most importantly, it will give you a clear plan to work with.

Thinking clearly under pressure

Another potentially debilitating symptom of becoming anxious is the loss of ability to think clearly when you are under pressure. This can affect your decision-making skills and cause you to do random, out of the ordinary things, which can have an effect on the outcome of the competition. To help prevent this happening means going back to having a clear system with self-created rules that you need to stick with when the pressure is on. This will help prevent you from being affected by what other competitors are doing on the day and questioning your own thoughts. Within your training, make sure that some pressure zone exercises are brought in so you can experience the pressures of competition, thereby preparing your mind and body to think quickly and react accordingly.

Learning to deal with your nerves at a competition

This one of the main skills any athlete has to bring into their training system. The first important aspect is recognising at what point your nerves kick in and to recognise the symptoms.

Is it prior to the competition day? If so, they are likely to be a different type of nerves that you have time to cope with and you should have a strict system in place to deal with these. It may be that you plan out your routine the week before the competition and write everything down with dates and times so you have a systematic routine to fall back on and follow.

Is it on the morning of the competition? If so, you should make sure that you have a good breakfast

187. A whiteboard in the lorry showing the day's times.

and plan your food and liquid intake for the day, with snacks to hand and cold drinks available. Make sure that you allow an extra 10 minutes for every single task, including course-walking, studding up, warm-up routines – everything! Some riders find it useful to have a whiteboard in their lorry with all the timings of the day on it so no one gets confused about where to be at what time. Politely ask your support staff to be aware of your time constraints so that someone being late doesn't contribute to your anxiety. Often, nerves can make athletes irritable so it would be important that support staff and owners are sensitive to this fact and stay neutral in their reactions.

Is it when you are about to mount your horse or, more likely, when you are about to perform? If so, having time to complete your breathing exercises is essential. It may be that you also use this time to visualise yourself riding the dressage test or your showjumping round, using 'real time', going through each element slowly and clearly in your head. Some people find it helps visualisation if they imagine that they are watching themselves on television, so they see from the 'outside' how well the test or course can be ridden. Others like actually to be 'inside their own head', looking through their eyes whilst visualising each movement or question as they ride through the process. Which technique works for you really depends on the type of learner you are. Either way, you will need peace and quiet and an extra 10 minutes preferably before you mount your horse.

Probably the most crucial aspect for a rider is recognising how nerves can affect their riding and developing a strategy to help cope with the symptoms. As described earlier, anxiety can put you into an incoherent state which, in turn, will affect the pressures applied to the horse – which is often why your horse might not perform as well in competition as he does at home when you are in a relaxed state.

The final aspect of dealing with nerves at a competition is a *body control check*. Whilst in the warm-up area a good technique is to take your body through a mind control check to test your pressures. Start with your head and take your eyes to look at a focal point. Every time you make a line or directional change, focus your eyes on an object to ride towards. Doing this will align your body and kick in your awareness of any asymmetry in your position, or alert you if your horse is not quite moving straight. It also stops other riders from bothering you as they will recognise that you are concentrating and don't want to be disturbed. Next, work through your arms and shoulders. First imagine that you are riding towards a mirror and 'look' at your shoulders to see if they are level. Feel where they are. Move them about. Do they feel stiff or awkward to move? Recognise how much weight of contact you have in each hand. Can you do a weight check and go through the process learned in training to freshen the contact with the 'soften' button? Are you using your biceps or triceps? Are your fingers tight? Are your elbows in front of or behind your hips? Crucially, are your upper arms tight or 'breathing'? Next, move through to the awareness of your seat bones and whether they are equally placed, light and moving with the movement of the horse. Finally allow your focus to concentrate on your weight distribution through to the stirrups and what sort of pressure aids you are applying with your legs. This procedure should only take a minute and can be a crucial part of aligning yourself into a focal zone.

10.6 Riding at a championship

Whether it is the Badminton Grassroots Championship, a Youth European Championship or even a Senior Championship, you have probably worked long and hard to get to that point, with many miles covered and lots of money spent. There can only be one winner and the knowledge that you have prepared to the best of your ability and performed to the highest of your level can be as rewarding as winning the competition.

10.6a Preparation leading up to a championship

Preparing for a big competition starts many weeks and months beforehand, so every aspect of preparation is taken care of. Your own and your horse's fitness work should have previously been planned and moved up to the level of the competition with a week to ten days to spare. This is in case you miss any fitness days as a result of something trivial, but it also gives you the opportunity to slightly taper your horse's work a few days prior to the competition so that he is physically and mentally in the right state to compete.

Your horse's passport, vaccination certificate and any other paperwork will need checking in plenty of time in case anything is out of date. Your Clean Sport rules should be adhered to all the time, but be extra careful with any supplements and feed that you are using and, if in doubt, cease feeding them or take samples of each batch and store them safely. If you use any human medications make sure you have enough packed for the duration if you are travelling out of the country. Do not purchase human medicines abroad as, although they have similar packaging, they may contain different active ingredients that may be on the prohibited list. For foreign trips ensure that your lorry is compatible with regulations and that all your horse's paperwork, veterinary tests and health papers have been looked into and booked.

Plan your horse's training workload leading up to the event with emphasis on confidence, correct riding and no mistakes. Be careful to not over-train, since this can lead to frustration and an unhappy horse. It is more useful to practise little achievable exercises, relevant to your performance, which will have a positive outcome.

10.6b At the event

If the championship is an International long format, try to arrive early enough to get your horse checked by the vet, settled in and with enough daylight to take him out for a quiet ride or training session if that is planned. You will be allocated a horse number, which will need to be on your horse every time he leaves the stable. This will be often changed when the competition begins, which can be a little confusing. Keeping your horse in a relaxed state is fundamental to his performance, so find enough time to take him out to graze and try to keep his days to as regular a routine as possible. Make sure that you graze in an area that has been allocated by the event organisers and ensure that it is free from acorns, sycamore seeds or other poisonous plants such as ragwort, deadly nightshade, etc. At one Irish event, in one of the riding areas that was also used for grazing, there were a lot of sycamore shoots that had started sprouting. Sycamore poisoning involves a toxin that affects the muscle metabolism in horses, producing a disease that can be rapidly fatal.

Another aspect of carrying out your riding sessions in the allocated areas is the need to be careful not to ride near the cross-country course at the risk of being eliminated. The officials at the event will be specific about where you are permitted to exercise as sometimes you will be allowed to ride across/near the course to get to a hacking route.

There will usually be a rider's briefing that will cover all rules and regulations and should offer an outline of the competition. If it is a championship that involves teams of different nations there will be a drawn order at the meeting of the *chefs d'equipe* on the day before the trot-up to decide the order of countries and create a running order. The members of the ground jury will walk with the course designer and the technical delegate, generally on the day before the trot-up, and make any last-minute alterations then open it for competitors to walk after that. It is advisable at a championship to walk the cross-country course at least three times – I used to walk Badminton and Burghley five times. Use your first walk as a first impression, looking 'through your horse's eyes' at what he will see at each fence. Take into consideration the topography, the 'feel' of the course and imagine how your horse will respond to the different questions. It's advisable to leave longer for your second walk as it is a good time to look at all the different lines and black flag routes available with all the 'what-if' reaction plans put in place. Your third walk should take into consideration measuring the track that you intend to ride, taking note of all the minute markers and which fences are in each minute so you can make a plan. Then, if you get a chance to do a final walk on the cross-country morning, it is good to walk or jog around by yourself, taking every eventuality into consideration.

10.6c The trot-up

The trot-up procedure should be well practised prior to the event; it is a crucial part of the competition. Arrive at the trot-up area approximately 20 minutes before your allotted time to walk and settle your horse. Use a snaffle bridle with reins rather than a double-linked leading chain as you can then influence the straightness if need be. Have the bridle number on the off-side as that's where the ground jury will be standing.

When you walk and stand up to the ground jury, be polite and try to stand slightly in front of your horse so the vet can look around for any skin rubs or obvious wounds before you move off in walk then trot. If you get sent to the holding box for any reason just follow the advice of the holding box vet, who will be your friend and act in the best interests of you and your horse. He will inspect your horse and question you about any previous history, which will be taken into consideration before re-inspection. This is a very nerve-racking time, both before and during the competition, and it is unfortunately something that most riders will probably experience at some point.

10.6d Dressage day

It is very important that the dressage day runs like clockwork and is free of stress. This requires some planning and keeping within a time frame, with everyone knowing what their job involves. Prior to the dressage make sure that all your tack, spurs and, most importantly, your bit is legal for the competition. If in any doubt, find the steward who will put your mind at rest and take away any stress or potential problems. After the dressage has started try to watch as many other riders as you can. I always like to take the youth riders to look at the arena to ride through the test in their heads. It is important to look at the measurements between the boards so you have all your focal points to help you ride an accurate test. Notice what is around the arena and where you enter, which will help you consolidate the plan prior to the bell going. Be aware that

188. The vet checking for obvious injuries at the second veterinary inspection.

if the bell goes as you are passing the A marker, you do not have enough time to trot all the way around a 60x20m arena within the 45 seconds allowed before entering the arena. You will need to double back or canter around the arena, otherwise you will be starting with a minus 2.

Note what happens in the collecting arena and where you will be allowed to work, as that can add stress to the warm-up routine if not pre-planned. Try to stick to your normal warm-up routine so that your horse knows what to expect and, if you are working with a coach, make sure that they know all the timings and plans. A decision on whether to wear working boots – which involves stopping work to take them off – is important as some combinations will need to keep in the zone right up into the field of play and not want their focus broken.

After your test the steward will want to check your horse's bit, ear covers and tack before you leave the area, so it is important that nobody touches the horse or tack before the steward does these checks. After that it is fairly important that you are able to cool your horse down as you would do at home, so take him back into the warm-up area and do his stretches and relaxation work so he leaves the area in a relaxed, stress-free state and his muscles have been cooled down properly.

189. Taking boots off and last-minute check before the dressage test.

10.6e Cross-country day

This is generally the most exciting day of the competition, filled with anticipation, nerves, excitement and hopefully elation. A well-oiled team is important so before the day you should have a 5-minute meeting with your helper(s), whether that is just one person or perhaps a team of people if you are riding more than one horse. Discussion points would be management of the horse prior to the cross-country, timings for the whole day, roles and responsibilities, tack and equipment checks and management of the horse after the cross-country. At a team championship there will often be three meetings, one for the riders, one for the support staff and one for the parents and owners, so absolutely everyone knows their role for the day and a plan has been put in place.

Start by looking at your start time and work backwards to establish timings for warm-up, mounting, tacking and studding-up, grazing or exercise prior to the cross-country and the initial feeding time in the morning. Make a note of those times and send them to all the members of your team and also put them on a white/blackboard in your lorry so no one makes any timing mistakes. Before smartphones came along it used to be crucial that the whole team set their own watches to the 'event time' so everyone was working from the same time. Nowadays, however, the event works from the time set by our computers and mobile devices. As a coach I will take responsibility to set the riders' stopwatches up correctly so that, whilst they are in the warm-up, they can check the time by switching their stopwatch mode to check the precise time. There is a very useful app called Atomic Clock Pro that gives you the World Time, showing the seconds counting, which is ideal for that precision timing.

Plan time to do a last course-walk by yourself so that you can go through the course in your head, just how you will ride it. Make sure that you know all of the minute markers, what you might do as a contingency plan at each combination fence, where the stopping points are and recap on all of the tightest racing lines available. You will need to have a clear idea about what happens if you don't quite go through the flags correctly at a narrow fence so you can instantly make a decision on whether you approach the fence again or carry on. If you see a fence judge waving a red flag for you to stop, ensure that you make a mental note of where you stop your stopwatch so that you can go back to full speed and restart it in the same place once you have been given the all-clear to restart.

Plan where you will put all of your equipment for washing and cooling your horse off in the area allocated at the finish. Try to choose somewhere in the shade if that's possible and make sure that your equipment is labelled and recognisable to all of your team.

Deciding whether to watch other riders jump the course before you do is a matter of personal preference. The knowledge that you have walked and planned your lines according to your understanding of your own horse is very valuable, but you can easily be swayed if you see other riders taking different lines and stride patterns. As a coach I like to take in as much information about the course as possible, but only feed the relevant information to my riders as I think will be useful.

Finally, before mounting, it is important for you to sit quietly and alone to go through the course and visualise yourself riding round successfully as planned. Whatever the length of the cross-country, it is important that your warm-up covers the slow build-up and normal stretching, the gymnastic element to make sure that your horse is fully on the aids and has warmed up all his muscles, then also some sprint work so that he is ready to go out of the start box at gallop. However, the precise way in which you cover these elements will need to be personal to each individual horse, as some horses can easily get tense and too excited, which gets their heart rate up too high too early. The 2018 World Champion Allstar B would get hugely excited in the warm-up area so he always worked and jumped early on the cross-country morning and then kept very quiet up to the start box to keep him as relaxed as possible.

After crossing the finish of the cross-country test it is essential that your full attention is on the welfare of your horse. Make a point of maintaining the rein contact and ride up correctly into a working canter before a transition to trot for a couple of 20m circles, making sure that your horse stays up to the bridle before making that transition to walk in order to prevent a last-minute injury resulting from a loss of balance. Care for your horse as necessary by having a team washing him in cold water and scraping the hot water that has been heated by horse's body temperature off so that the surrounding air can help cool him. Keep your horse walking as he is being cooled to help remove the

190. Allstar B having a morning cross-country warm-up in Tokyo.

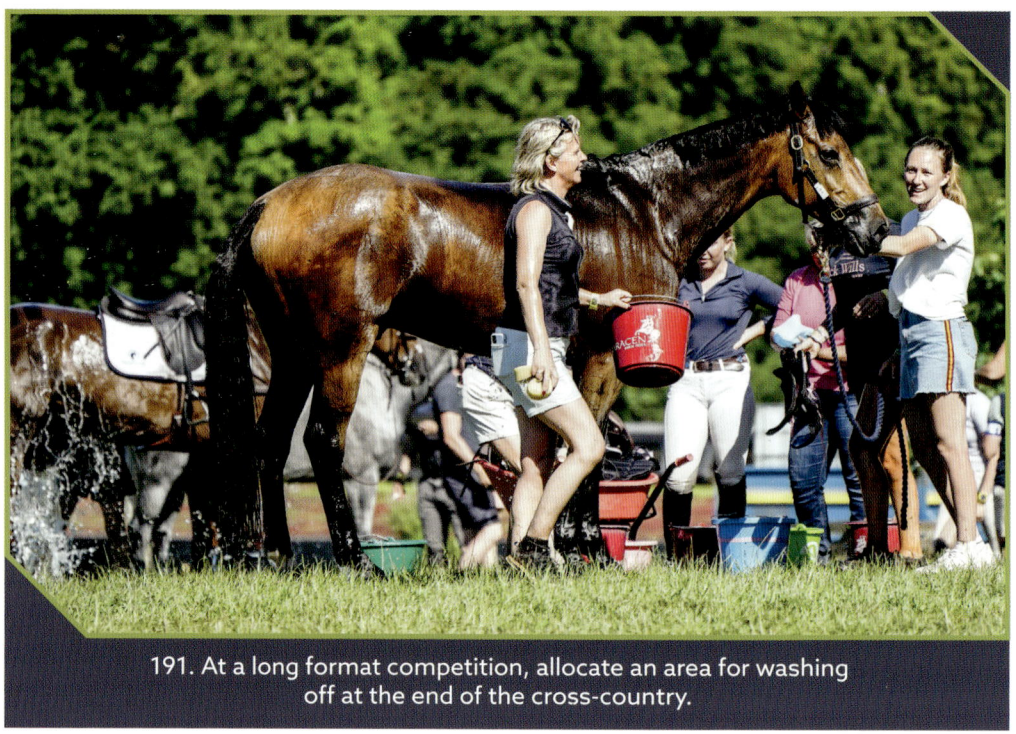
191. At a long format competition, allocate an area for washing off at the end of the cross-country.

192. The cooling-off area at Tokyo Olympics with fans and mist.

lactic acid build-up in the big skeletal muscles, which could potentially cause stiffness later on. Cooling the horse's legs as early as possible is also important. A good way is having some J-cloths to hand, which can go directly onto the horse's legs below the knee, followed by some disposable ice packs and then pop the cross-country boots back on top to hold the ice in place. This makes a very inexpensive but highly effective cooling system that is quick and easy to use at a competition.

An ideal way of allowing good recovery after the cross-country is to give the horse a quiet period in his stable, then a little grazing time before bedtime. If you are worried about any injuries it is wise to speak to the FEI official treating vet, who will advise you accordingly.

10.6f Showjumping day

The stables are normally busy very early on the showjumping morning and it's important to get to them early enough that your horse isn't fretting about not being fed as others are around him. After feeding, check for any injuries that may have come to light overnight before getting your horse out for a walk in hand and a trot-up to see if there is any soreness from the day before. After the trot-up is a good time to walk the showjumping course. First ensure that the course has been passed for walking by the ground jury. Take advantage of having time to walk the course at least three times. Take into consideration the starting gates, the tighter lines necessary to avoid time penalties, where the entrance is in relationship to any of the fences and gradients within the distances. The course design will often lead the horse into getting longer in his frame, so when walking the course plan where you can rebalance the horse sufficiently.

Having a routine warm-up plan is crucial and keeping the jumps to a minimum can often be beneficial at a long format event, so your horse is not fatigued before he goes into the arena. Some riders like to use the official jumping arenas before the jumping starts to do some gymnastic exercises, which can help mentally and physically to bring the horse into a shorter frame after galloping and jumping at speed the previous day. This work in the arena will have to be observed by an FEI steward and will often need to be arranged the evening before.

After the showjumping you may get asked to go with a doping official to get tested – either just yourself or your horse. You will need to go with the official immediately and they will escort you to the testing area and explain the procedure as you go through it. It is all very simple but can be nerve-racking if you're experiencing it for the first time. After the competition allow your horse to settle well, drink plenty and be relaxed before travelling, especially if you have a long distance to go.

Enjoy and good luck!

Training to Win

INDEX

A
aids 29–31, 49–50, 70–1, 73, 87, 90, 93–4, 96–7, 101, 138–42
Allstar B 11, 212, 233
Alogo 195
angled fence 145–9
ascending spread 110, 187
athlete's philosophy 27–44
Atomic Clock 232
attention to detail 18, 45, 48, 50

B
balance 29, 65, 70–5, 88–9, 94–105, 130–3
bascule 204
basics 45, 48, 107, 142, 189
body control check 227
bounce 99–102, 157–8
building block system 21–4, 46–8, 73, 95, 116, 149
building distance 74

C
canter
  collected 76–8, 80, 109, 200–3
  working 75–80, 82, 115
  medium 77–80, 109, 115, 122–3, 153, 203
  extended 76, 109
  counter 108, 115–18, 128, 139–42, 208
  jumping 31, 80–1, 143–4, 180, 196
canter poles 77–8, 196, 200
cavalletti 54, 80–1, 99–104, 153–5, 206–7
centre line 86, 89, 132–6, 164
challenge 19–21, 26, 48–50, 200
champion 15–19, 94, 189
Chef d'equipe 229
circles 77, 82, 116–17, 122–3, 132–3
circuit training 57

Clean Sport 221–2, 228
coach 16, 19, 27–8, 38, 46, 190–5
collection 33, 78, 132, 157
competition
  planning 209
  aims 210
confidence 15, 21, 26, 48, 57, 155, 164, 168–9, 173–7
contact 31, 70, 127, 170–1
conformation 38–9, 45, 125
corner cup 53
core strength 40
course design 211, 215
crooked 36
cross-country fences
  arrowhead 159–62
  box corner 151
  bullfinch 111
  coffin 111, 177
  corner fence 149–56
  ditches 22–5, 105, 111, 161, 177–80
  drop 169–70, 179
  gate 217
  high sided brush corner 151
  leaf pit 179–81
  open corner 149–50
  shoulder brush 111, 163–7
  table 111, 160, 180
  water 34–5, 111, 160, 173–7, 179–80, 211, 217

D
dehydrated 215
deliberate practice 21, 27, 48
directional change 73, 90, 97–8, 100, 102, 104, 153–5
downhill slope 160, 171, 172
dressage
  boards 52–3, 98
  test 35, 60, 80, 132–3, 138
dressing 211

E

Equine Anti-Doping Programme 221
equine passport 228
Equine Prohibited Substance List 221
evasion 50, 86, 127
expression 118
eyes 59, 66–8, 72, 78, 93, 97, 99, 102, 118, 144, 169–71
  training of 40, 42

F

fast work 55, 59–62
fatigue 40, 50, 115, 123, 184, 235
feedback 38, 48, 60–1, 125, 190–1, 194
feed batch number 222
FEI International Equestrian Federation 62, 132, 205, 211, 221, 235
FEI Anti-Doping and Controlled Medication Regulations 221
first minute 111, 183–4
fitness
  aerobic 40
  anaerobic 40
  equine 50, 55, 57, 59–62, 75, 209, 211, 228
  human 17, 40, 43
flags 53, 90, 92, 95, 149, 151, 161–2, 174, 179, 217, 232
floor plan 57, 74, 93, 118, 121, 123, 130, 132, 134–5
flying change 109, 117–18, 132, 138–42, 208
focal point 17, 65–6, 72, 86–7, 118, 134, 137, 216–18

G

gait 31, 65, 73, 81, 108, 115
gears 59, 72, 74, 111, 143, 157, 211
GPS watch 220
gradient 104, 111, 159, 169, 170–2, 182, 211–12
ground rail 153, 180, 187

H

half-halt 31, 49, 72, 80, 87, 98, 109, 118, 130, 137
halt 17, 63, 73, 84, 108, 123–8
head 66–8, 71, 157, 227
health 17, 40, 45, 228
holding a line 73, 109, 111, 153, 206
hoof-brain coordination 73, 84, 102, 105
hoof-pastern axis 39

I

international competition 187, 193, 205, 220–1
impulsion 31, 33

L

last minute 111, 184
learning 16, 19, 27, 38, 45–8, 55, 61, 66, 107, 138, 187, 226
leg-yield 89, 95–9, 108, 122, 136–41, 146, 153, 164–5
lift 98, 122, 137, 204, 206–8
light conditions 213
long format 50, 58, 62–3, 110, 186, 204, 211, 215, 220, 228, 235
lower leg 59, 67, 70–2, 127, 140, 157, 164, 171

M

marginal gains 17, 189
MIMclip 150, 219
Minimum Eligibility Requirement (MER) 38, 210
minute markers 218, 220, 229, 232
mistake 37–8, 46–9, 93, 184, 190, 194, 223, 228, 232

N

National competition 187
nausea 44, 225
nerves 20, 187, 223–7, 232
  creating a strategy 223
  breathing 224–7
no-excuse culture 19, 37
nutrition, human 43–4

P

parallel 84–5, 100–2, 110, 113, 115–16, 118, 121–4, 134, 144–7, 186–8, 200, 204–5
patience 45
performance over outcome 38, 189
performance goal 38, 190
performance profiling 189, 190
planning 55, 74, 194, 209–10, 230
podium mentality 15–19, 126
pole
  zigzag 87–8, 153
  wooden 50
  plastic 50
  narrow 89
  half-round 51, 89, 113, 129
pole raiser 51–2, 84
position 45, 59, 65–72, 80–1, 84, 86, 96–8, 118–19, 129, 153, 180, 182, 203
positive mindset 15, 19
power 49, 72, 74, 103, 140, 143, 161, 168, 170, 172, 180, 192, 194–5, 205–6
practice, deliberate 21, 27, 48
precision training 202
preparation point 59, 72, 217
pressure 20, 26, 36, 45, 47, 49, 65, 73–4, 87, 93–4, 127, 139–42, 147, 194–6, 223–8
process goal 190

Q

quality 17, 27, 48–50, 59, 72, 104, 118–19, 122–3, 191–4, 204

R

reaction training 157
recreational riding 55
reflection 38, 46–7, 61, 74, 128
reins
  length 169
  single bridge 70, 110
rein back 35, 84, 127–8
related distance 80, 110, 158–9, 164–6, 179–80, 193
reprimand 46–7
resistance training 40
response 50, 96, 225
responsibility 15, 19–20, 27, 43, 65, 157–8, 221
reward 26, 45–7, 49, 65, 73, 87, 127
rhythm 29, 74–5, 111, 130–1
  fence 215, 182–4
routine 57, 109–11, 185–6, 226–7, 231

S

scales of training 27–35
seat position
  top speed 180, 182
  preparation point 59, 72
  landing 66
serpentine 77, 96, 98, 108
short format 58, 61
shoulder-in 89, 109, 118–22, 130–1,

Index

counter 136–7
showjumping
  warm up 185–8
  course 192–3, 235
  chunking 193
simple change 109, 132–3, 136
simulated cross country fence 53
skills 16, 21, 26, 48–9, 58, 111, 142–3, 189–90
soft profile fences 180, 182, 220
soundness 38
spring preparation 59
square exercise
  parallel poles 113–23
  short side training 128–33
start box 111, 179, 183–4, 220
stirrup length 70–1
straightness 33, 86–94, 136, 139, 163, 196
stretching 57, 108, 134
stride length, variation 33, 72, 74–5, 80, 143, 164–5, 168, 170–2, 194–5, 205, 214
suppleness 29–30, 84–5, 115, 139

T

tapering 57, 62
task-load 196, 225
telescopic training wings 53
terrain 72, 104–6, 143
time management 39–40
topography 143, 179, 182, 211–12, 214
training system 15–16, 27, 138, 209
training journal 37
tramlines 53, 87–8, 146–7
transitions 78–83
  canter–walk–canter 132–3, 140–1
  centre line 136
  halt 125
  within a gait 57, 73, 122–3
travers 89, 109, 131, 139, 141
trot
  collected 135
  working 82, 114, 116, 134, 137
  medium 108, 121–2, 131, 137
  extended 32, 109, 122
trotting poles 82, 97, 146, 153
trot up 63, 229, 230, 235
turning point 72, 217–18

V

vaccination 228
vertical 186–8

veterinary check 229–30
visualisation skills 111, 218, 227

W

walk
  collected 109
  medium 107
  extended 107
walk pirouette 109
water, depth of 177, 182
wing weights 51
winter work 57–9
work ethic 49–50, 59, 61

Z

zones
  comfort 19, 48, 55, 57, 190
  training 48
  pressure 26, 49, 194–5, 226